I do actually have some hobbies, but none worth talking about. Just little things that I dabble in.

In short, *Dragon Ball* is the only thing I can talk to people about.

—Toyotarou, 2020

Toyotarou

Toyotarou created the manga adaptation for the *Dragon Ball Z* anime's 2015 film, *Dragon Ball Z: Resurrection F*. He is also the author of the spin-off series *Dragon Ball Heroes: Victory Mission*, which debuted in *V-Jump* in Japan in November 2012.

Akira Toriyama

Renowned worldwide for his playful, innovative storytelling and humorous, distinctive art style, Akira Toriyama burst onto the manga scene in 1980 with the wildly popular *Dr. Slump*. His hit series *Dragon Ball* (published in the U.S. as *Dragon Ball* and *Dragon Ball Z*) ran from 1984 to 1995 in Shueisha's *Weekly Shonen Jump* magazine. He is also known for his design work on video games such as *Dragon Quest*, *Chrono Trigger*, *Tobal No. 1* and *Blue Dragon*. His recent manga works include *COWA!*, *Kajika*, *Sand Land*, *Neko Majin*, *Jaco the Galactic Patrolman* and a children's book, *Toccio the Angel*. He lives with his family in Japan.

SHONEN JUMP Manga Edition

STORY BY **Akira Toriyama**
ART BY **Toyotarou**

TRANSLATION **Caleb Cook**
LETTERING **Brandon Bovia**
DESIGN **Joy Zhang**
EDITOR **Rae First**

DRAGON BALL SUPER © 2015 BY BIRD STUDIO, Toyotarou
All rights reserved. First published in Japan in 2015 by SHUEISHA Inc., Tokyo.
English translation rights arranged by SHUEISHA Inc.

Printed in Italy

Published by VIZ Media, LLC
P.O. Box 77010
San Francisco, CA 94107

10 9 8 7 6 5
First printing, March 2021
Fifth printing, February 2024

viz.com

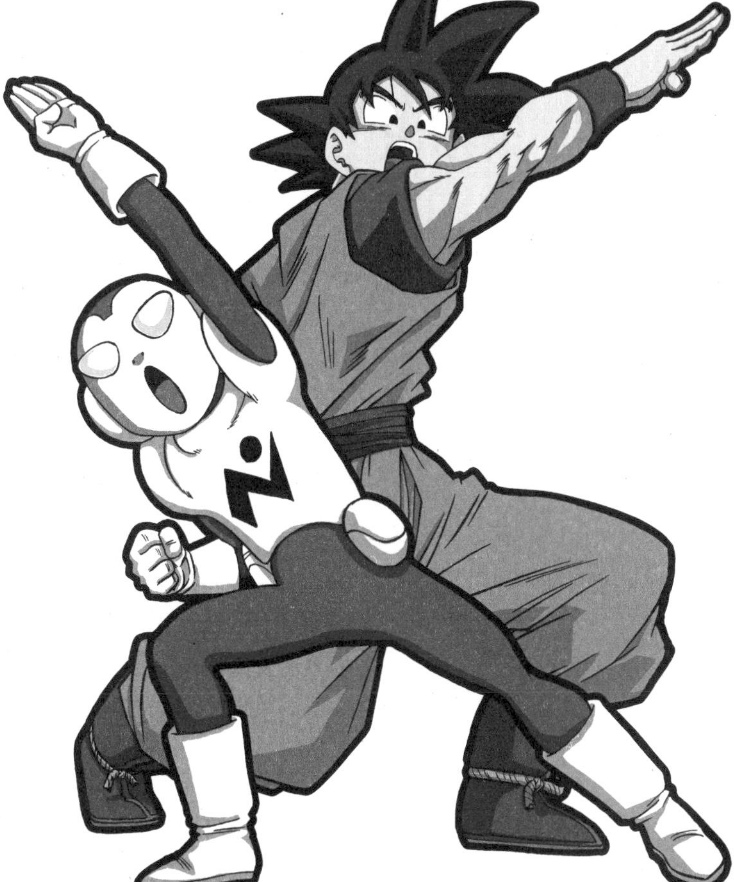

DRAGON BALL SUPER

MERUS'S TRUE IDENTITY

12

STORY BY
Akira Toriyama

ART BY
Toyotarou

CAST OF CHARACTERS

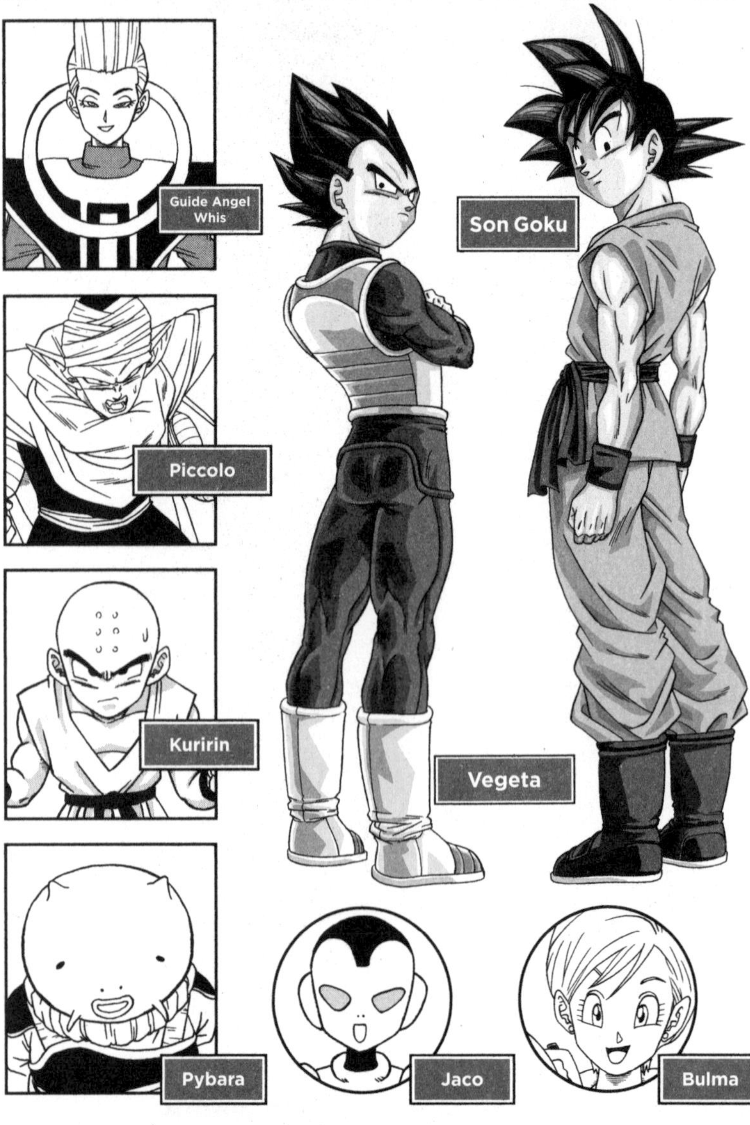
Son Goku
Vegeta
Guide Angel Whis
Piccolo
Kuririn
Pybara
Jaco
Bulma

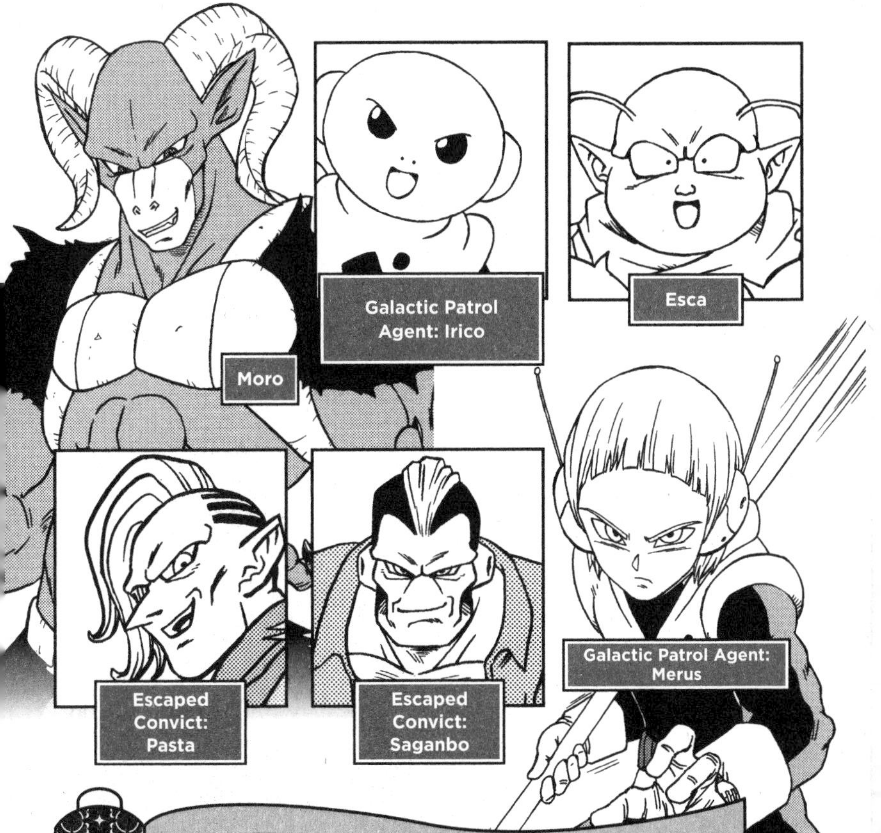
Moro
Galactic Patrol Agent: Irico
Esca
Galactic Patrol Agent: Merus
Escaped Convict: Pasta
Escaped Convict: Saganbo

STORY THUS FAR

A long, long time ago, Son Goku left on a journey in search of the legendary Dragon Balls—a set of seven balls that, when gathered, would summon the dragon Shenlong to grant any wish. After a great adventure, he collects them all. Later, he becomes the apprentice of Kame-Sen'nin, fights a number of vicious enemies, defeats the great Majin Boo and restores peace on Earth. Some time passes, and then Lord Beerus, the God of Destruction, suddenly awakens and sets out in search of the Super Saiyan God. Goku, by becoming the Super Saiyan God, manages to stop Beerus from destroying the Earth and starts training under him with Vegeta. After some time, the ancient villain Moro escapes from the Galactic Prison and goes off to search for the Dragon Balls in new Namek, where Goku and the Galactic Patrol confront him. However, Moro's ability to absorb life energy is too much for them, and Moro manages to make his wishes. After retreating, Goku travels to a distant planet to train with Merus, while Vegeta goes to Yardrat to learn about spirit techniques that could defeat Moro. Meanwhile, Moro himself has freed a gang of convicts from the Galactic Prison and is commanding them to attack planets across the galaxy. Now, his evil may threaten Earth as well...

12

DRAGON★BALL SUPER

TABLE • OF • CON-TENTS

DRAGON BALL SUPER

CHAPTER 53: SAGANBO'S GALACTIC BANDIT BRIGADE

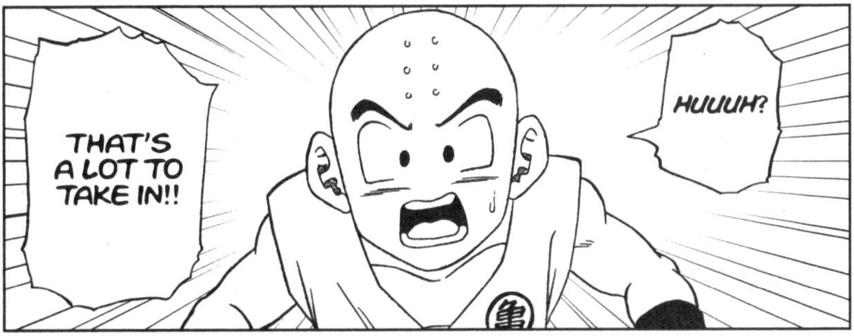
HUUUH?
THAT'S A LOT TO TAKE IN!!

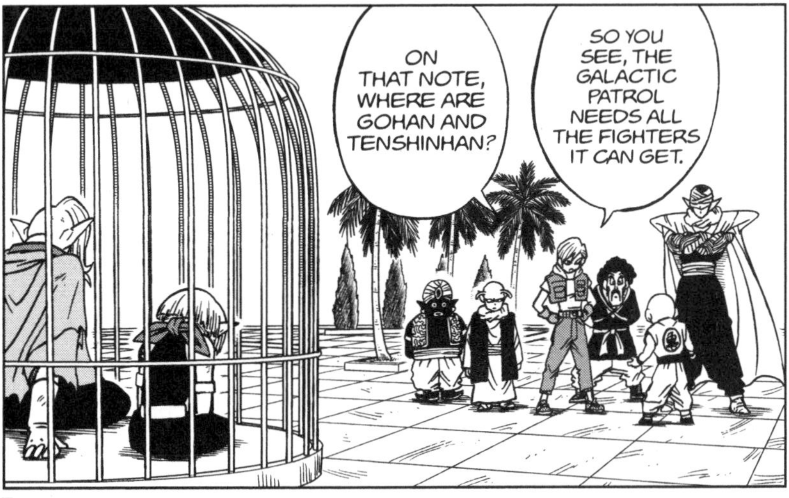
SO YOU SEE, THE GALACTIC PATROL NEEDS ALL THE FIGHTERS IT CAN GET.
ON THAT NOTE, WHERE ARE GOHAN AND TENSHINHAN?

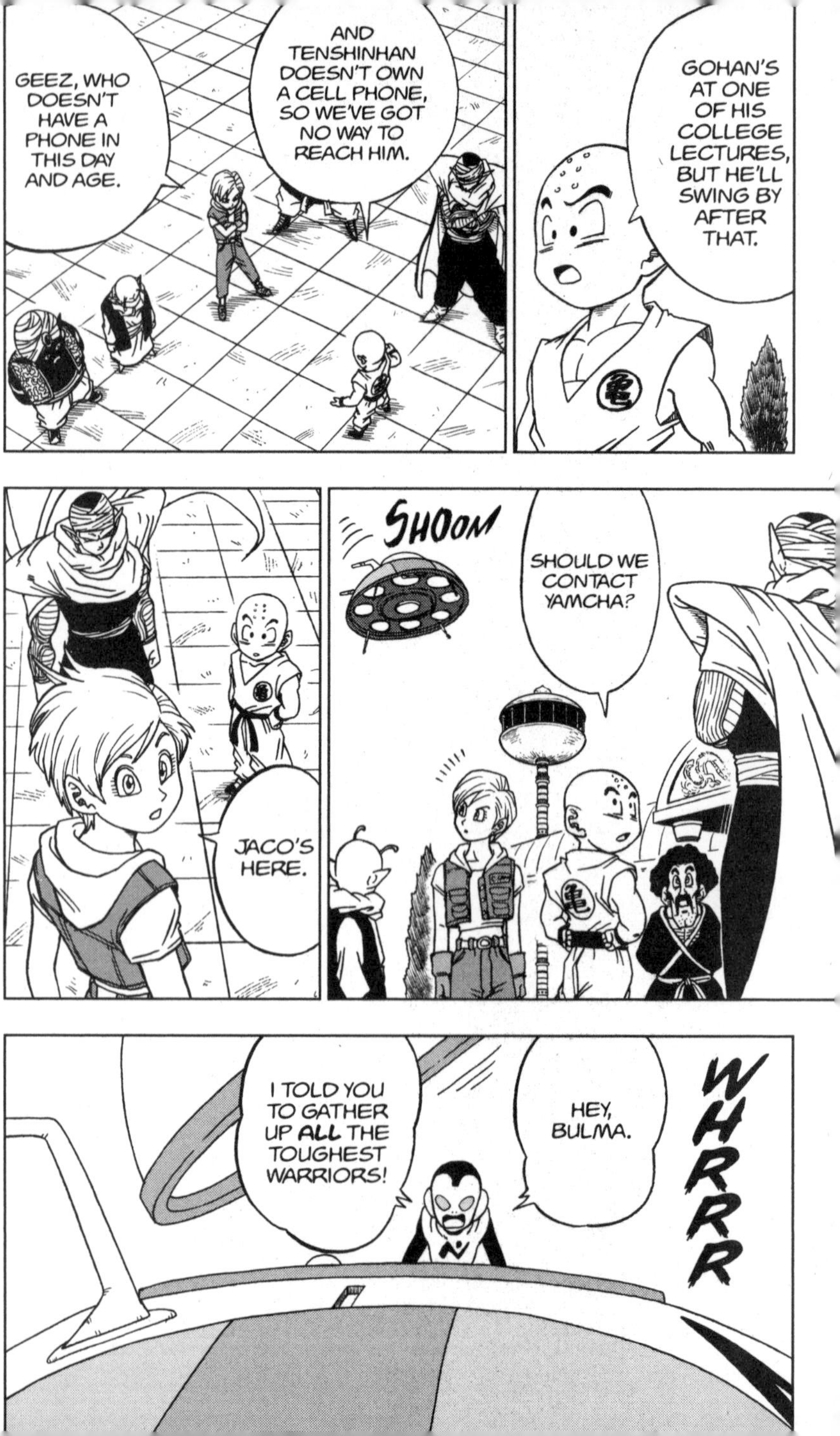
GOHAN'S AT ONE OF HIS COLLEGE LECTURES, BUT HE'LL SWING BY AFTER THAT.
AND TENSHINHAN DOESN'T OWN A CELL PHONE, SO WE'VE GOT NO WAY TO REACH HIM.
GEEZ, WHO DOESN'T HAVE A PHONE IN THIS DAY AND AGE.
SHOOM
SHOULD WE CONTACT YAMCHA?
JACO'S HERE.
WHRRR
HEY, BULMA.
I TOLD YOU TO GATHER UP **ALL** THE TOUGHEST WARRIORS!

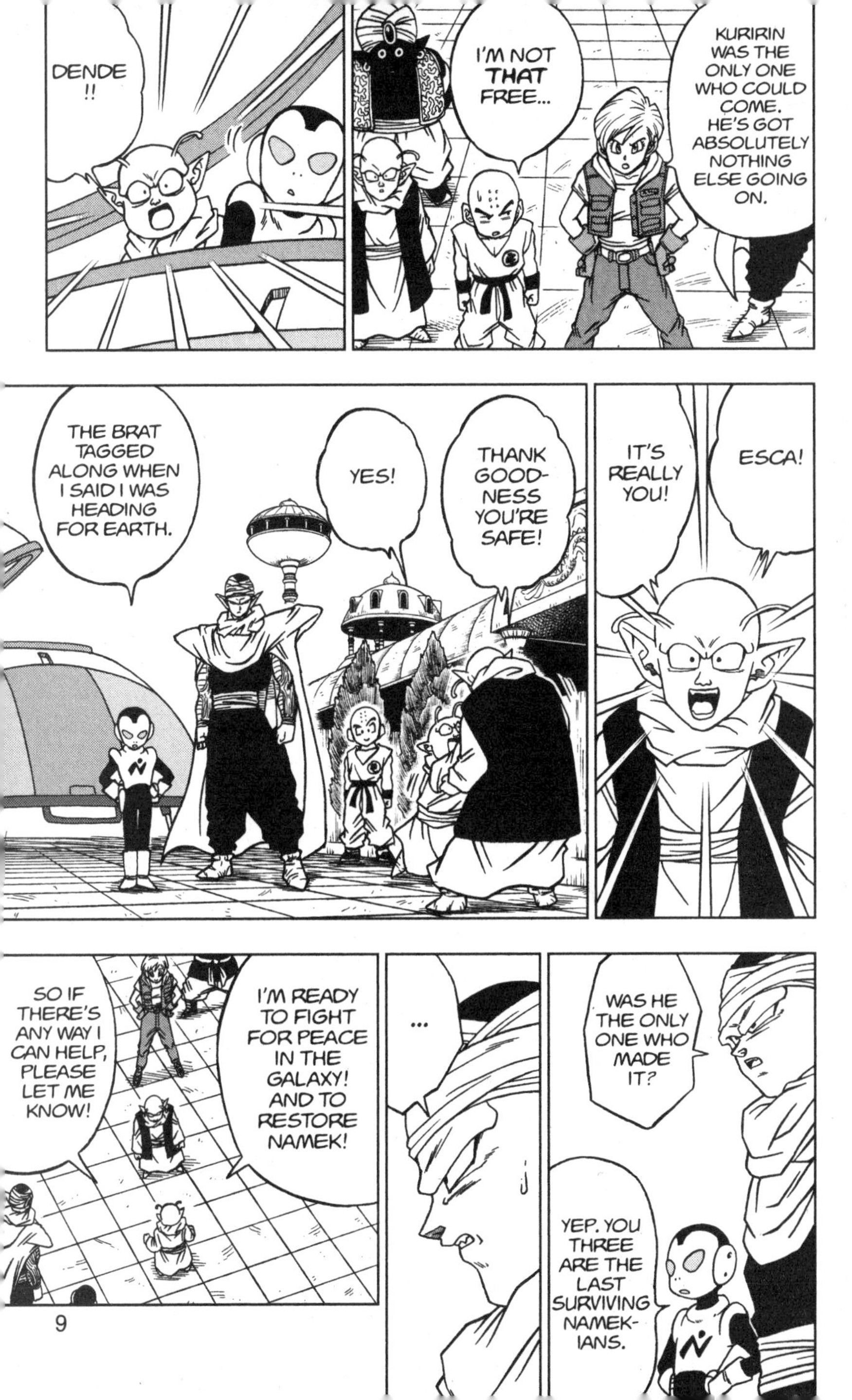
KURIRIN WAS THE ONLY ONE WHO COULD COME. HE'S GOT ABSOLUTELY NOTHING ELSE GOING ON.
I'M NOT **THAT** FREE...
DENDE !!
ESCA!
IT'S REALLY YOU!
THANK GOOD-NESS YOU'RE SAFE!
YES!
THE BRAT TAGGED ALONG WHEN I SAID I WAS HEADING FOR EARTH.
WAS HE THE ONLY ONE WHO MADE IT?
YEP. YOU THREE ARE THE LAST SURVIVING NAMEK-IANS.
...
I'M READY TO FIGHT FOR PEACE IN THE GALAXY! AND TO RESTORE NAMEK!
SO IF THERE'S ANY WAY I CAN HELP, PLEASE LET ME KNOW!

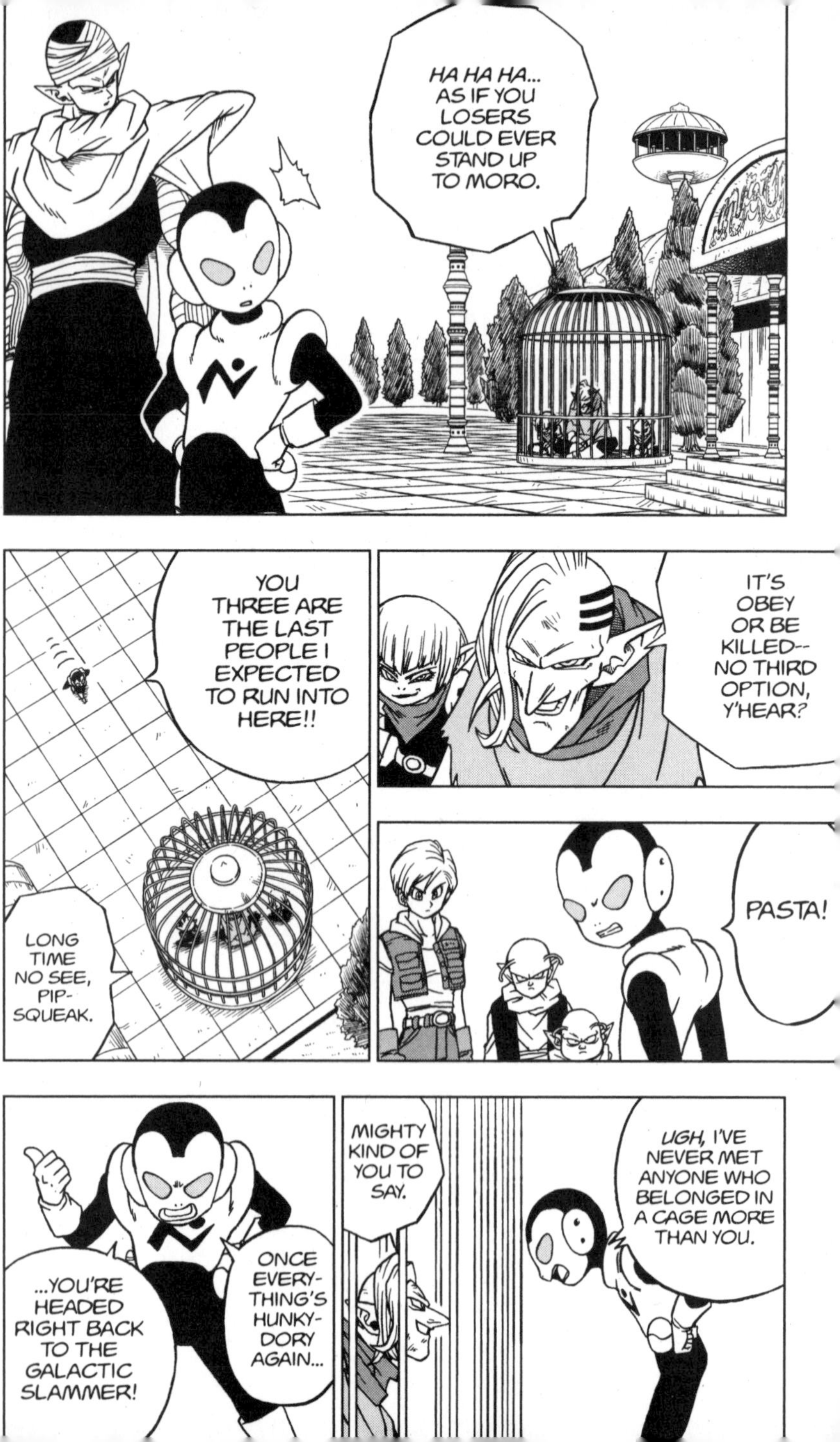
HA HA HA... AS IF YOU LOSERS COULD EVER STAND UP TO MORO.
IT'S OBEY OR BE KILLED-- NO THIRD OPTION, Y'HEAR?
PASTA!
YOU THREE ARE THE LAST PEOPLE I EXPECTED TO RUN INTO HERE!!
LONG TIME NO SEE, PIP-SQUEAK.
UGH, I'VE NEVER MET ANYONE WHO BELONGED IN A CAGE MORE THAN YOU.
MIGHTY KIND OF YOU TO SAY.
ONCE EVERY-THING'S HUNKY-DORY AGAIN...
...YOU'RE HEADED RIGHT BACK TO THE GALACTIC SLAMMER!

YOU LET THEM CONTACT MORO?!

WHAT?!

HA HA HA, YOU STILL DON'T GET IT--THE MAIN FORCE IS GONNA SWOOP DOWN TO RESCUE US ANY DAY NOW.

T-TRY LEADING WITH THAT NEXT TIME!

I'D BETTER ASK HQ TO CONFIRM WHO EXACTLY'S COMING OUR WAY!

NOD

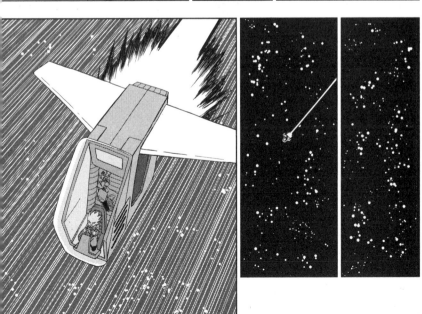

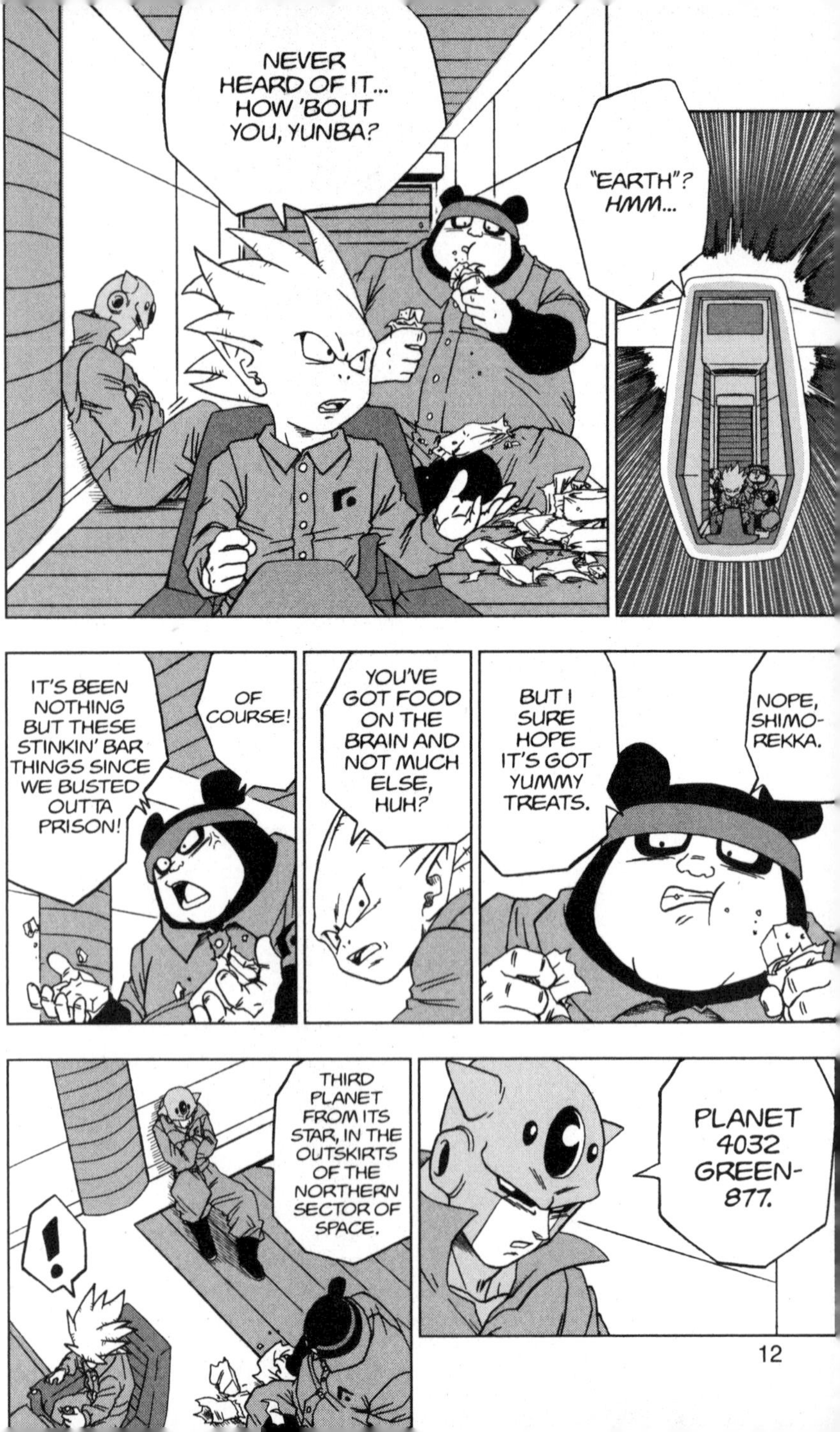
"EARTH"? HMM...
NEVER HEARD OF IT... HOW 'BOUT YOU, YUNBA?
NOPE, SHIMO-REKKA.
BUT I SURE HOPE IT'S GOT YUMMY TREATS.
YOU'VE GOT FOOD ON THE BRAIN AND NOT MUCH ELSE, HUH?
OF COURSE!
IT'S BEEN NOTHING BUT THESE STINKIN' BAR THINGS SINCE WE BUSTED OUTTA PRISON!
PLANET 4032 GREEN-877.
THIRD PLANET FROM ITS STAR, IN THE OUTSKIRTS OF THE NORTHERN SECTOR OF SPACE.
!

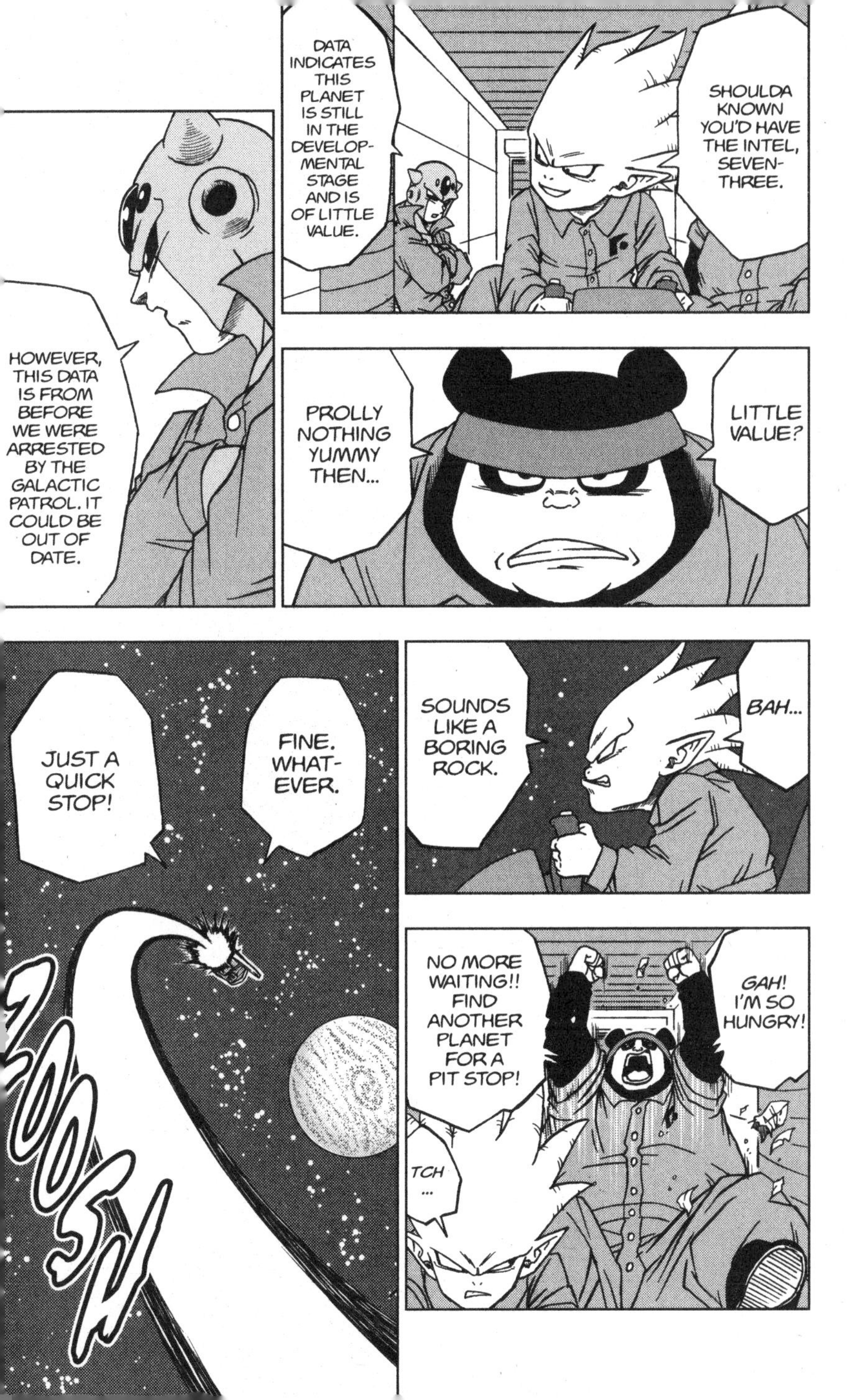
DATA INDICATES THIS PLANET IS STILL IN THE DEVELOPMENTAL STAGE AND IS OF LITTLE VALUE.
SHOULDA KNOWN YOU'D HAVE THE INTEL, SEVEN-THREE.
LITTLE VALUE?
PROLLY NOTHING YUMMY THEN...
HOWEVER, THIS DATA IS FROM BEFORE WE WERE ARRESTED BY THE GALACTIC PATROL. IT COULD BE OUT OF DATE.
BAH...
SOUNDS LIKE A BORING ROCK.
GAH! I'M SO HUNGRY!
NO MORE WAITING!! FIND ANOTHER PLANET FOR A PIT STOP!
TCH ...
FINE. WHATEVER.
JUST A QUICK STOP!
ZOOOSH

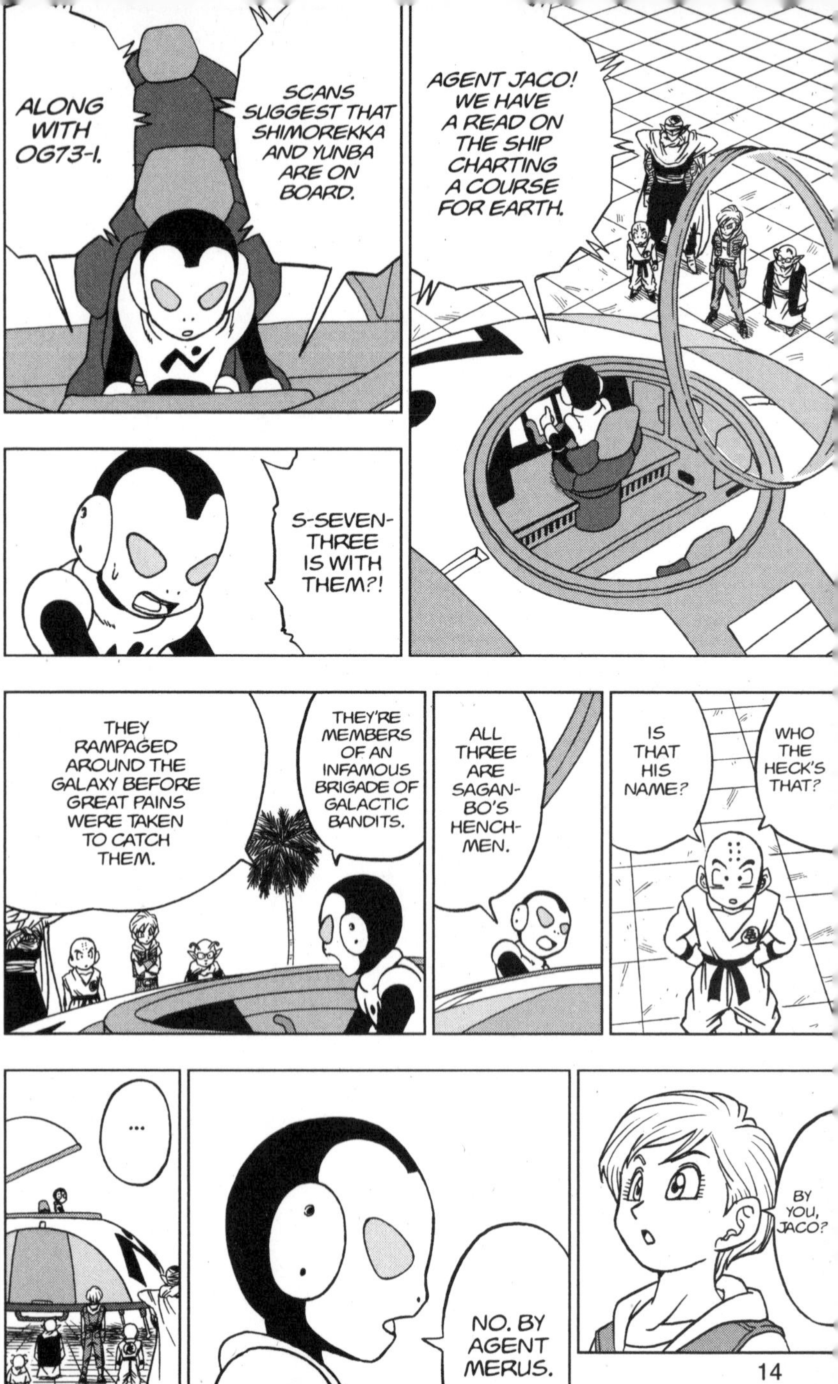
AGENT JACO! WE HAVE A READ ON THE SHIP CHARTING A COURSE FOR EARTH.
SCANS SUGGEST THAT SHIMOREKKA AND YUNBA ARE ON BOARD.
ALONG WITH OG73-1.
S-SEVEN-THREE IS WITH THEM?!
WHO THE HECK'S THAT?
IS THAT HIS NAME?
ALL THREE ARE SAGAN-BO'S HENCH-MEN.
THEY'RE MEMBERS OF AN INFAMOUS BRIGADE OF GALACTIC BANDITS.
THEY RAMPAGED AROUND THE GALAXY BEFORE GREAT PAINS WERE TAKEN TO CATCH THEM.
BY YOU, JACO?
NO. BY AGENT MERUS.
...

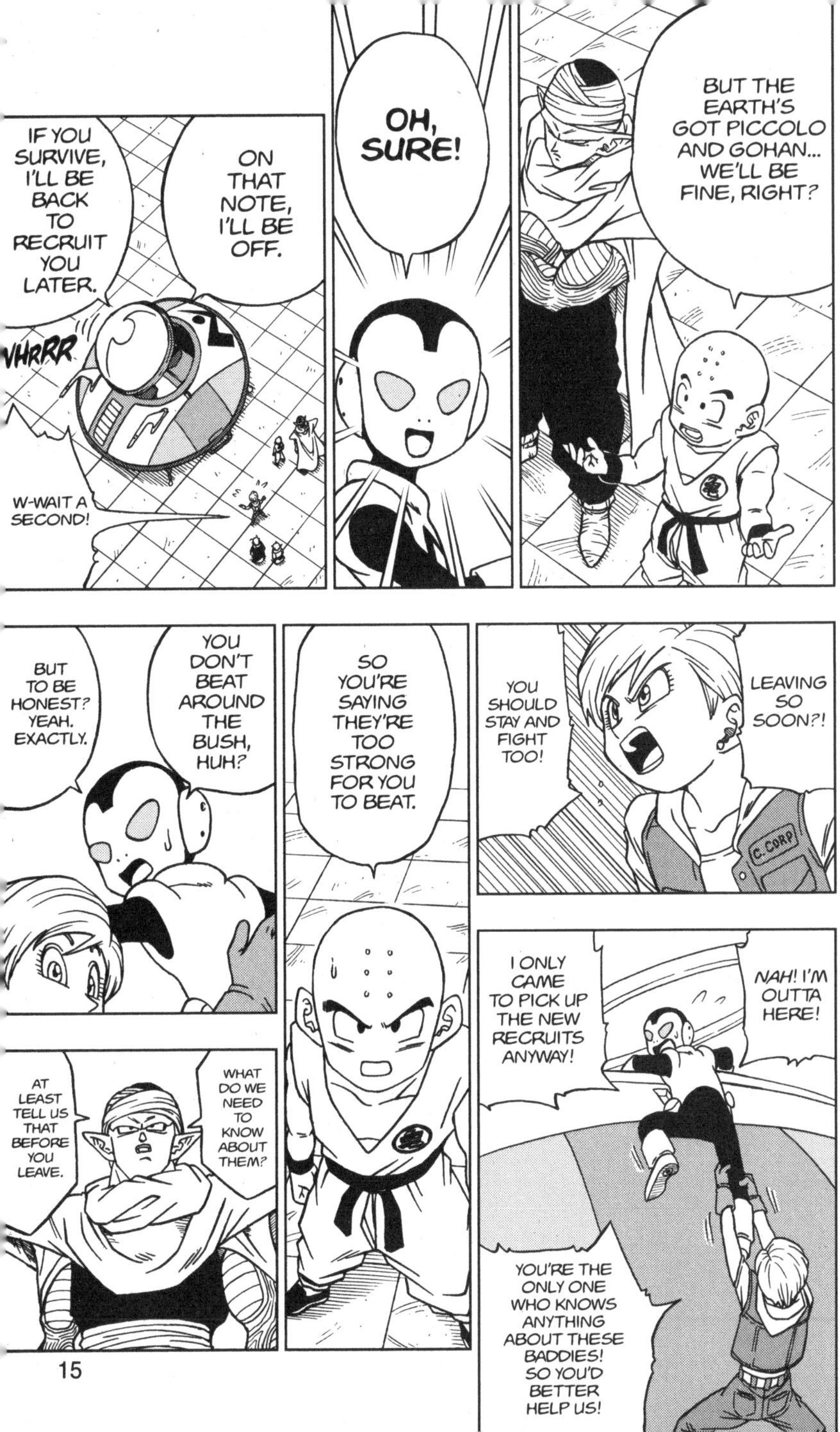
BUT THE EARTH'S GOT PICCOLO AND GOHAN... WE'LL BE FINE, RIGHT?
OH, SURE!
ON THAT NOTE, I'LL BE OFF.
IF YOU SURVIVE, I'LL BE BACK TO RECRUIT YOU LATER.
VHRRR
W-WAIT A SECOND!
LEAVING SO SOON?!
YOU SHOULD STAY AND FIGHT TOO!
C. CORP
NAH! I'M OUTTA HERE!
I ONLY CAME TO PICK UP THE NEW RECRUITS ANYWAY!
YOU'RE THE ONLY ONE WHO KNOWS ANYTHING ABOUT THESE BADDIES! SO YOU'D BETTER HELP US!
SO YOU'RE SAYING THEY'RE TOO STRONG FOR YOU TO BEAT.
YOU DON'T BEAT AROUND THE BUSH, HUH?
BUT TO BE HONEST? YEAH. EXACTLY.
WHAT DO WE NEED TO KNOW ABOUT THEM?
AT LEAST TELL US THAT BEFORE YOU LEAVE.

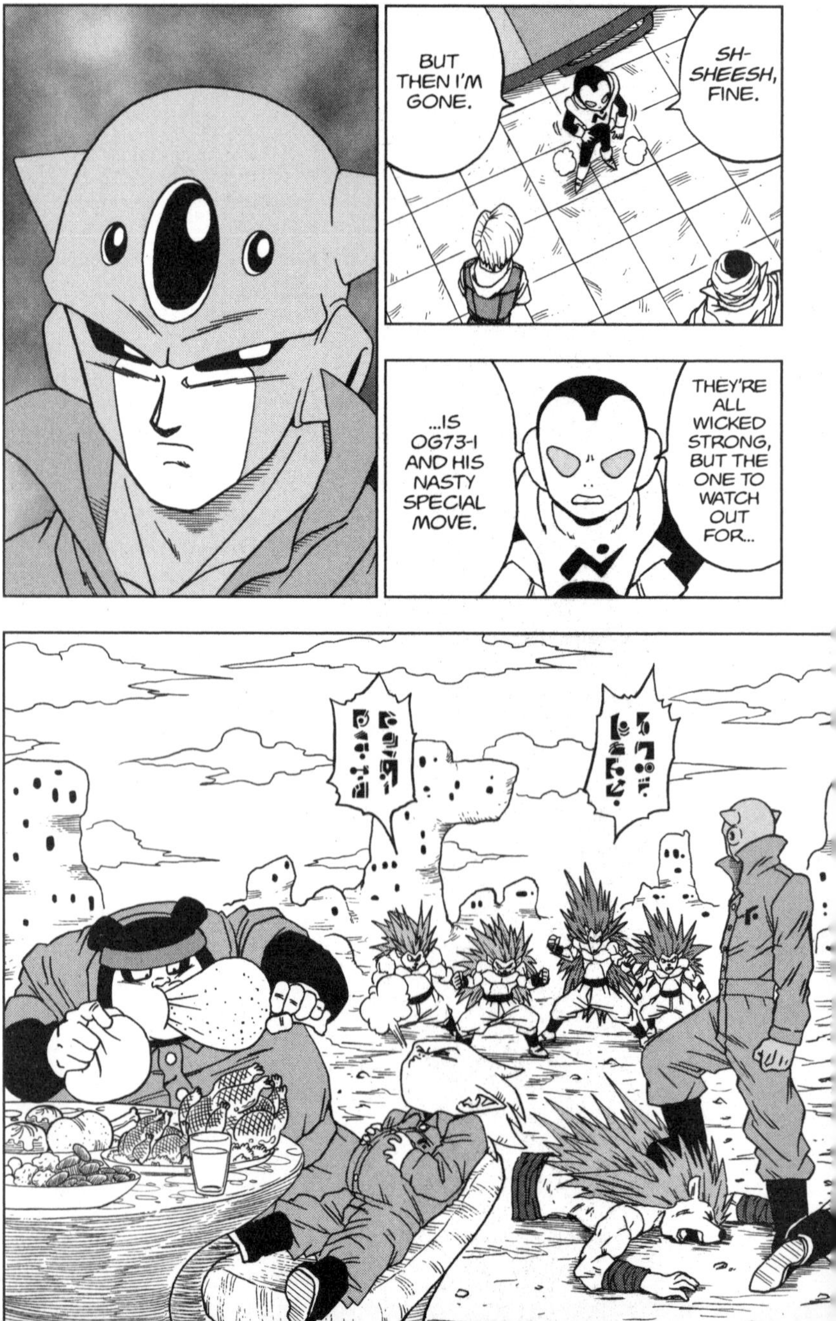
SH-SHEESH, FINE.
BUT THEN I'M GONE.
THEY'RE ALL WICKED STRONG, BUT THE ONE TO WATCH OUT FOR...
...IS OG73-1 AND HIS NASTY SPECIAL MOVE.

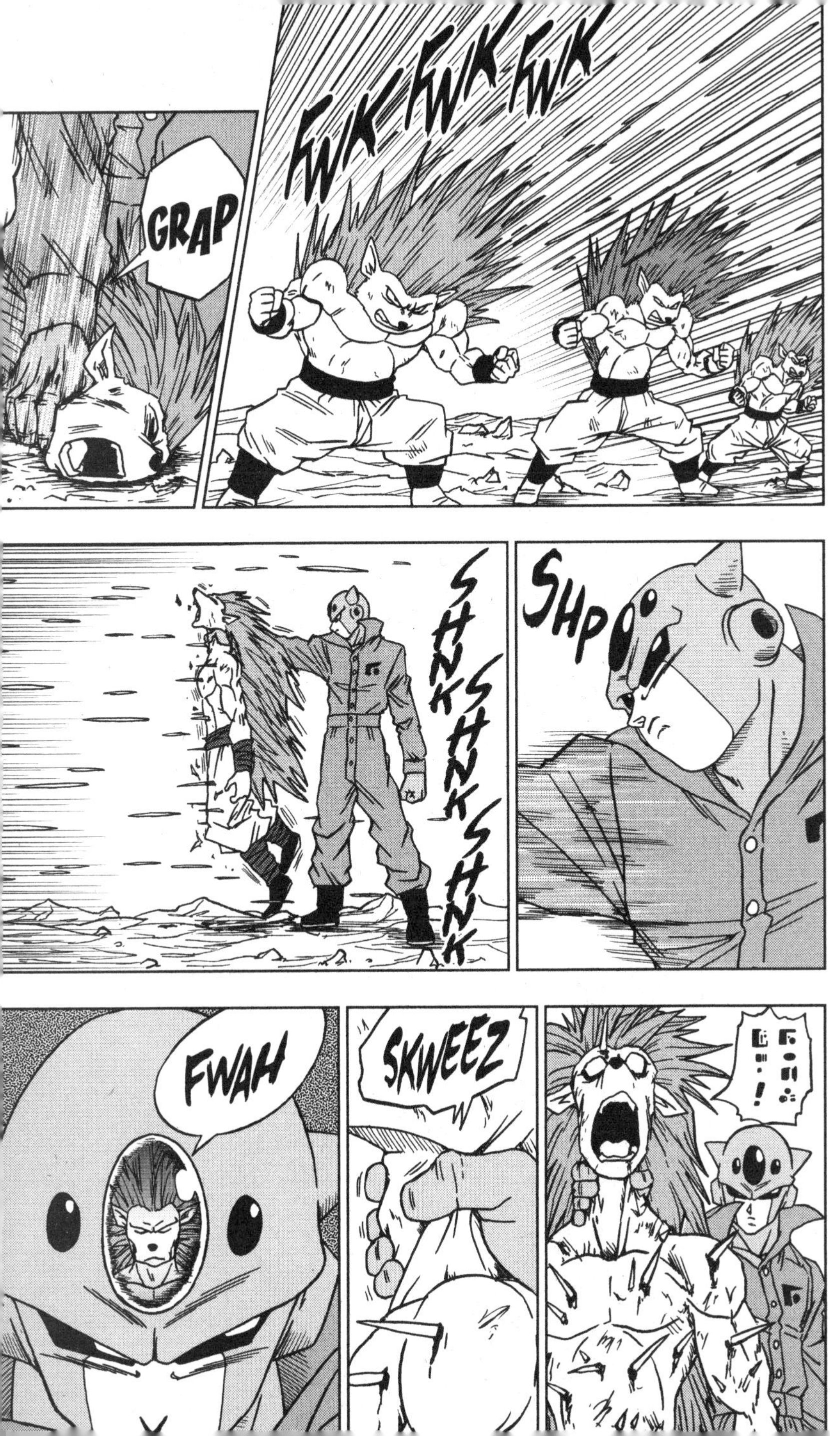
FWK FWK FWK
GRAP
SHP
SHNK SHNK SHNK
SKWEEZ
FWAH

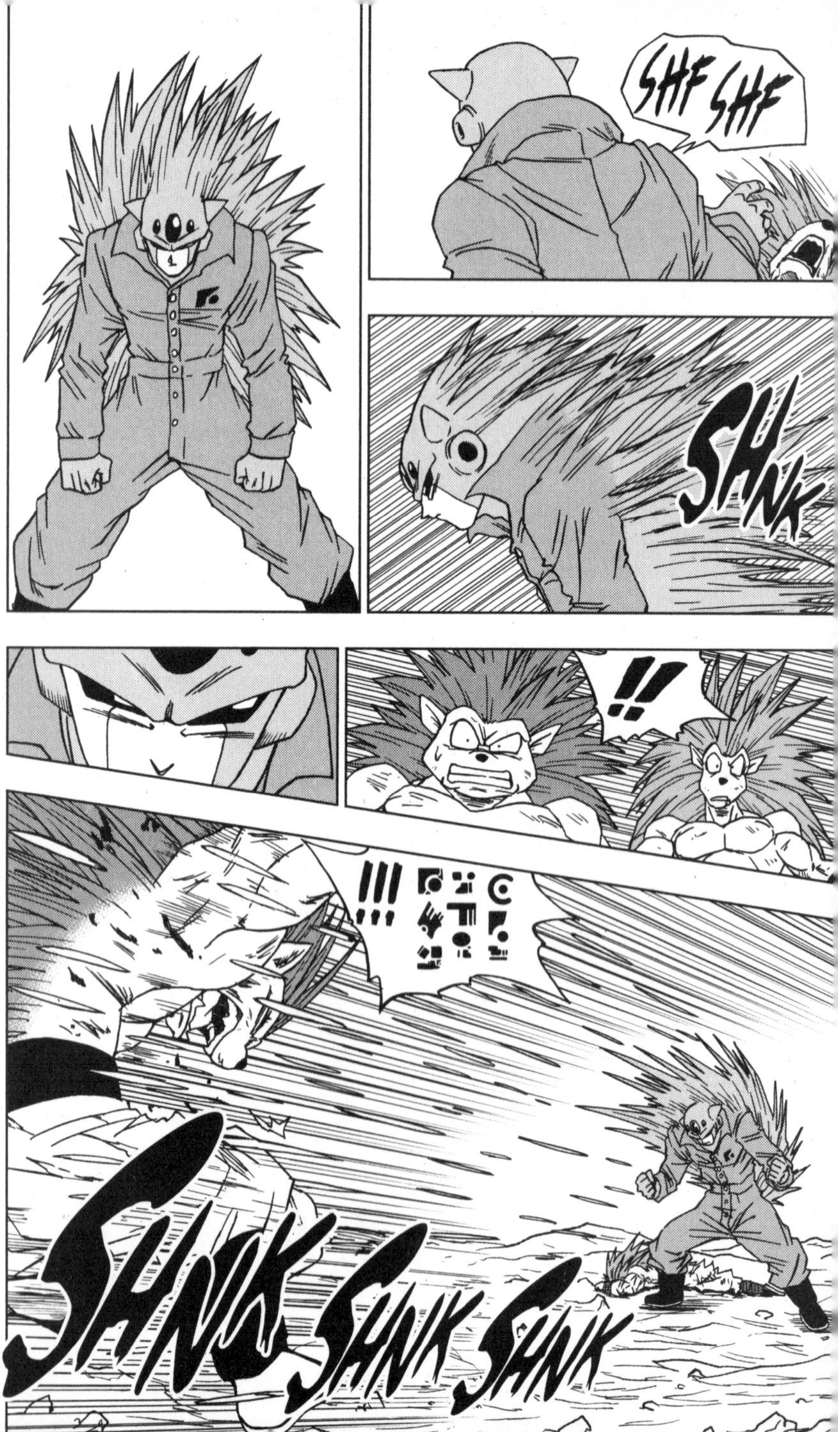
SHF SHF
SHNK
!!
!!!
SHNK SHNK SHNK

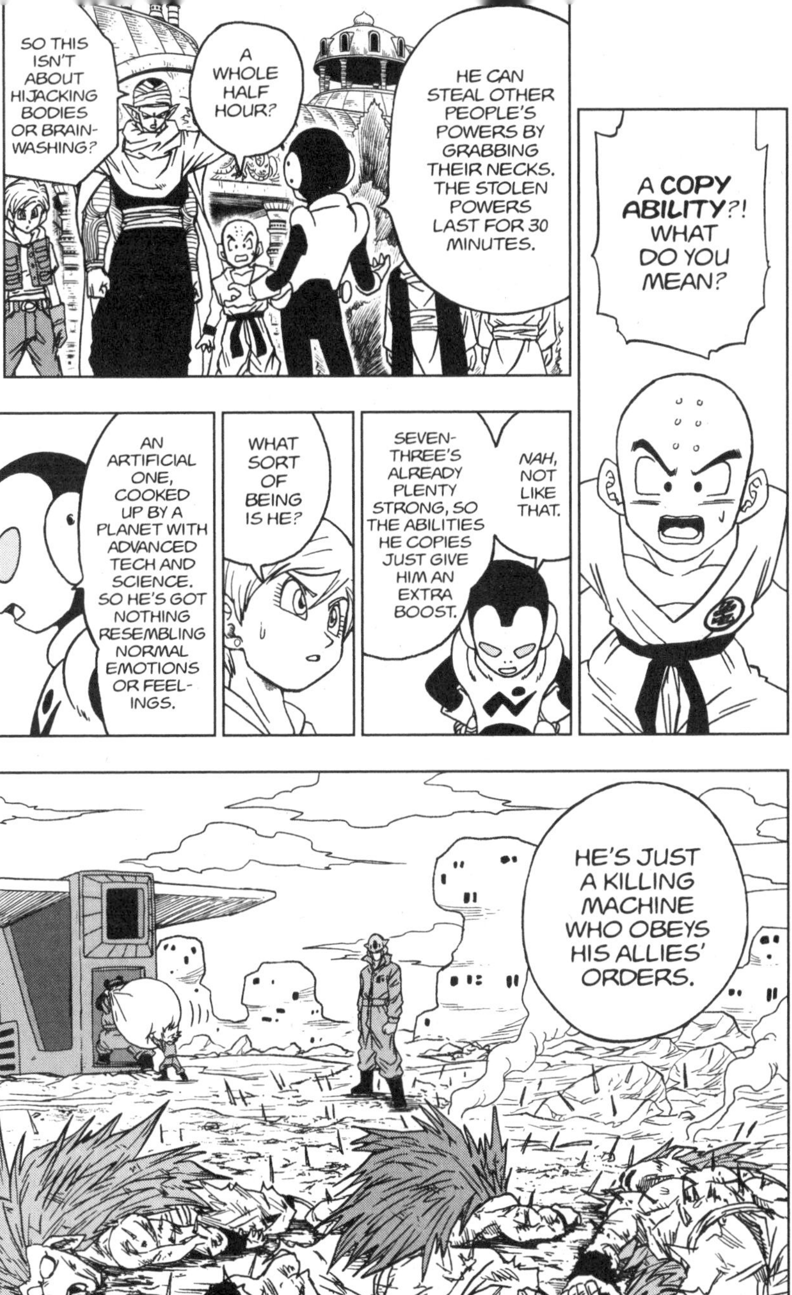
A **COPY ABILITY**?! WHAT DO YOU MEAN?
HE CAN STEAL OTHER PEOPLE'S POWERS BY GRABBING THEIR NECKS. THE STOLEN POWERS LAST FOR 30 MINUTES.
A WHOLE HALF HOUR?
SO THIS ISN'T ABOUT HIJACKING BODIES OR BRAIN-WASHING?
NAH, NOT LIKE THAT.
SEVEN-THREE'S ALREADY PLENTY STRONG, SO THE ABILITIES HE COPIES JUST GIVE HIM AN EXTRA BOOST.
WHAT SORT OF BEING IS HE?
AN ARTIFICIAL ONE, COOKED UP BY A PLANET WITH ADVANCED TECH AND SCIENCE. SO HE'S GOT NOTHING RESEMBLING NORMAL EMOTIONS OR FEEL-INGS.
HE'S JUST A KILLING MACHINE WHO OBEYS HIS ALLIES' ORDERS.

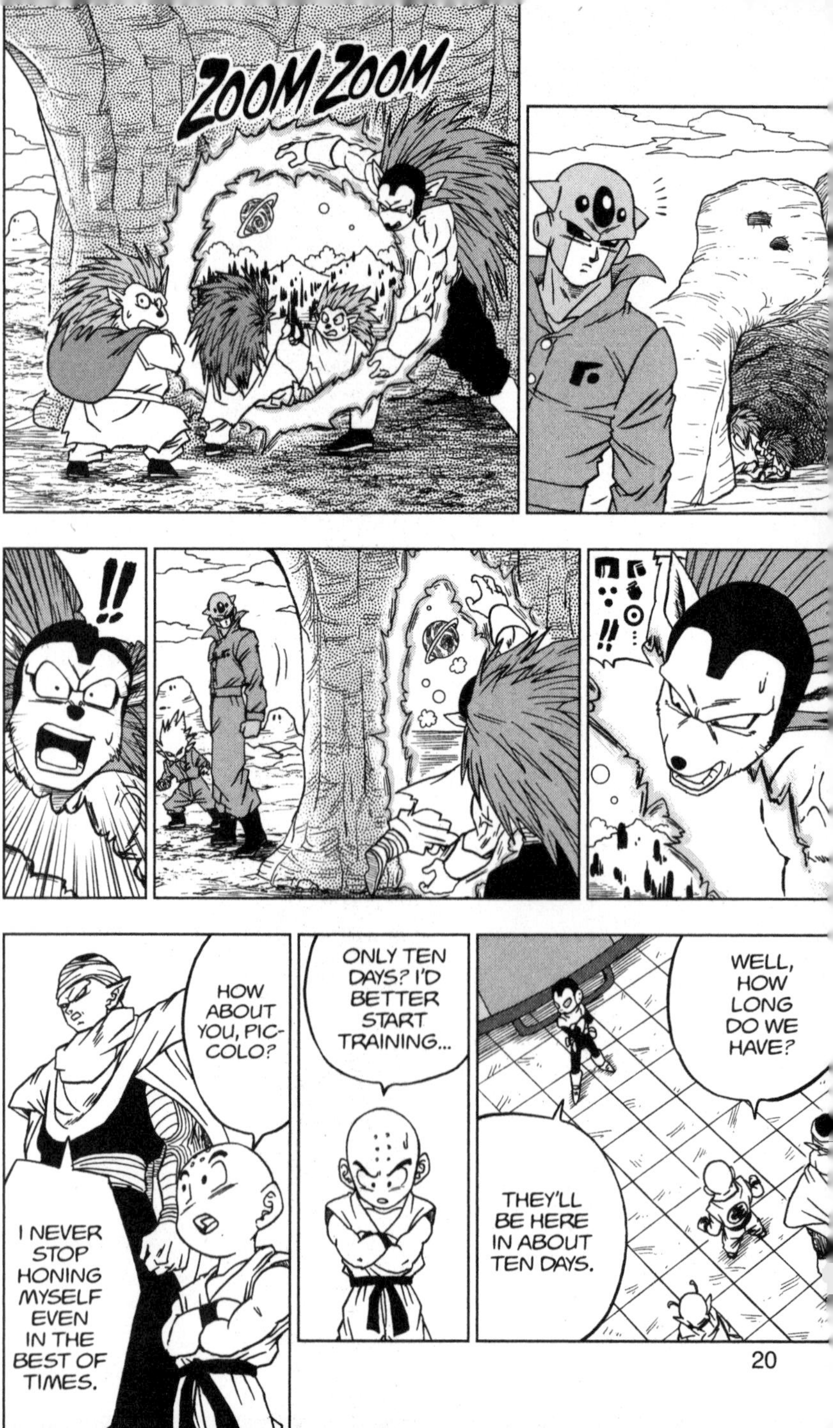
ZOOM ZOOM
!!
!!
WELL, HOW LONG DO WE HAVE?
THEY'LL BE HERE IN ABOUT TEN DAYS.
ONLY TEN DAYS? I'D BETTER START TRAINING...
HOW ABOUT YOU, PICCOLO?
I NEVER STOP HONING MYSELF EVEN IN THE BEST OF TIMES.

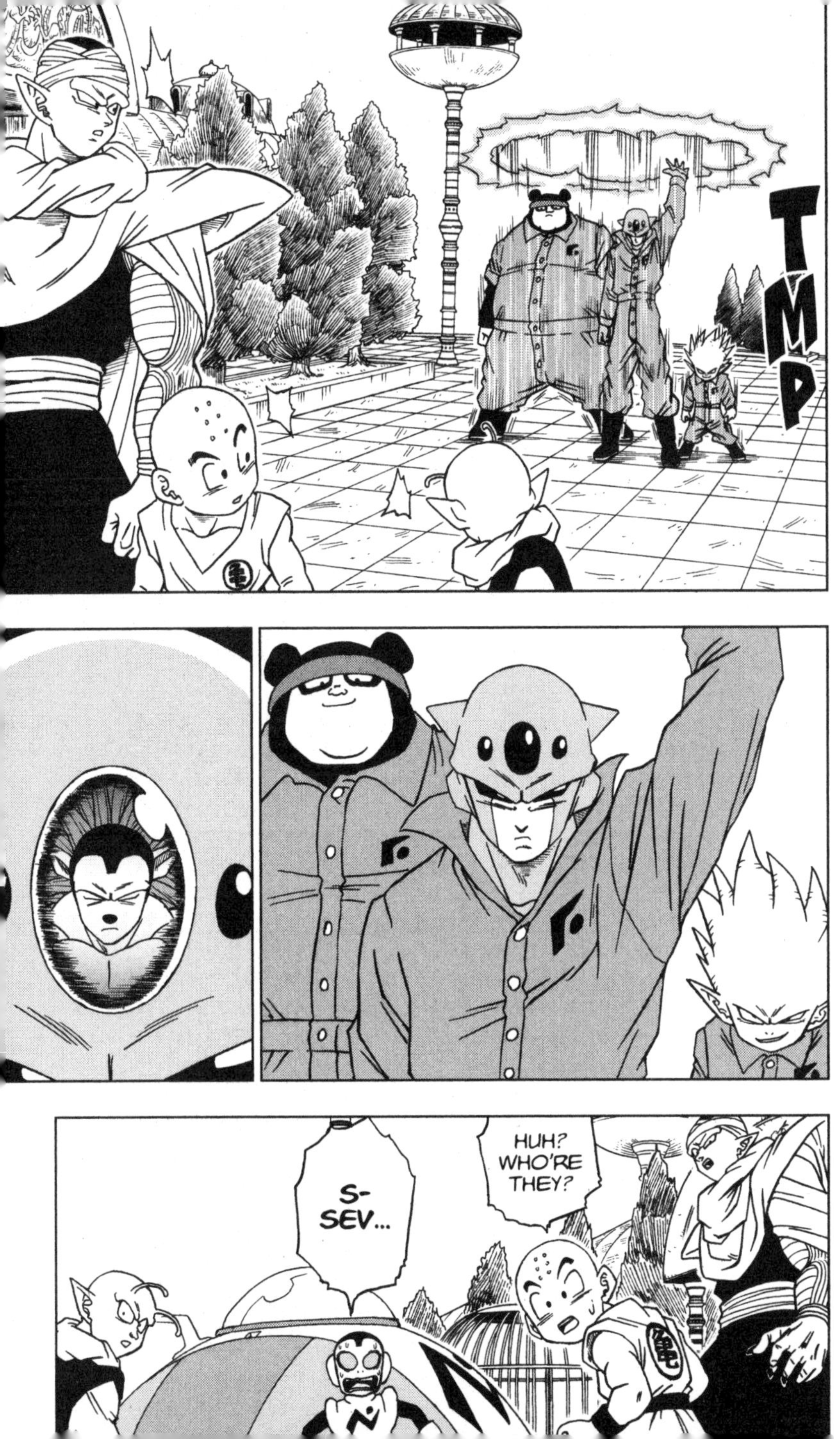
TMP
HUH? WHO'RE THEY?
S-SEV...

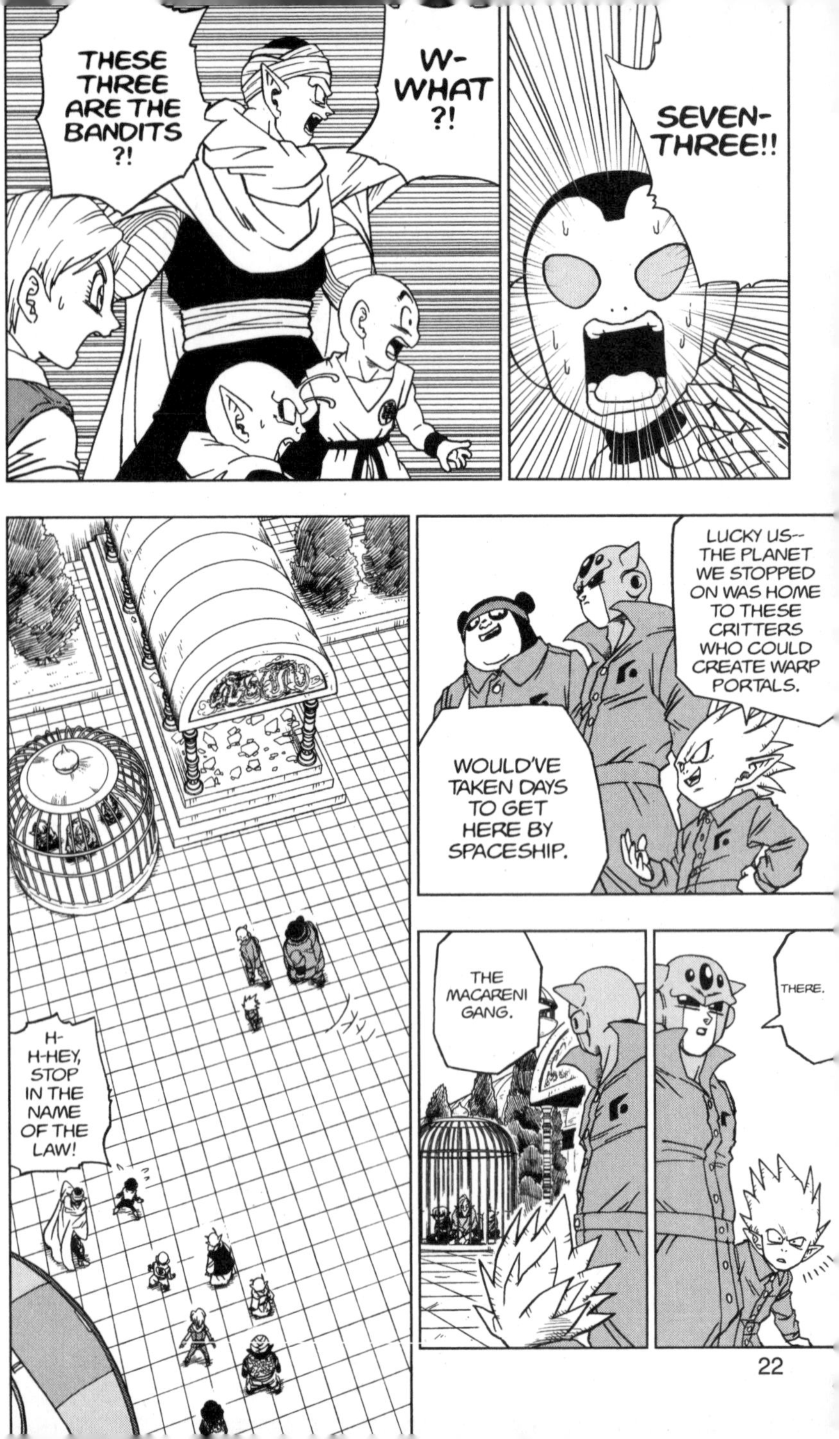
SEVEN-THREE!!
W-WHAT?!
THESE THREE ARE THE BANDITS?!
LUCKY US-- THE PLANET WE STOPPED ON WAS HOME TO THESE CRITTERS WHO COULD CREATE WARP PORTALS.
WOULD'VE TAKEN DAYS TO GET HERE BY SPACESHIP.
THERE.
THE MACARENI GANG.
H-H-HEY, STOP IN THE NAME OF THE LAW!

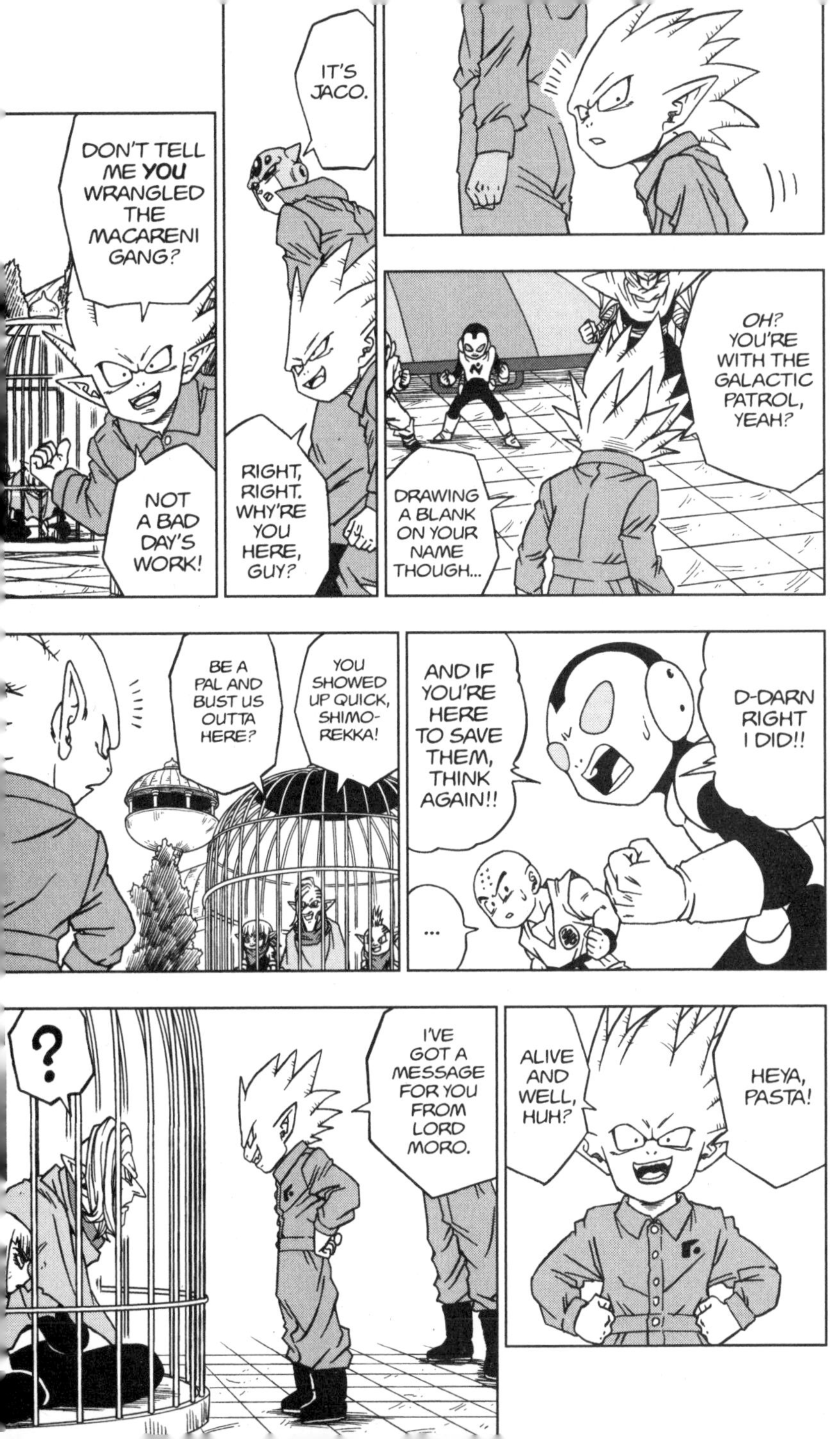

OH? YOU'RE WITH THE GALACTIC PATROL, YEAH?
DRAWING A BLANK ON YOUR NAME THOUGH...
IT'S JACO.
RIGHT, RIGHT. WHY'RE YOU HERE, GUY?
DON'T TELL ME **YOU** WRANGLED THE MACARENI GANG?
NOT A BAD DAY'S WORK!
D-DARN RIGHT I DID!!
AND IF YOU'RE HERE TO SAVE THEM, THINK AGAIN!!
...
YOU SHOWED UP QUICK, SHIMO-REKKA!
BE A PAL AND BUST US OUTTA HERE?
HEYA, PASTA!
ALIVE AND WELL, HUH?
I'VE GOT A MESSAGE FOR YOU FROM LORD MORO.
?

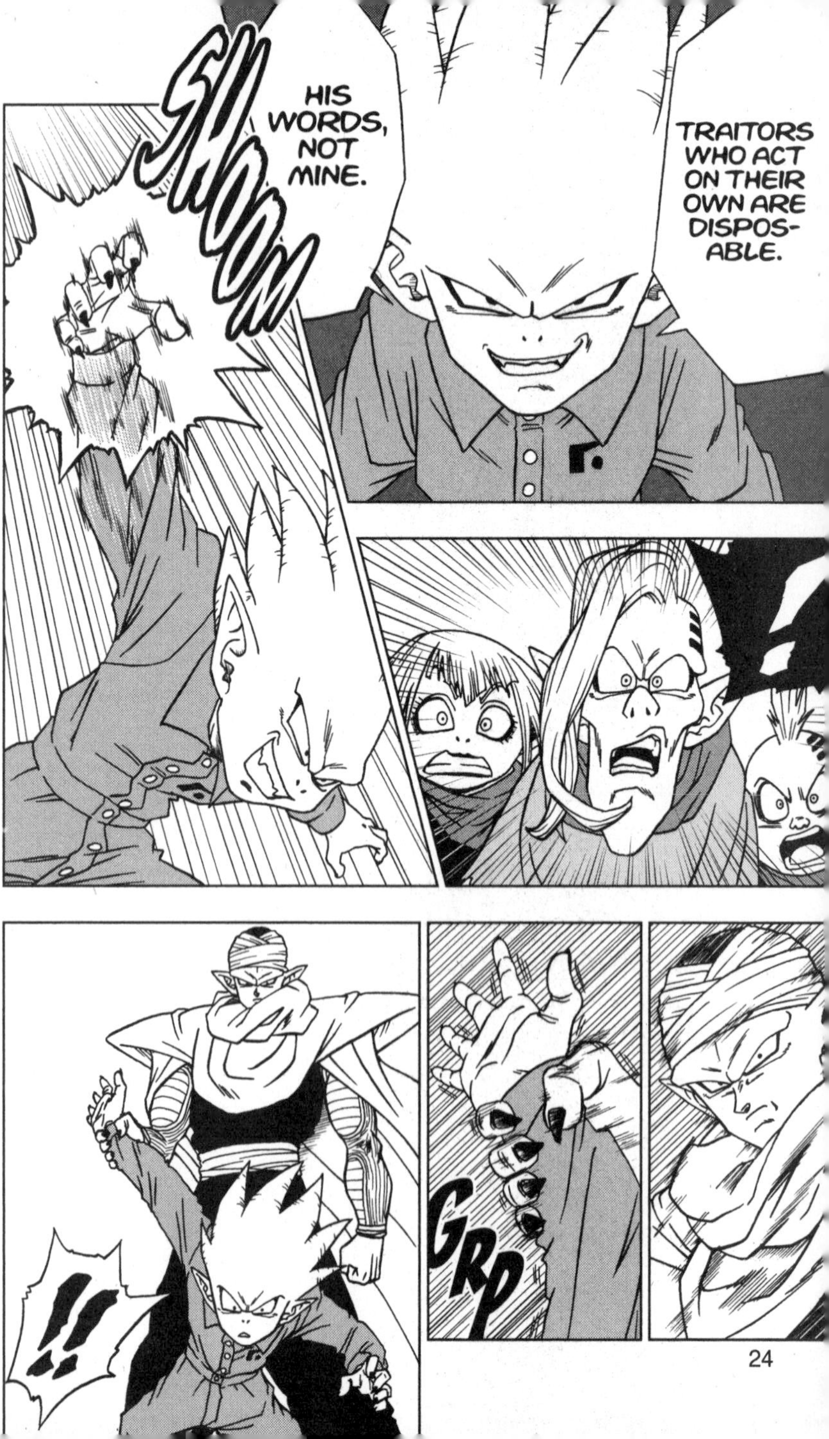

TRAITORS WHO ACT ON THEIR OWN ARE DISPOSABLE.
HIS WORDS, NOT MINE.
SHOOOM
GRP
!!

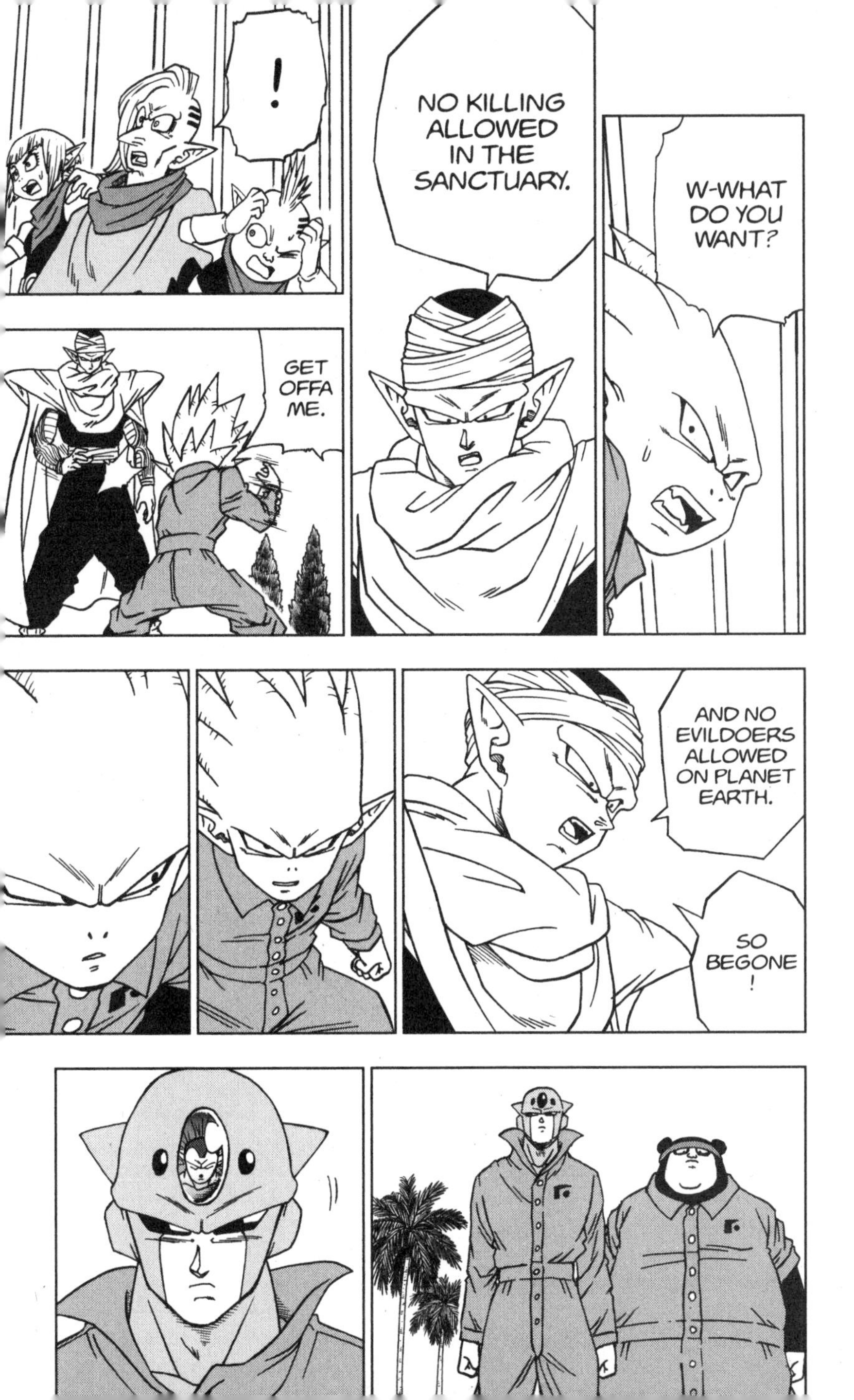
!
GET OFFA ME.
NO KILLING ALLOWED IN THE SANCTUARY.
W-WHAT DO YOU WANT?
AND NO EVILDOERS ALLOWED ON PLANET EARTH.
SO BEGONE !

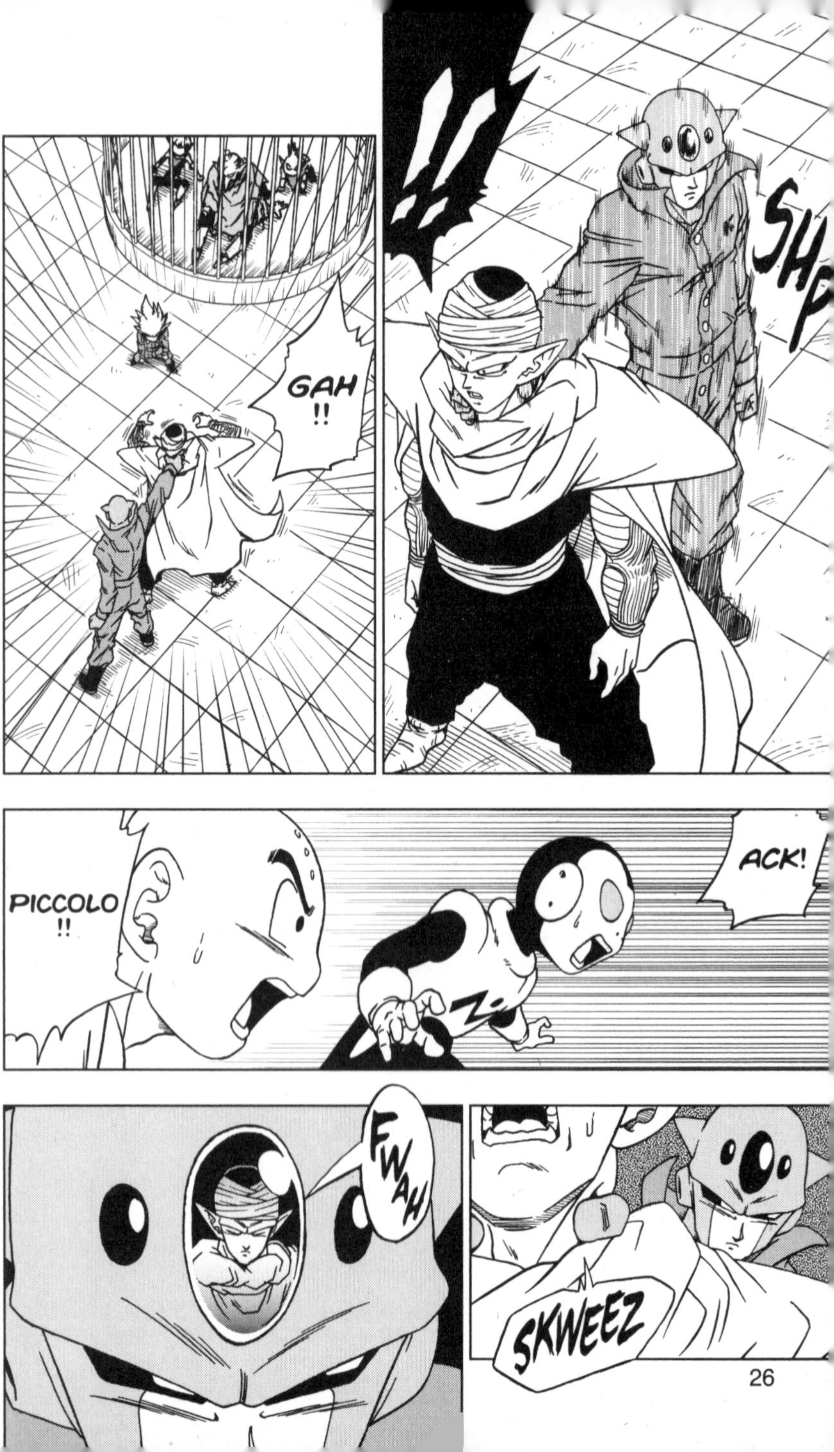
SHP
!!
GAH !!
ACK!
PICCOLO !!
SKWEEZ
FWAH

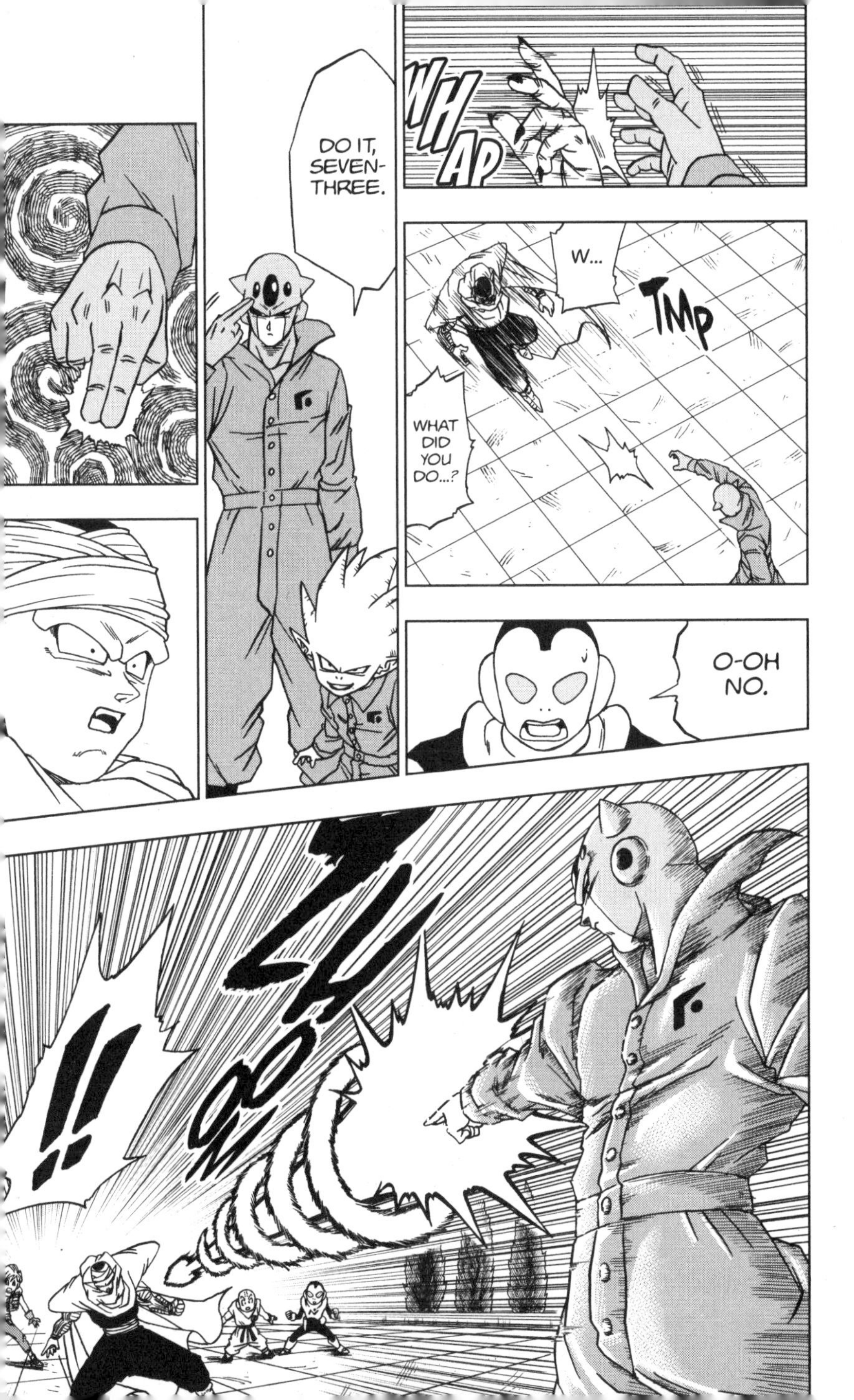
WHAP
W...
TMP
WHAT DID YOU DO...?
O-OH NO.
DO IT, SEVEN-THREE.
!!

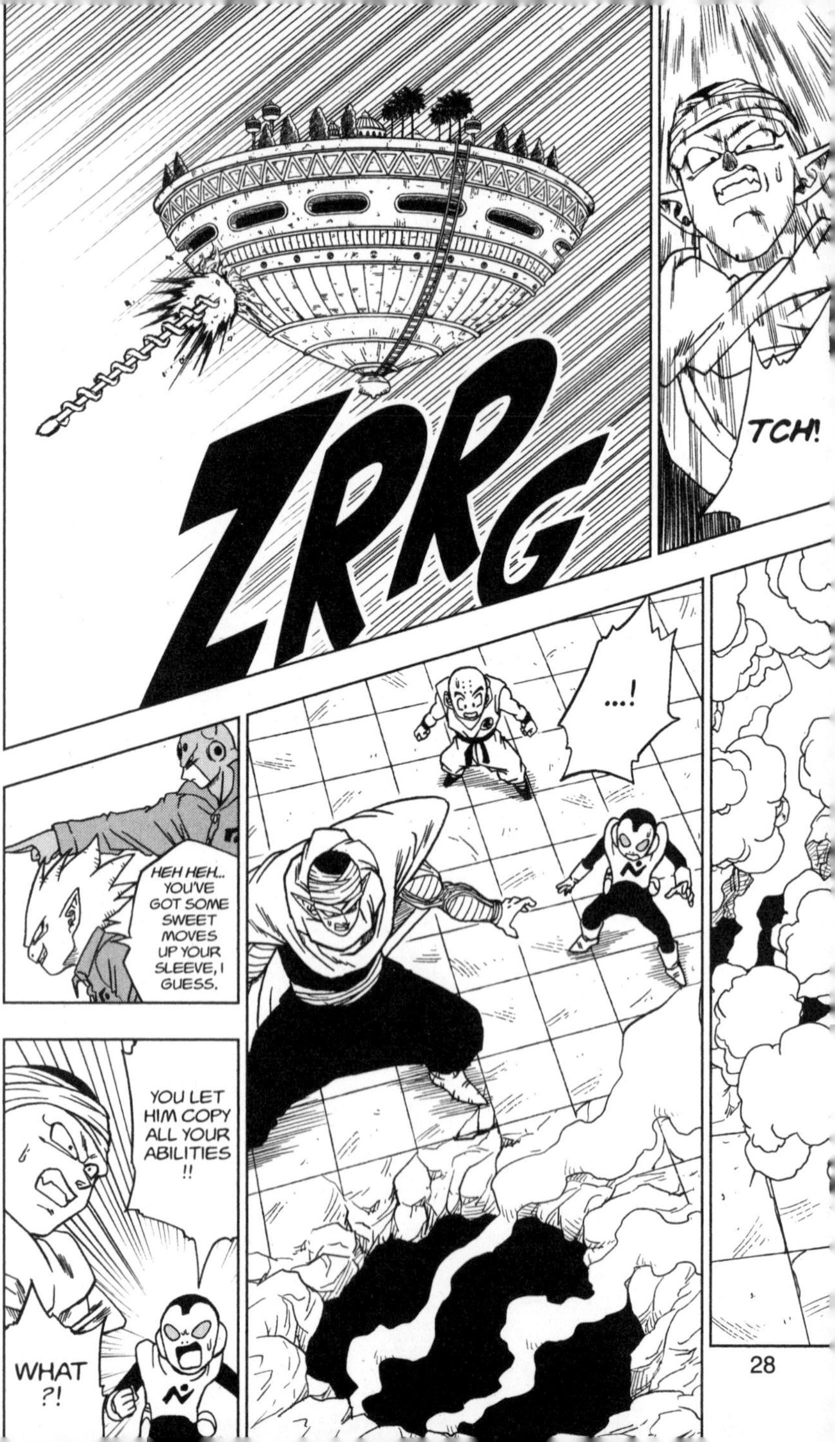
TCH!
ZRRG
...!
HEH HEH... YOU'VE GOT SOME SWEET MOVES UP YOUR SLEEVE, I GUESS.
YOU LET HIM COPY ALL YOUR ABILITIES !!
WHAT ?!

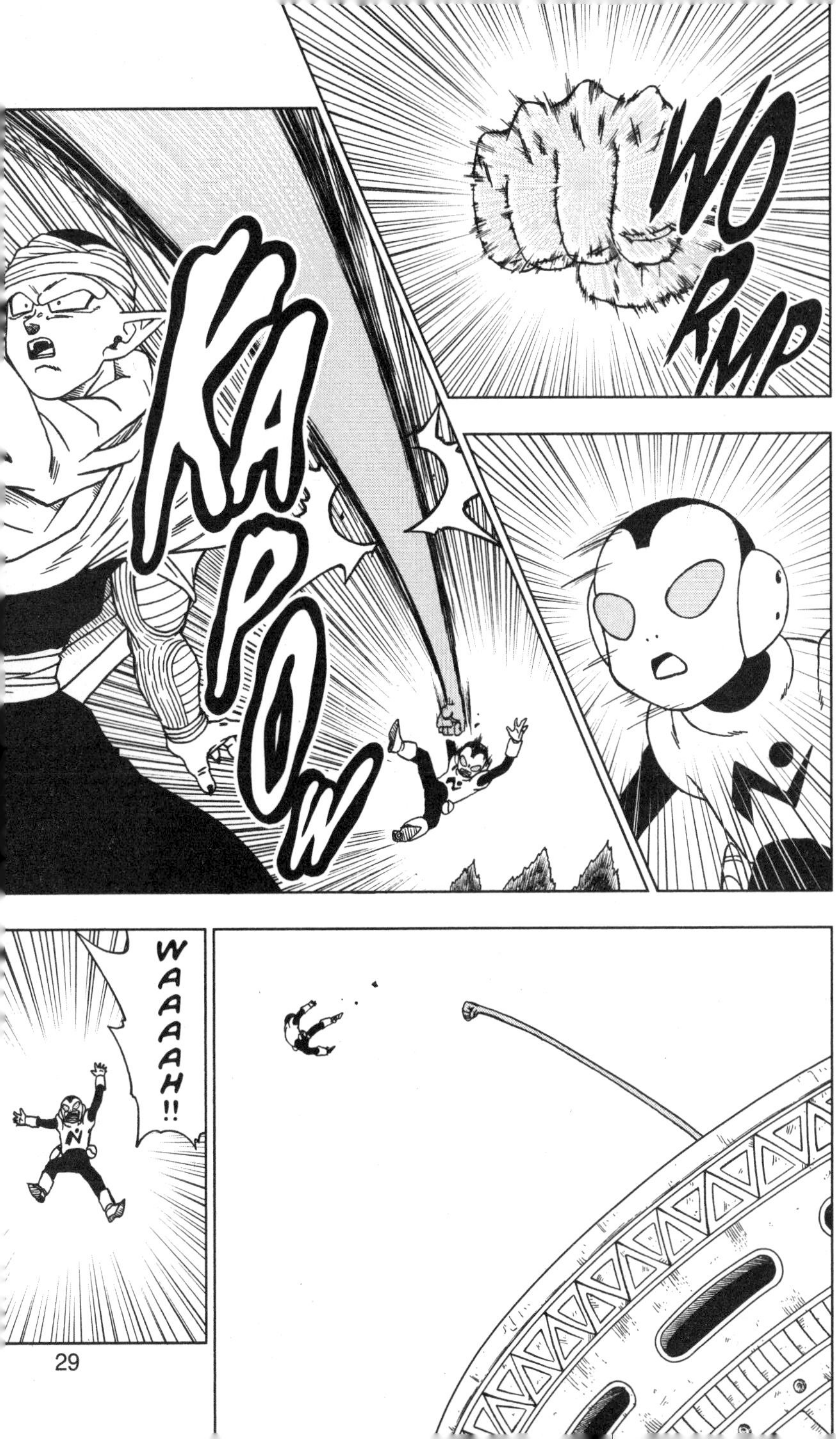
WORMP
KAPOW
WAAAAAH!!

JACO
!!

AFTER
THEM.

ZOOM

GRP

W-
WAIT
UP!

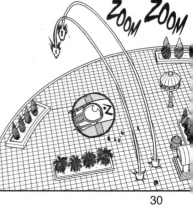

ZOOM ZOOM

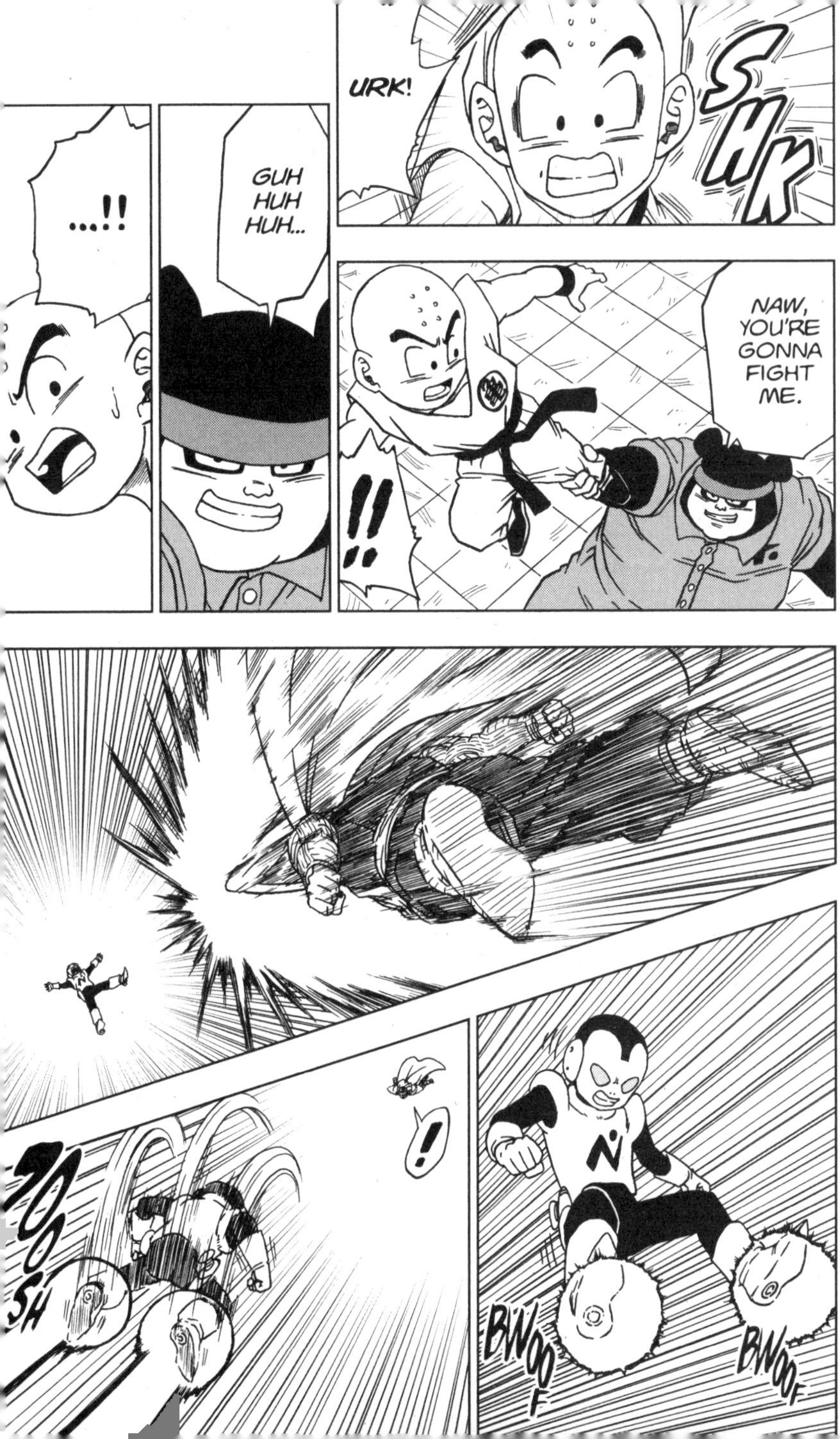
URK!
SHK
NAW, YOU'RE GONNA FIGHT ME.
!!
GUH HUH HUH...
...!!
BWOOF
BWOOF
!
WOOSH

FOR SHORT BURSTS, YEAH.

YOU COULD FLY ALL ALONG?

SKSHH

SORRY... THAT WAS SLOPPY.

YOU JUST *HAAAD* TO GO AND LET HIM GRAB YOU EVEN AFTER MY WARNING ABOUT HIS ABILITY?

TMP

TMP

MEANING, THAT ONE HE FIRED OFF WAS BASICALLY NO DIFFERENT THAN IF YOU'D DONE IT.

WELL, THE COPIED MOVES ARE JUST AS STRONG AS THE ORIGINALS.

BUT TELL ME HOW BEST TO FIGHT HIM.

RIGHT, I UNDERSTAND.

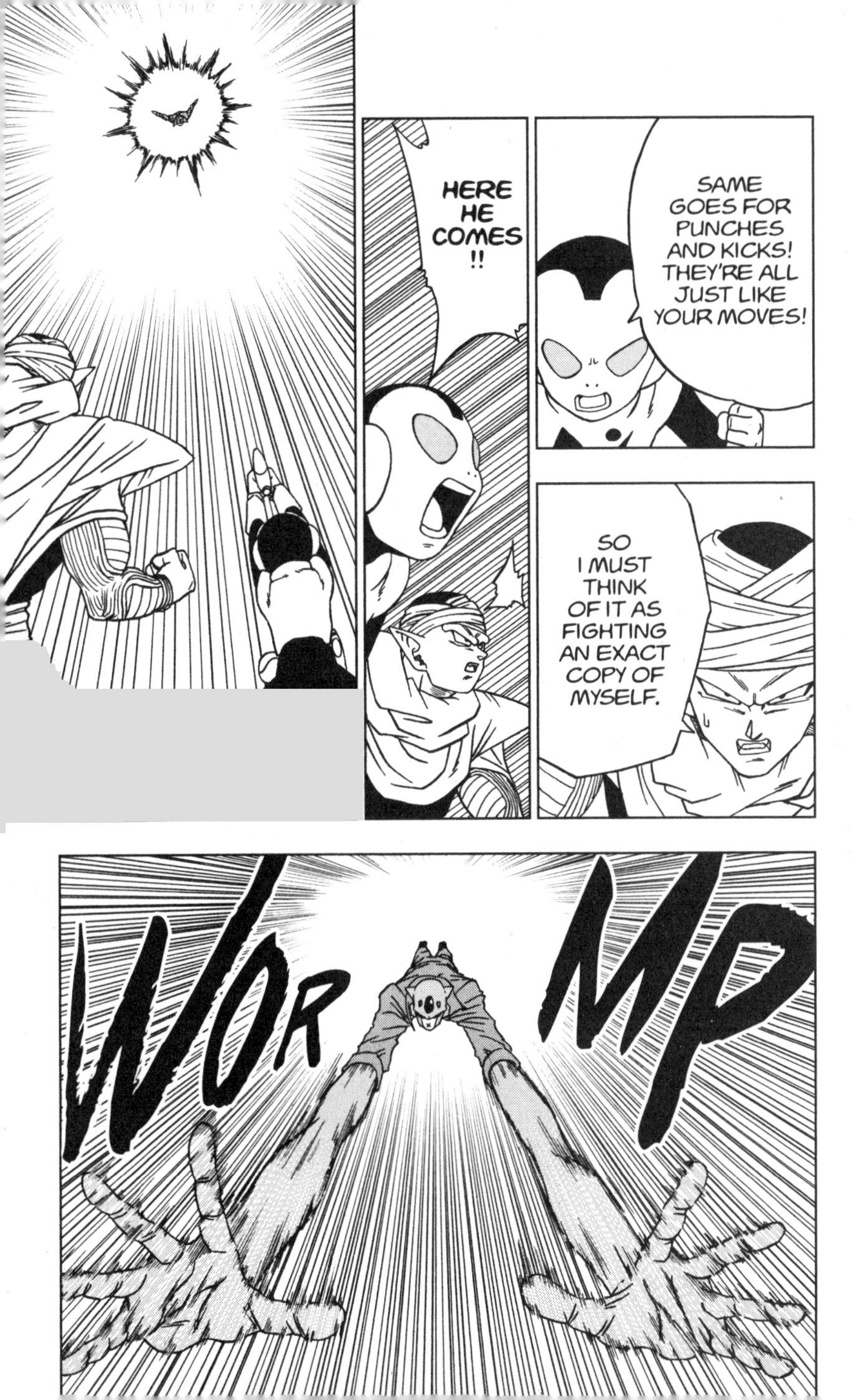
SAME GOES FOR PUNCHES AND KICKS! THEY'RE ALL JUST LIKE YOUR MOVES!
SO I MUST THINK OF IT AS FIGHTING AN EXACT COPY OF MYSELF.
HERE HE COMES!!
WORMP

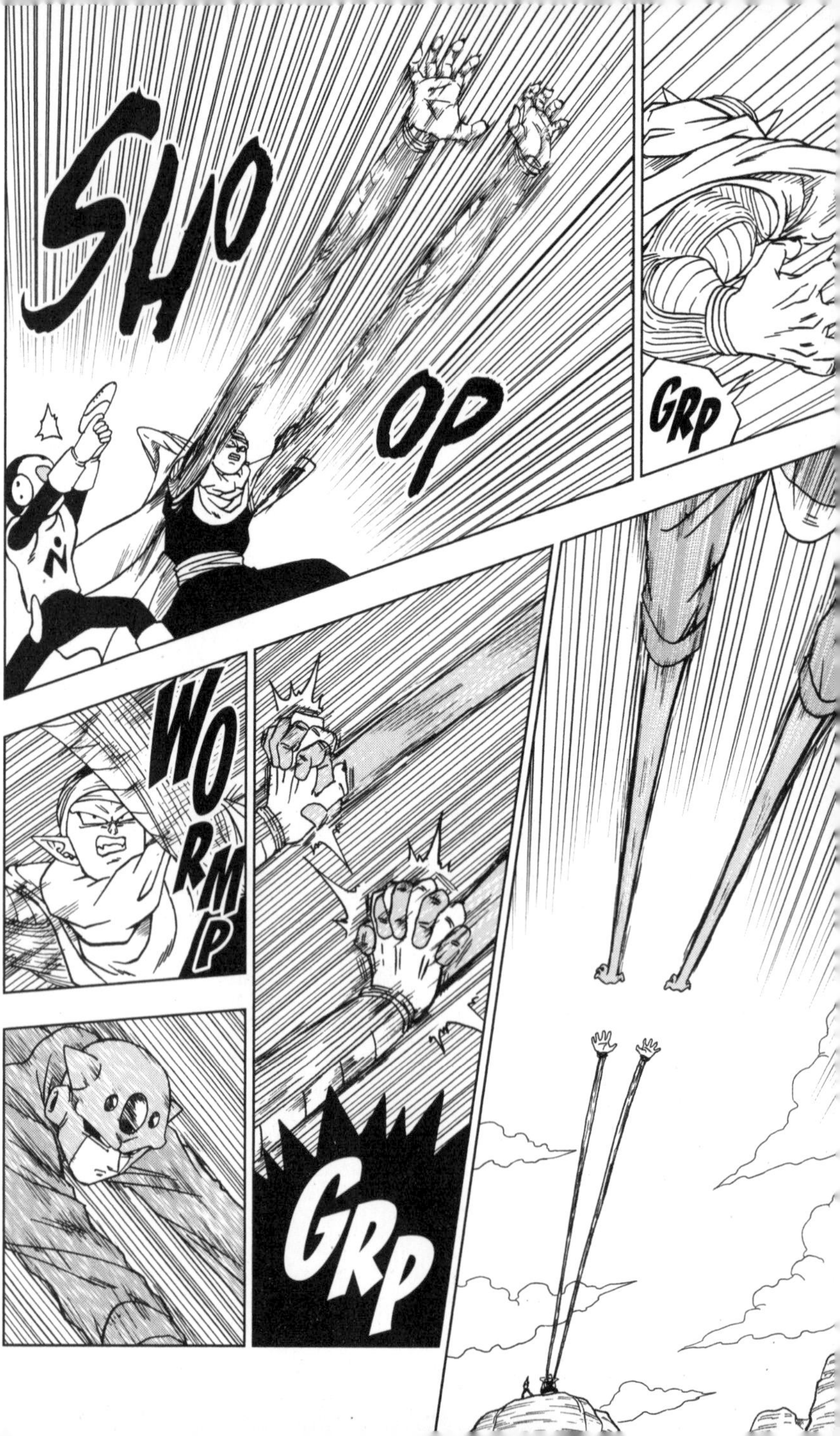
GRP
SHOOP
GRP
WORMP

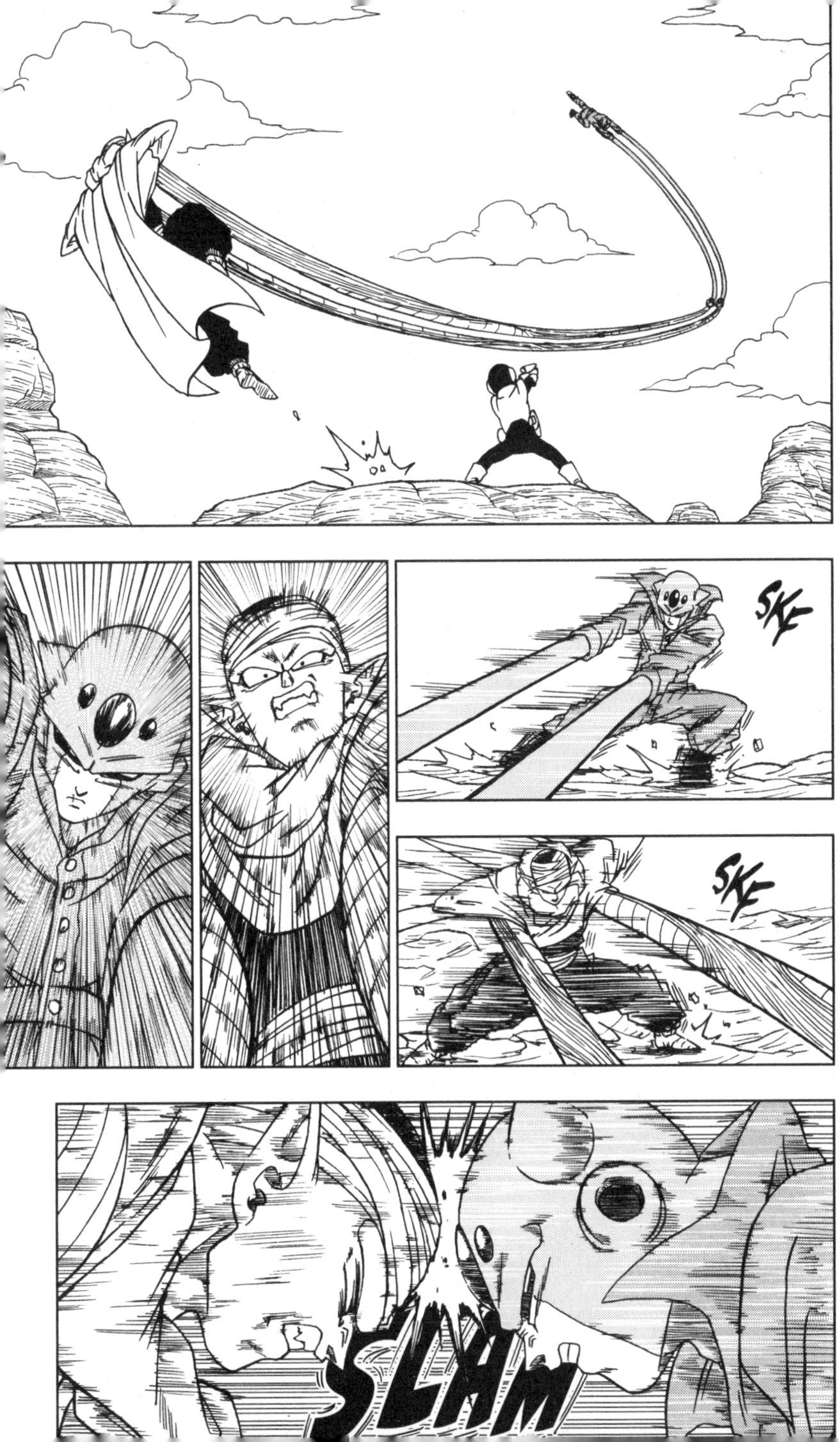
SKF
SKF
SLAM

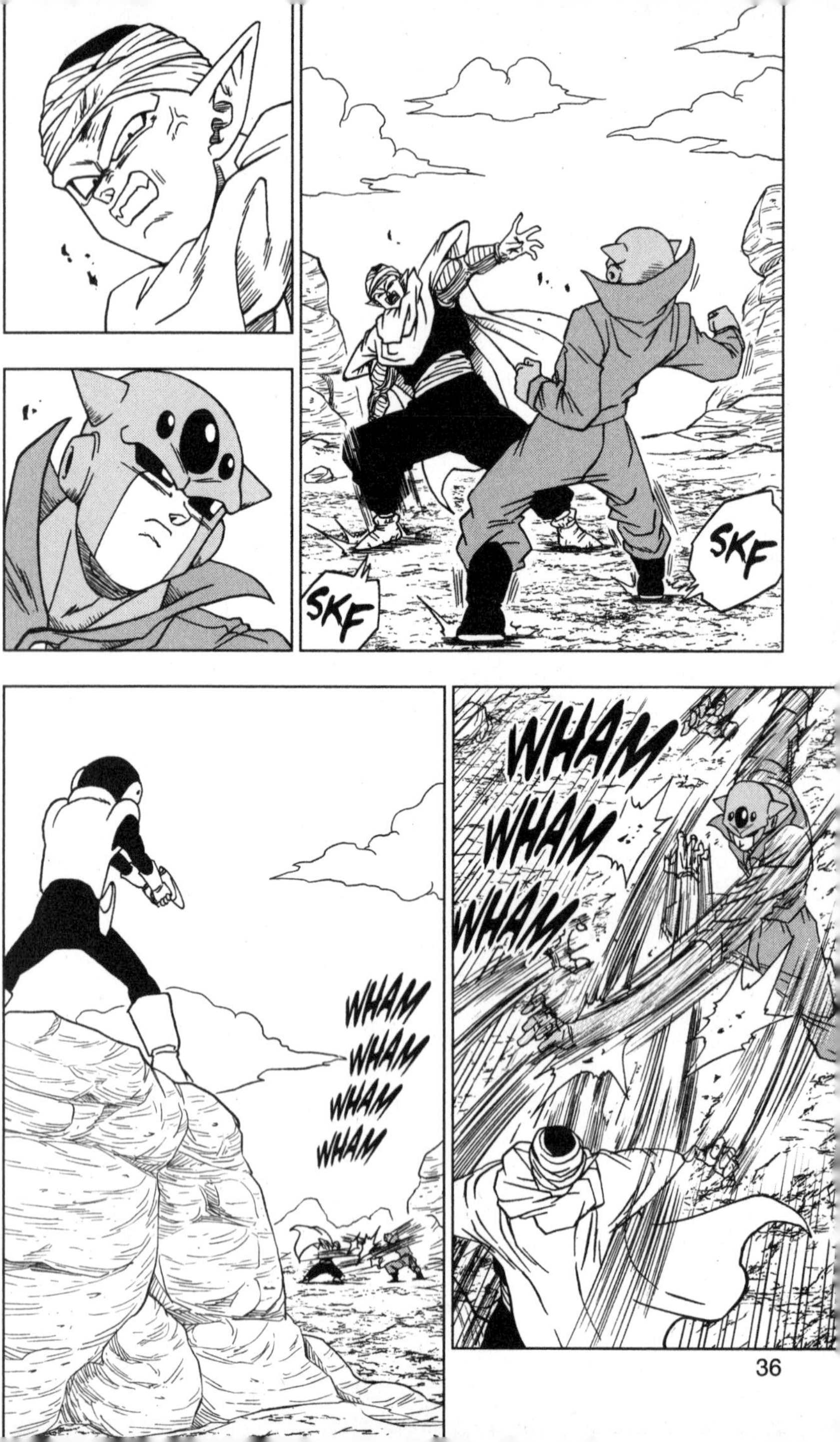
SKF
SKF
WHAM
WHAM
WHAM
WHAM
WHAM
WHAM
WHAM

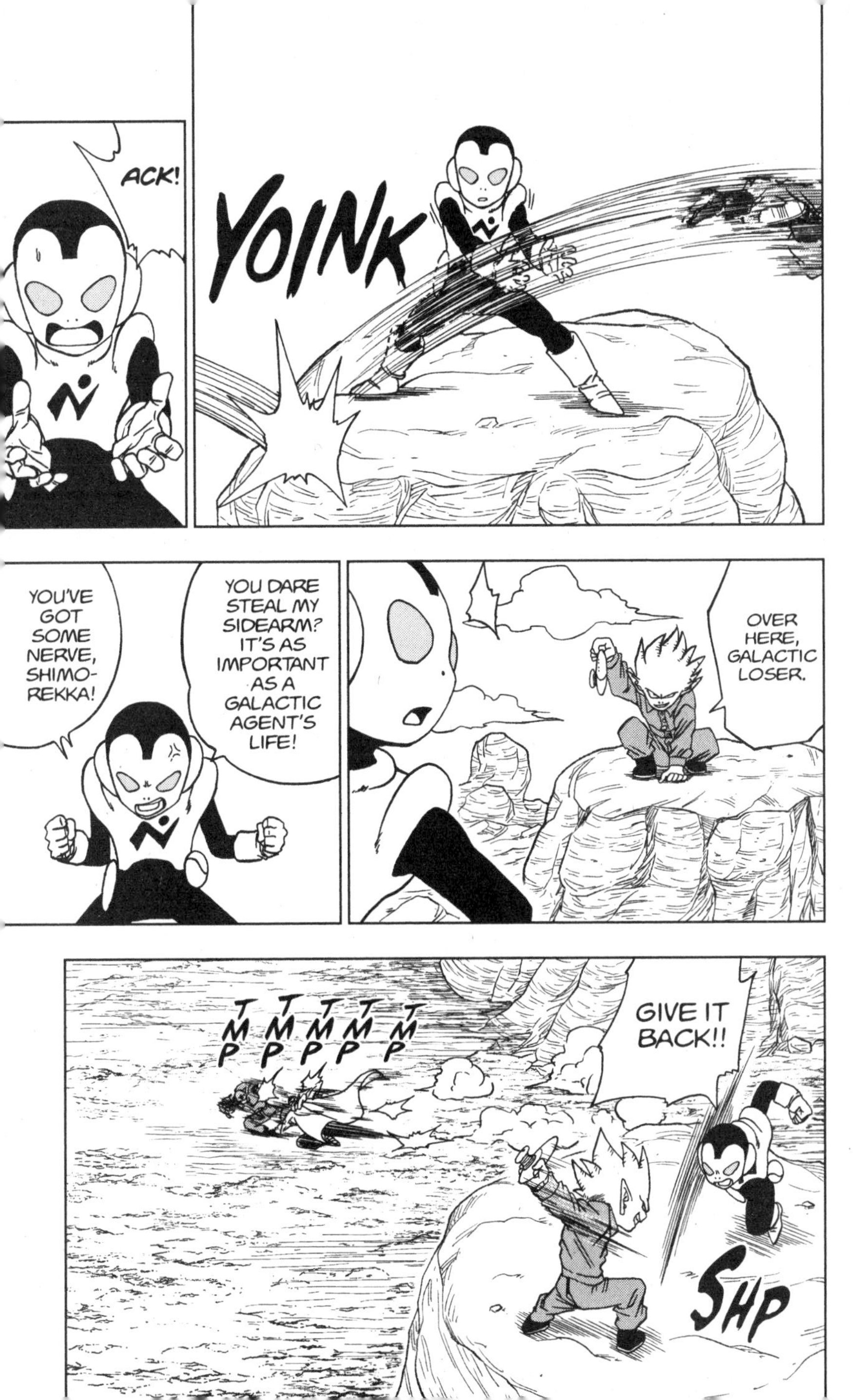
YOINK
ACK!
OVER HERE, GALACTIC LOSER.
YOU DARE STEAL MY SIDEARM? IT'S AS IMPORTANT AS A GALACTIC AGENT'S LIFE!
YOU'VE GOT SOME NERVE, SHIMO-REKKA!
GIVE IT BACK!!
TMP TMP TMP TMP TMP TMP
SHP

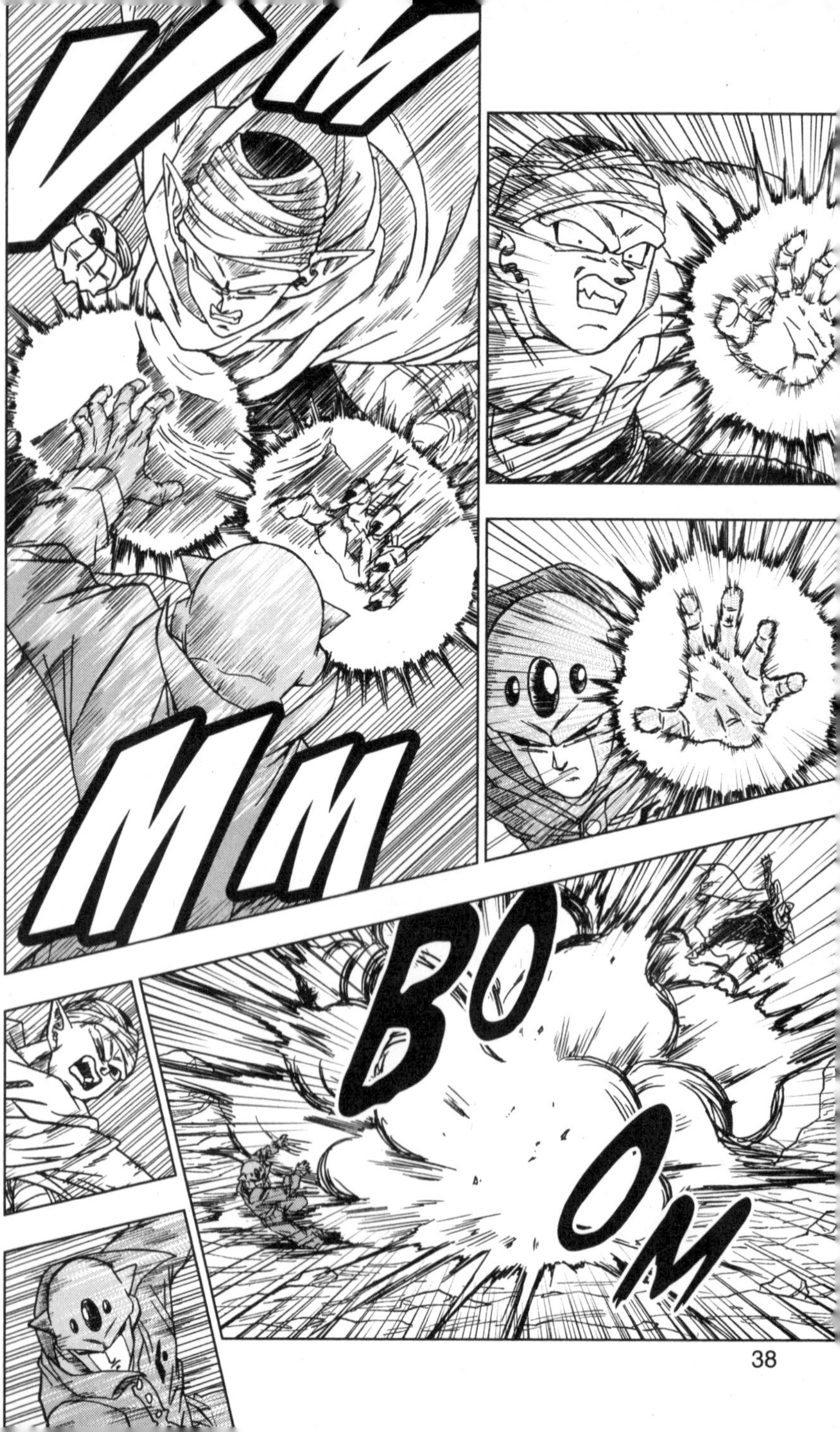
MM
BOOM

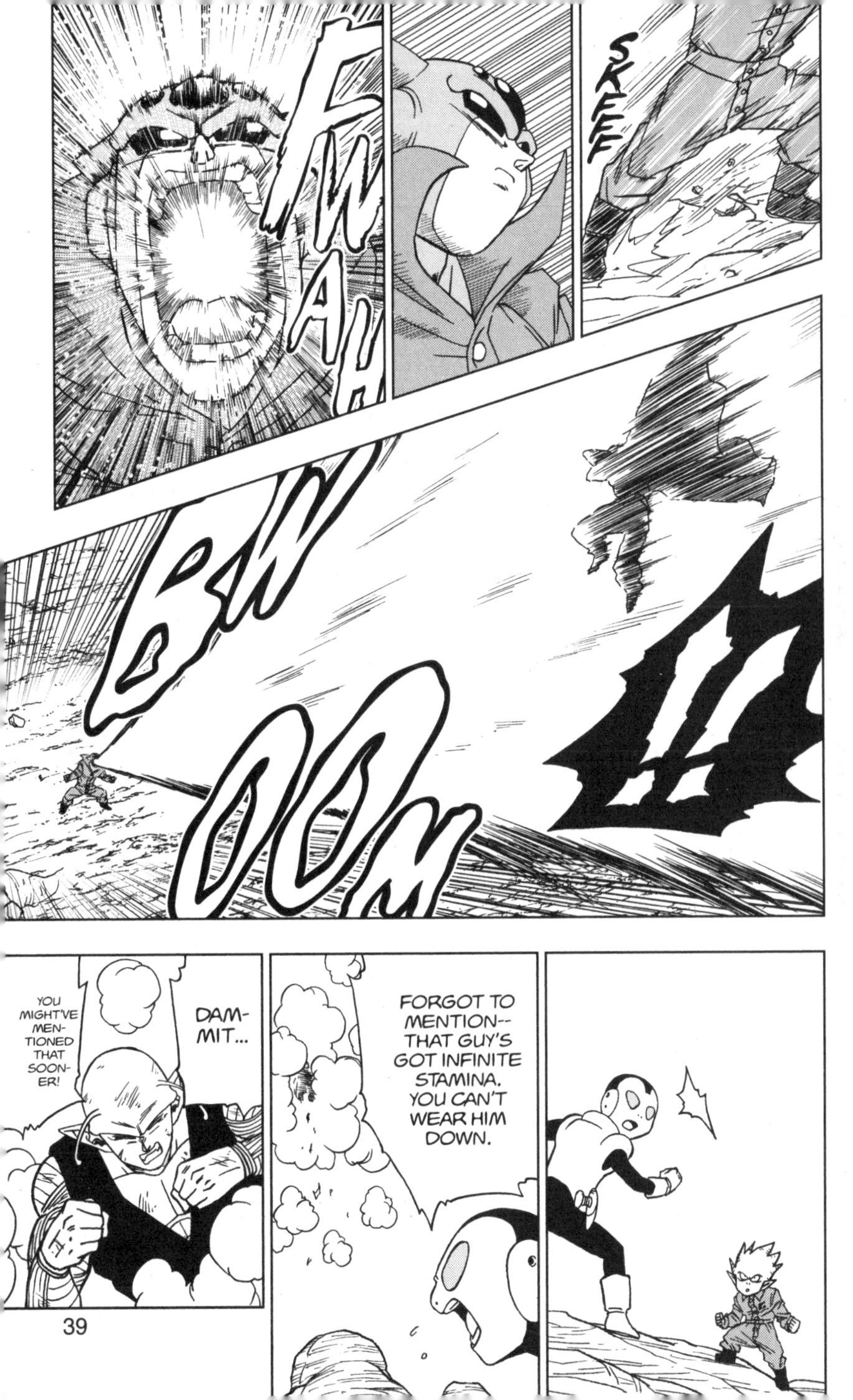
SKEFF
FWAAH
BWOOM
FORGOT TO MENTION-- THAT GUY'S GOT INFINITE STAMINA. YOU CAN'T WEAR HIM DOWN.
DAM-MIT...
YOU MIGHT'VE MEN-TIONED THAT SOON-ER!

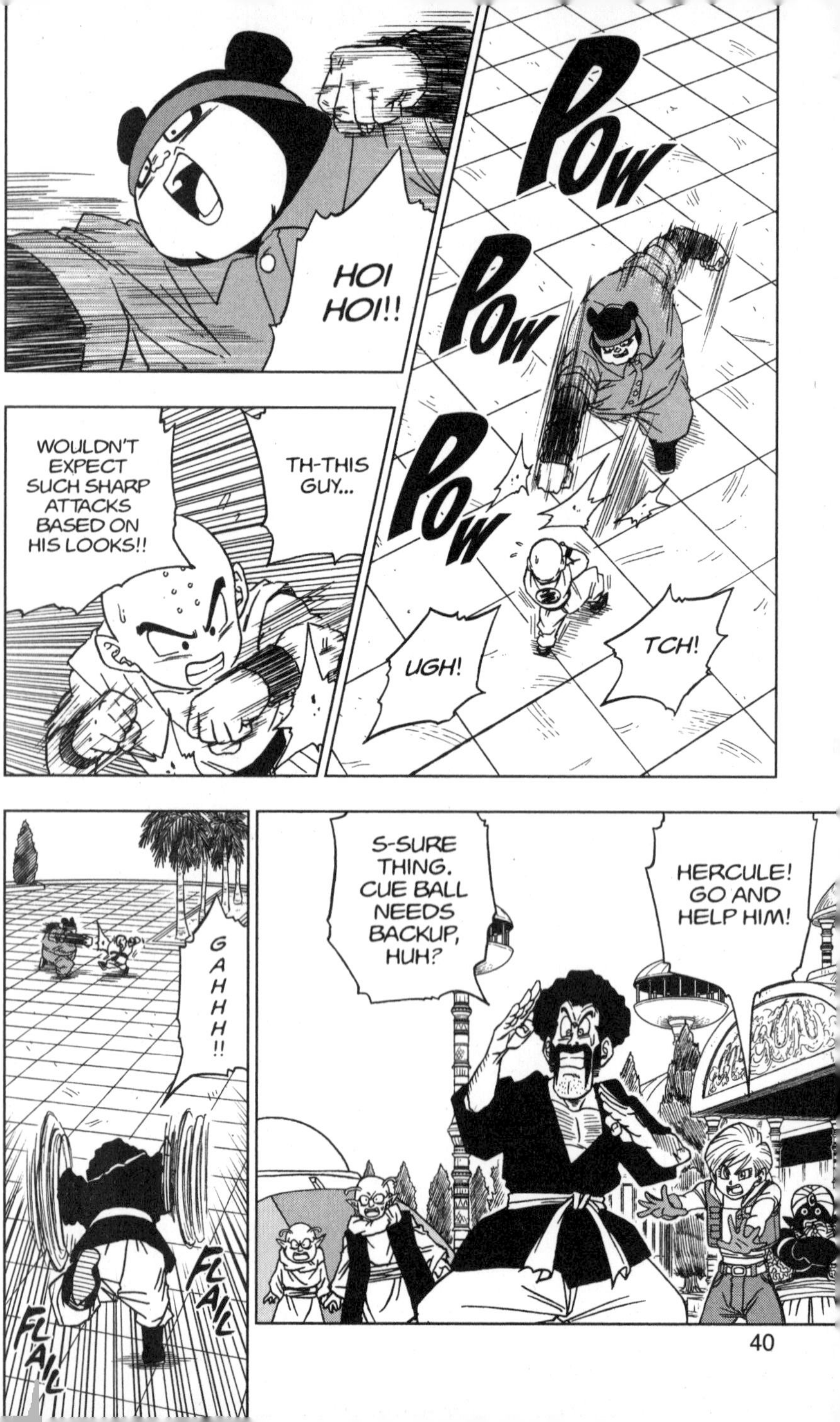
POW
POW
POW
TCH!
UGH!
HOI HOI!!
TH-THIS GUY...
WOULDN'T EXPECT SUCH SHARP ATTACKS BASED ON HIS LOOKS!!
HERCULE! GO AND HELP HIM!
S-SURE THING. CUE BALL NEEDS BACKUP, HUH?
GAHHH!!
FLAIL
FLAIL

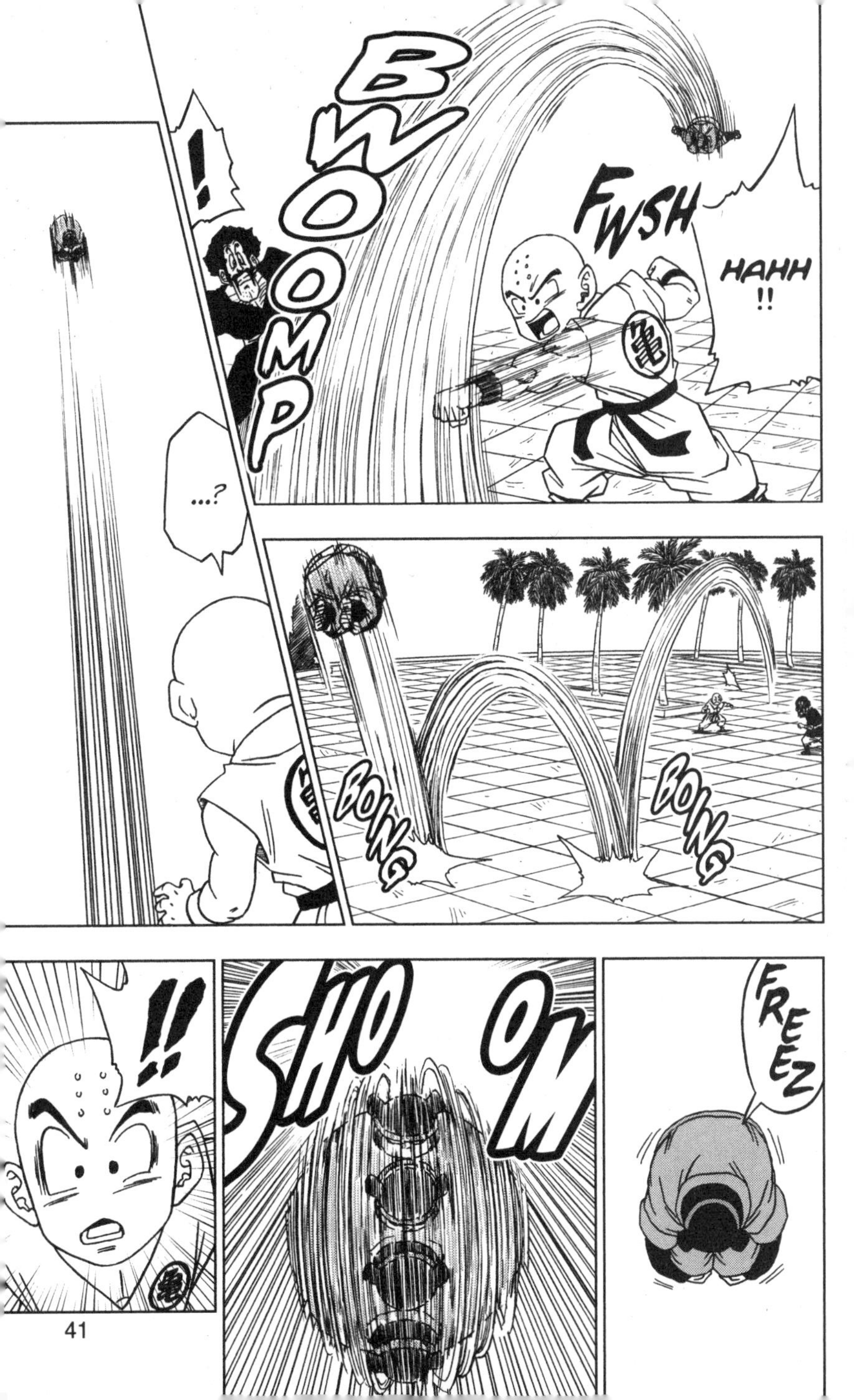
FWSH
HAHH!!
BWOOMP
!
BOING
BOING
...?
FREEZ
SHOOM
!!

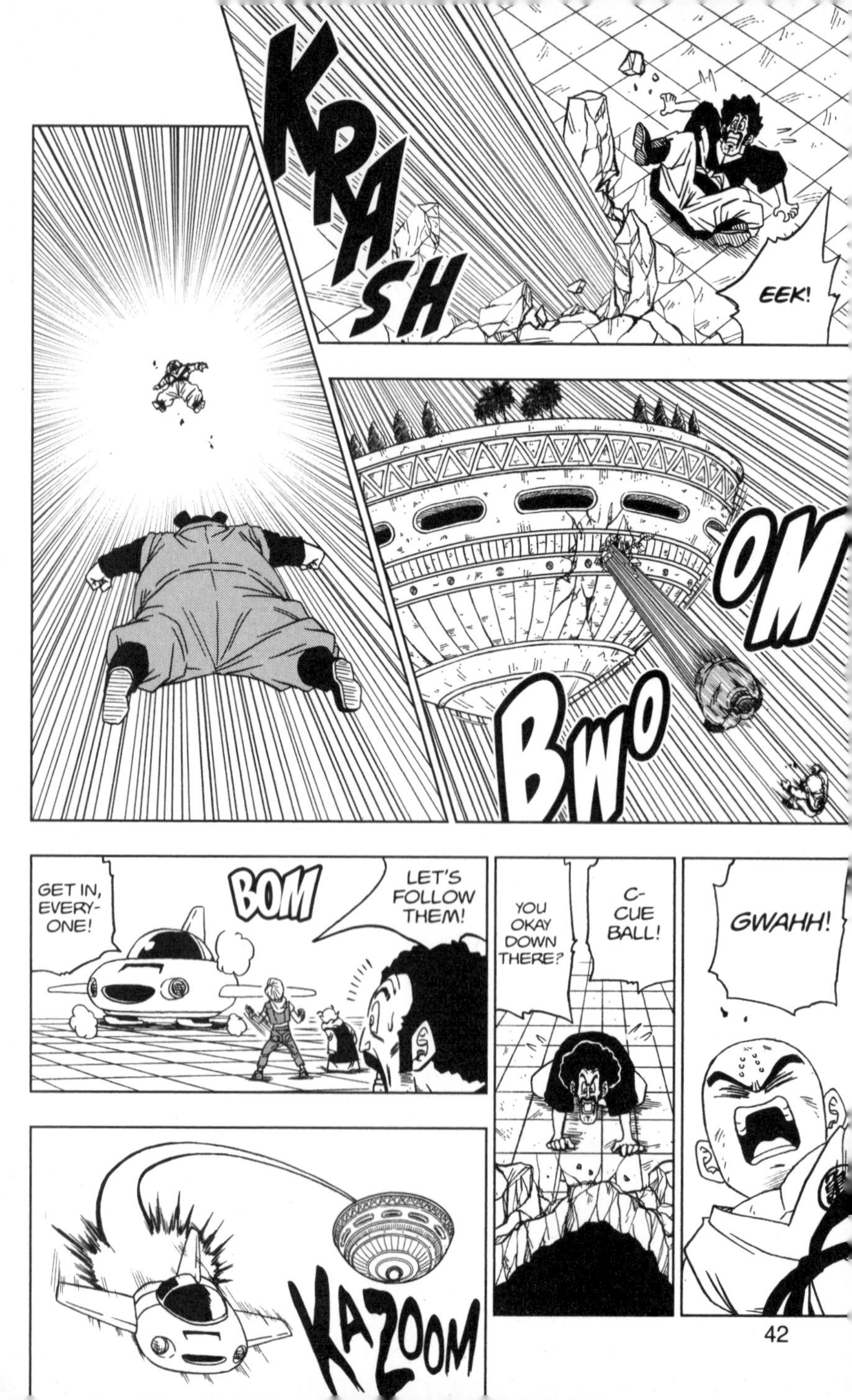
KRASH
EEK!
BWOOM
GWAHH!
C- CUE BALL!
YOU OKAY DOWN THERE?
LET'S FOLLOW THEM!
BOM
GET IN, EVERY-ONE!
KAZOOM

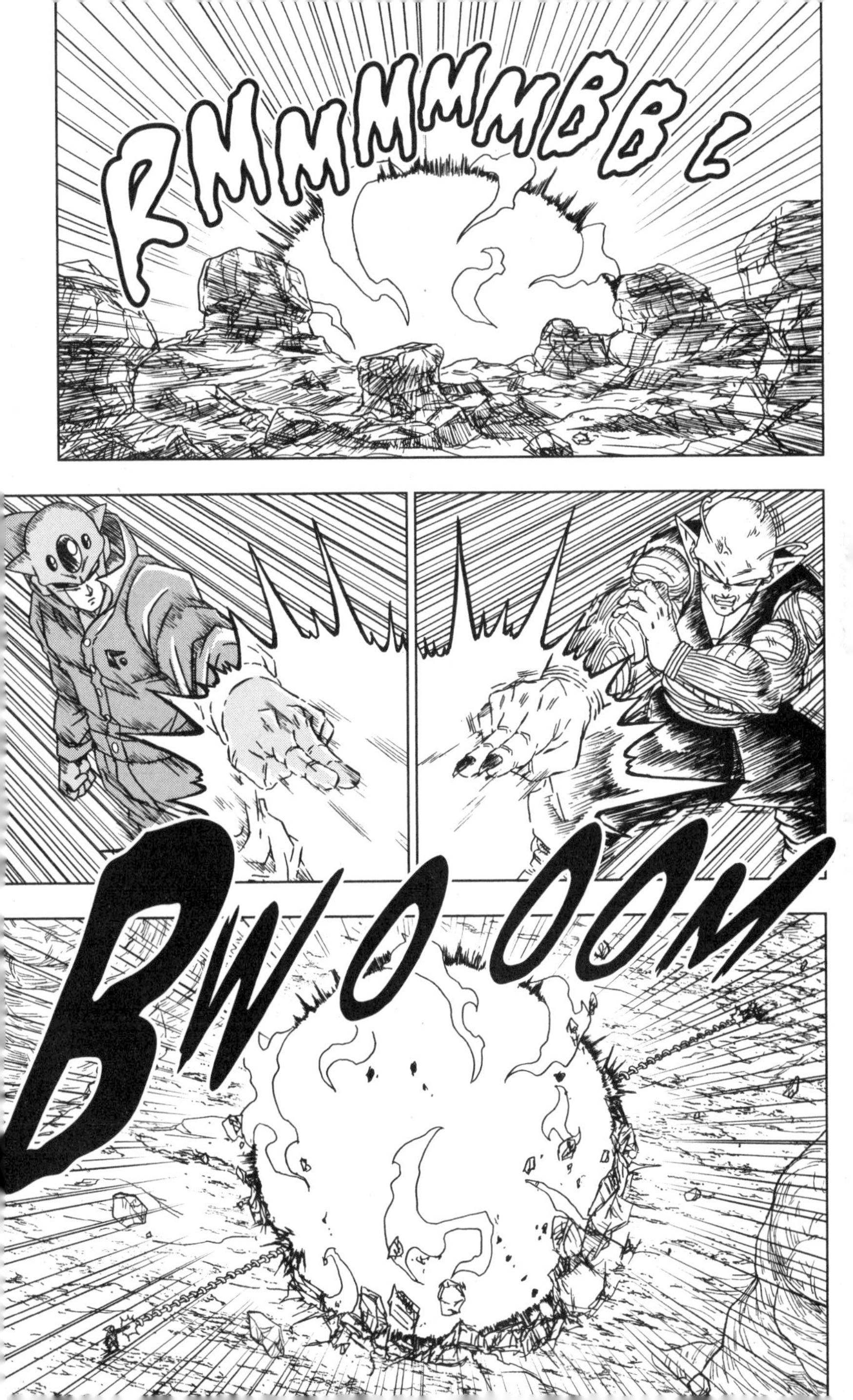
RMMMMMBBL
BWOOOM

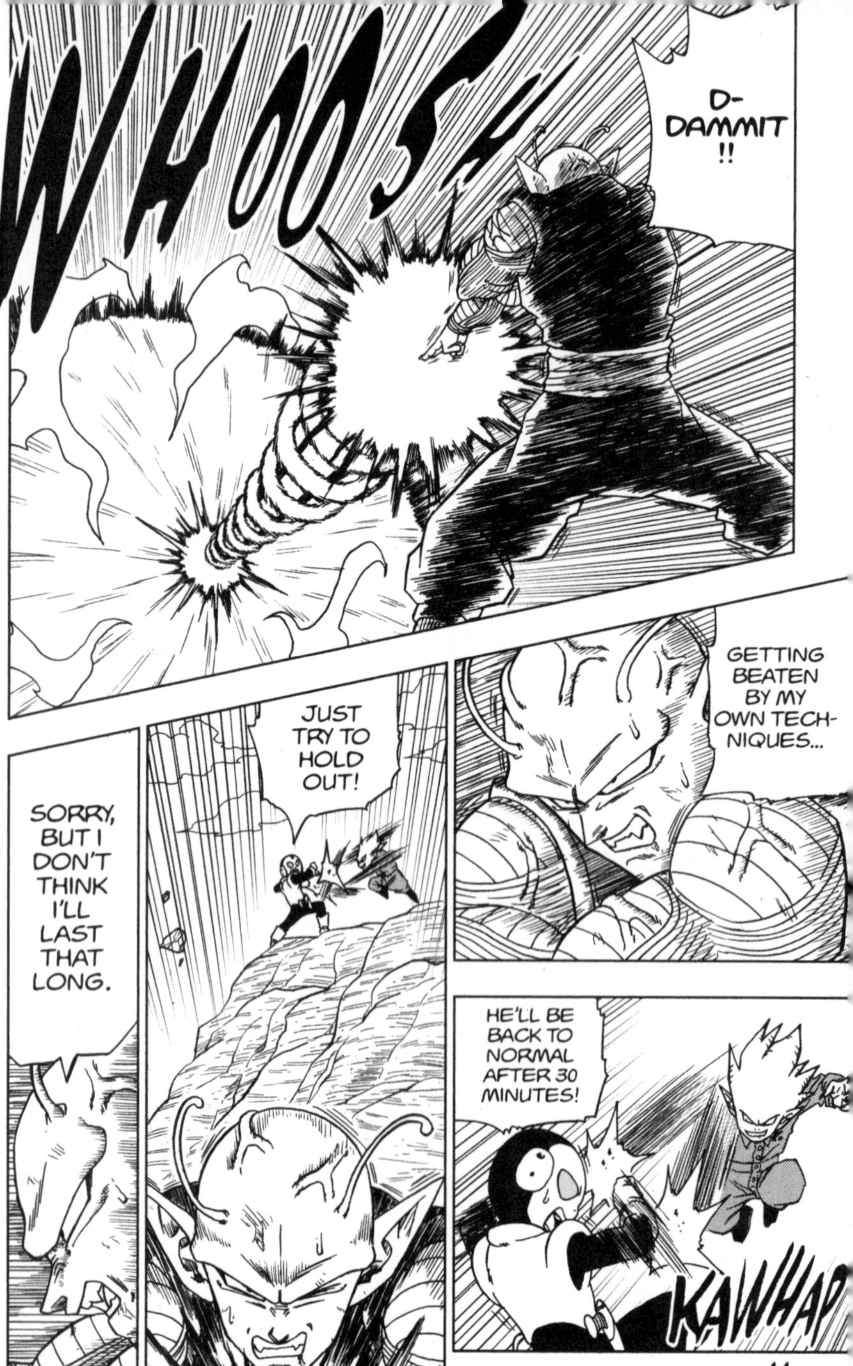
WHOOSH
D-DAMMIT!!
GETTING BEATEN BY MY OWN TECHNIQUES...
HE'LL BE BACK TO NORMAL AFTER 30 MINUTES!
KAWHAP
JUST TRY TO HOLD OUT!
SORRY, BUT I DON'T THINK I'LL LAST THAT LONG.

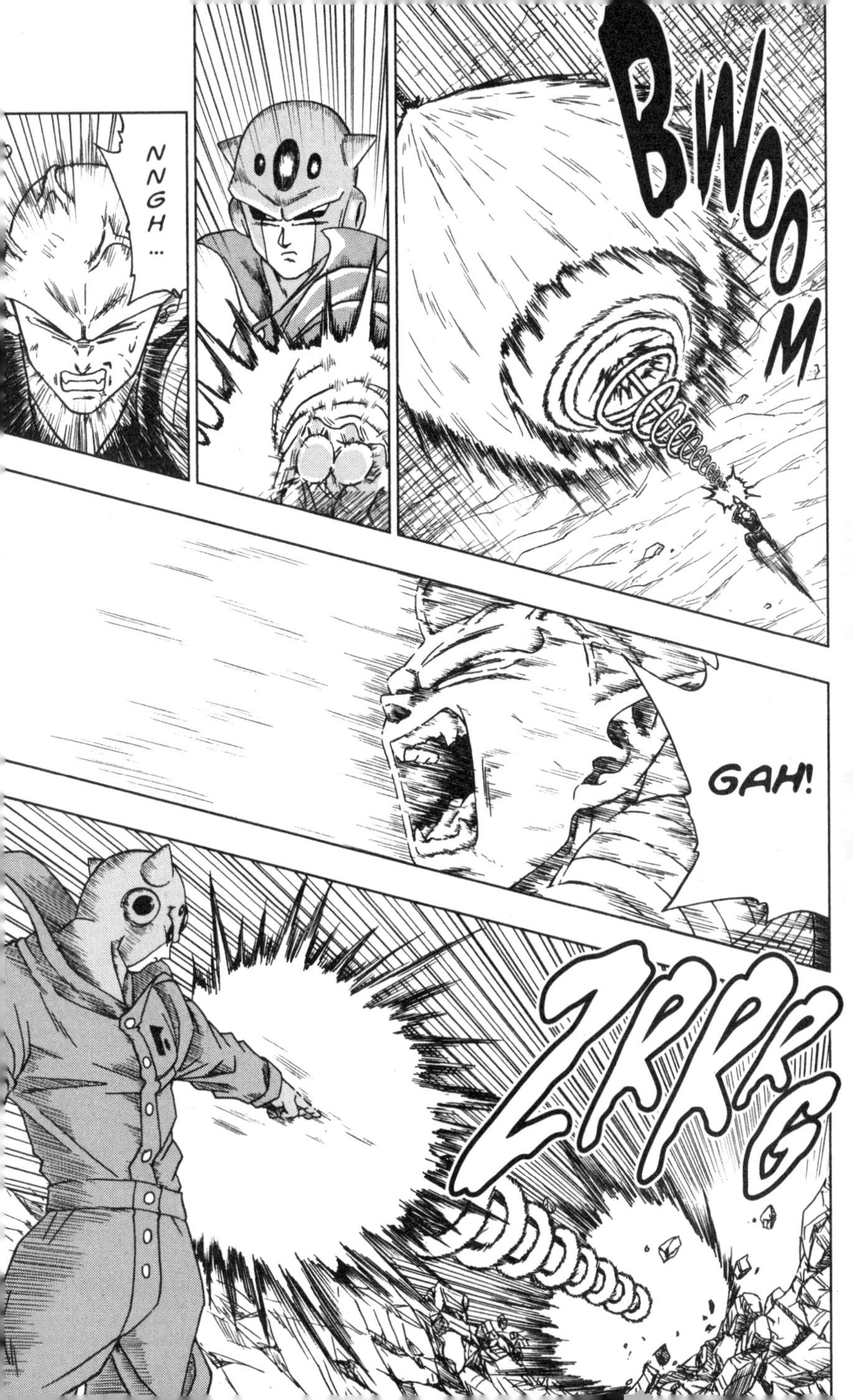
BWOOM
NNGH...
GAH!
ZPPPG

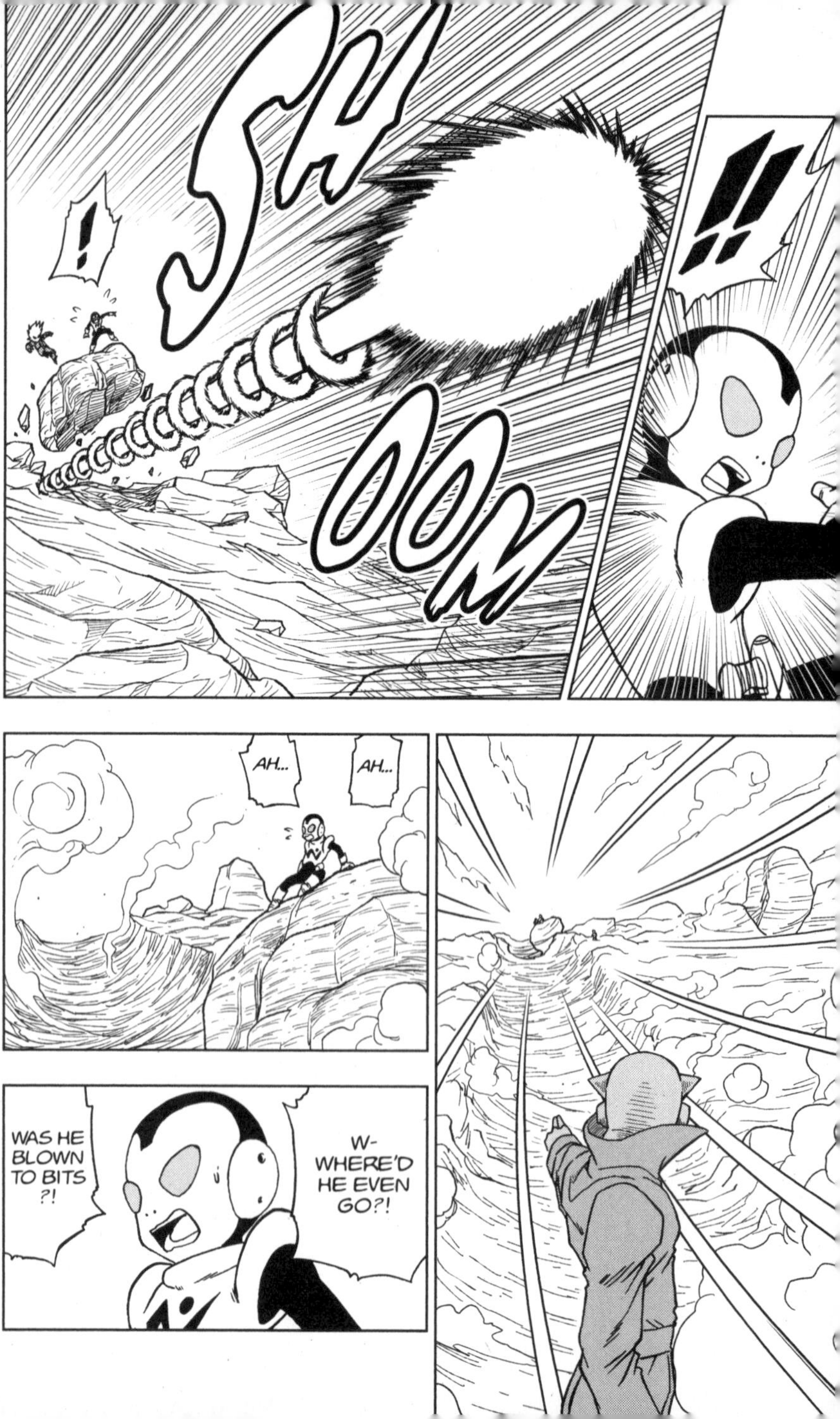
!!
!
SHOOM
AH...
AH...
W- WHERE'D HE EVEN GO?!
WAS HE BLOWN TO BITS ?!

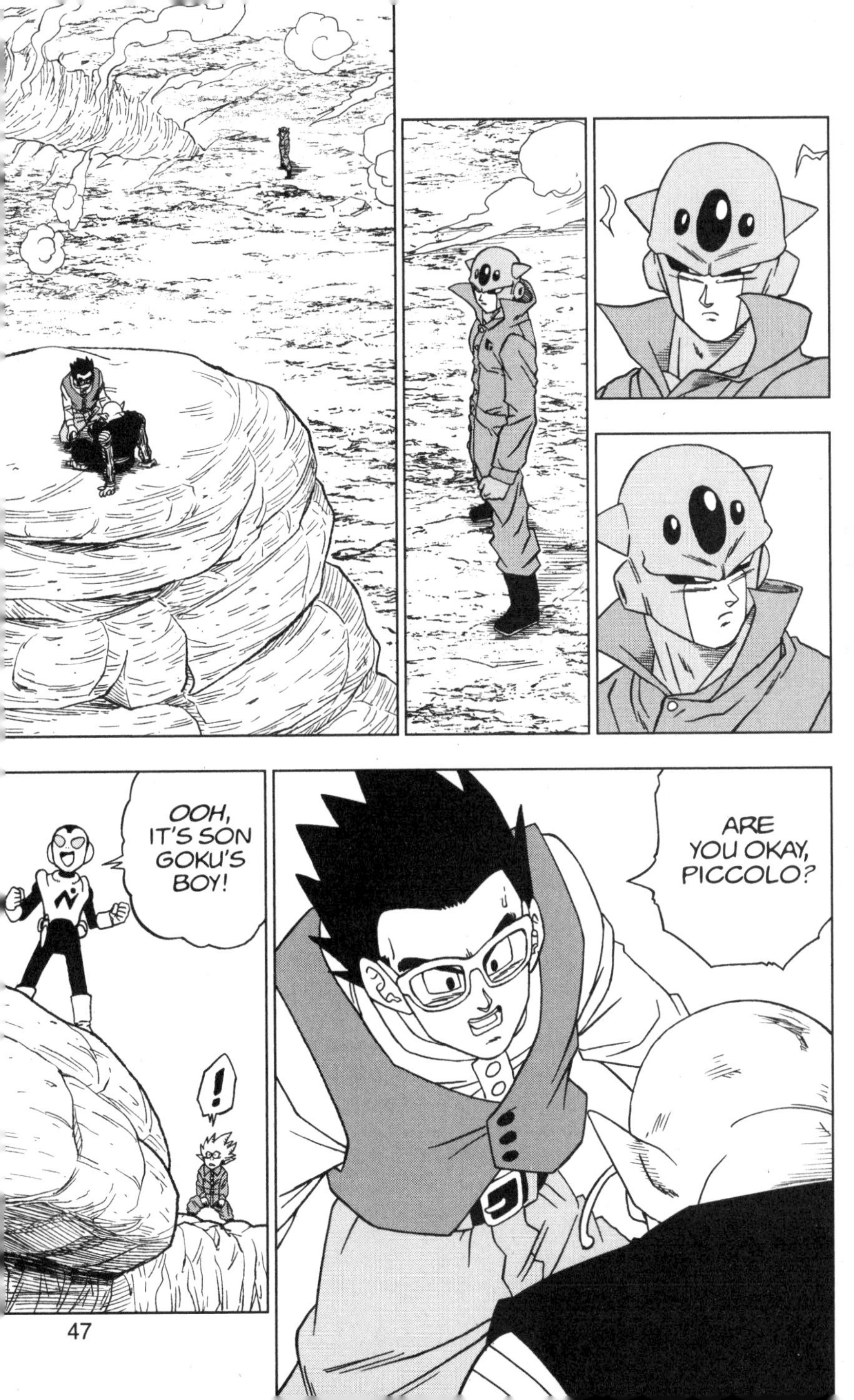
ARE YOU OKAY, PICCOLO?
OOH, IT'S SON GOKU'S BOY!
!

...

BUT WHAT'S GOING ON? WHO ARE THOSE GUYS ?!

I'M SORRY I'M SO LATE.

THANKS FOR THE SAVE, GOHAN.

SO MY DAD AND VEGETA MUST BE OFF WORLD?

RIGHT NOW, YOU'RE THE STRONGEST FIGHTER WE'VE GOT ON EARTH.

COPY ?!

I'LL SAVE THE LONG VERSION FOR LATER. FOR NOW, GOHAN, JUST DON'T LET THAT ONE GRAB YOU BY THE NECK, OR ELSE HE'LL COPY YOUR POWERS.

FAR, FAR FROM EARTH, ON AN UN-INHABITED PLANET

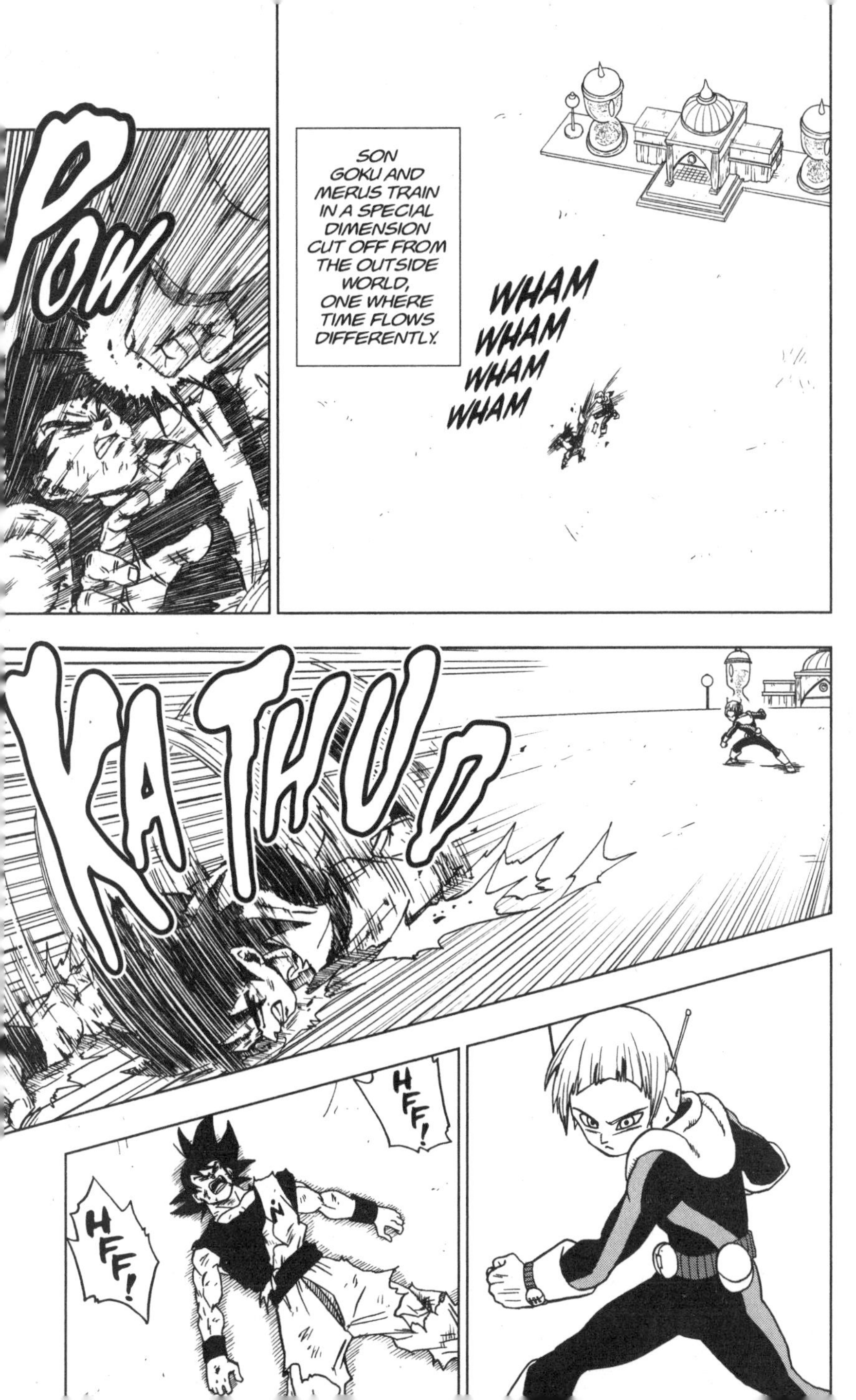
SON GOKU AND MERUS TRAIN IN A SPECIAL DIMENSION CUT OFF FROM THE OUTSIDE WORLD, ONE WHERE TIME FLOWS DIFFERENTLY.
WHAM WHAM WHAM WHAM
POW
KA THUD
HFF!
HFF!

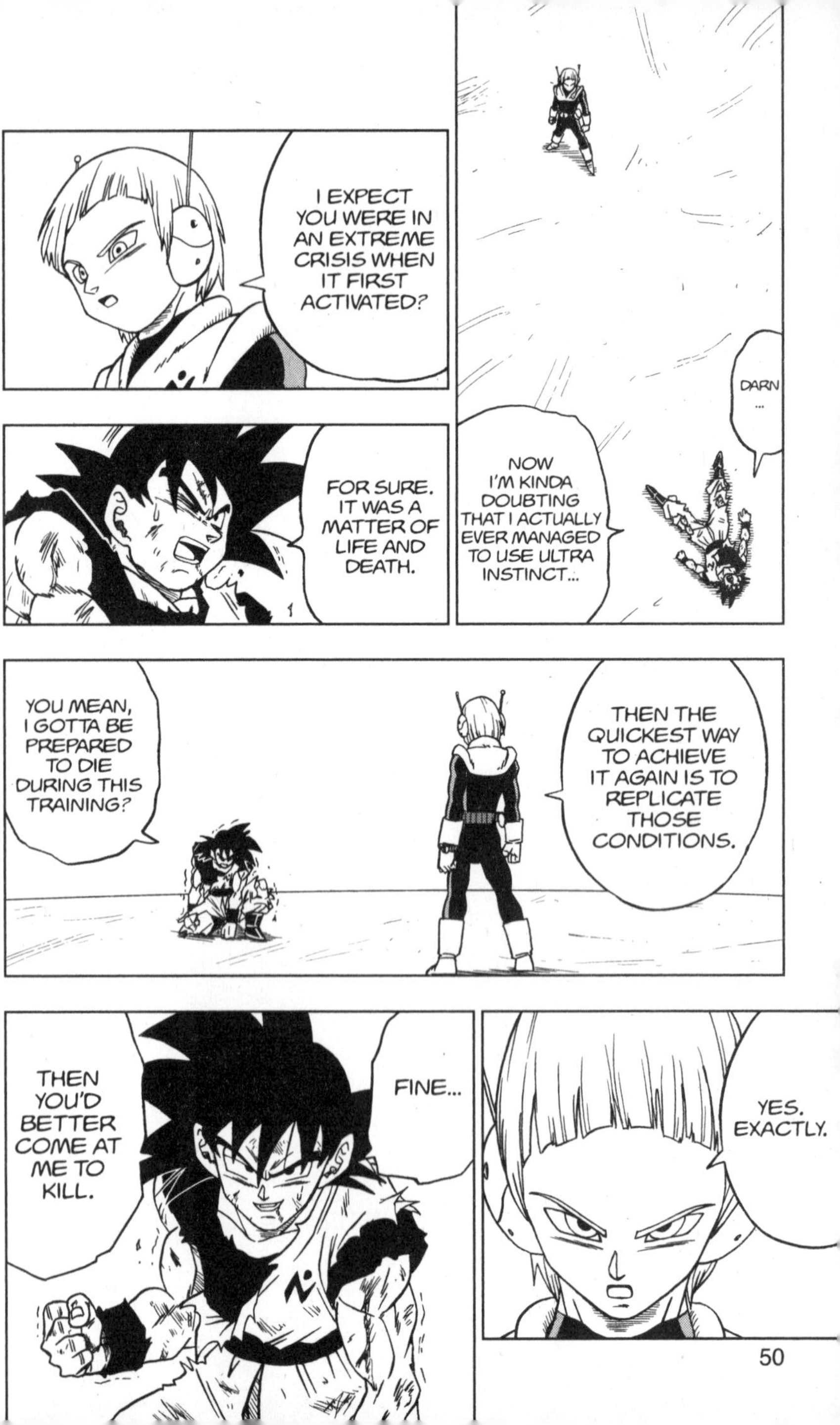
DARN...
NOW I'M KINDA DOUBTING THAT I ACTUALLY EVER MANAGED TO USE ULTRA INSTINCT...
I EXPECT YOU WERE IN AN EXTREME CRISIS WHEN IT FIRST ACTIVATED?
FOR SURE. IT WAS A MATTER OF LIFE AND DEATH.
THEN THE QUICKEST WAY TO ACHIEVE IT AGAIN IS TO REPLICATE THOSE CONDITIONS.
YOU MEAN, I GOTTA BE PREPARED TO DIE DURING THIS TRAINING?
YES. EXACTLY.
FINE...
THEN YOU'D BETTER COME AT ME TO KILL.

PLANET YARDRAT

I'M STARTING TO REGRET EVER COMING TO THIS ROCK...

DAMMIT...

FIRST, YOU MUST ACHIEVE BALANCE IN BODY AND MIND.

YOUR SPIRIT IS EVEN LESS STABLE THAN GOKU'S WAS.

HEY... HOW MANY MORE DAYS OF THIS?

YOUR BALANCE IS ALL DISRUPTED, AGAIN.

UGH... GRR...

BY THE WAY, GOKU WAS UP THERE FOR 150 DAYS.

FOR 150 DAYS?!

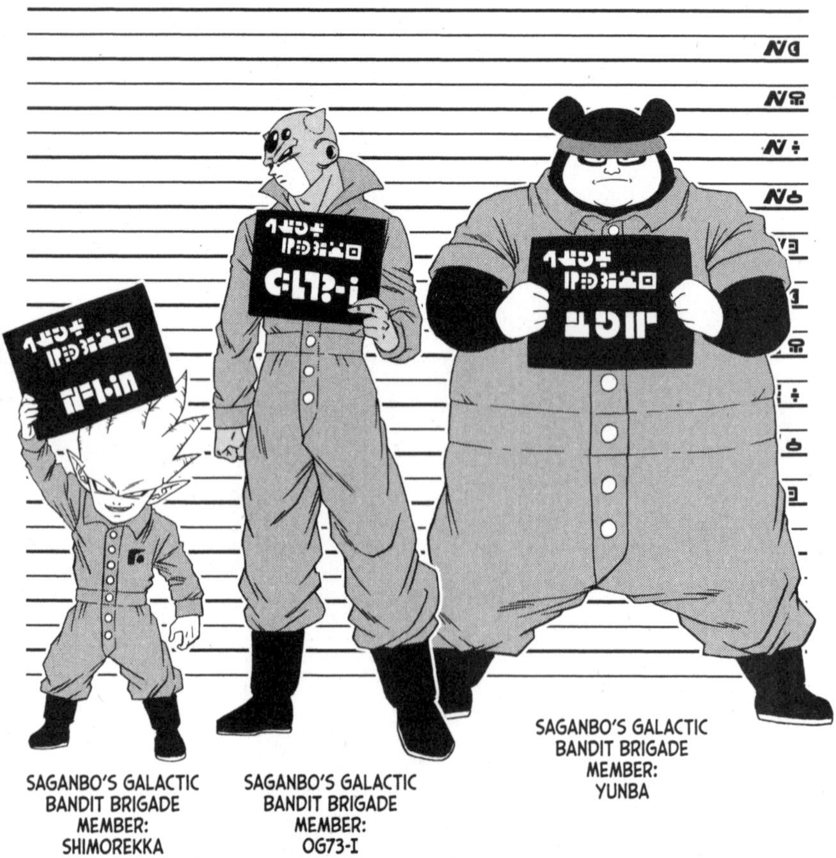
SAGANBO'S GALACTIC BANDIT BRIGADE MEMBER: SHIMOREKKA
SAGANBO'S GALACTIC BANDIT BRIGADE MEMBER: OG73-I
SAGANBO'S GALACTIC BANDIT BRIGADE MEMBER: YUNBA

DRAGON BALL SUPER

CHAPTER 54: GOHAN VS. SEVEN-THREE

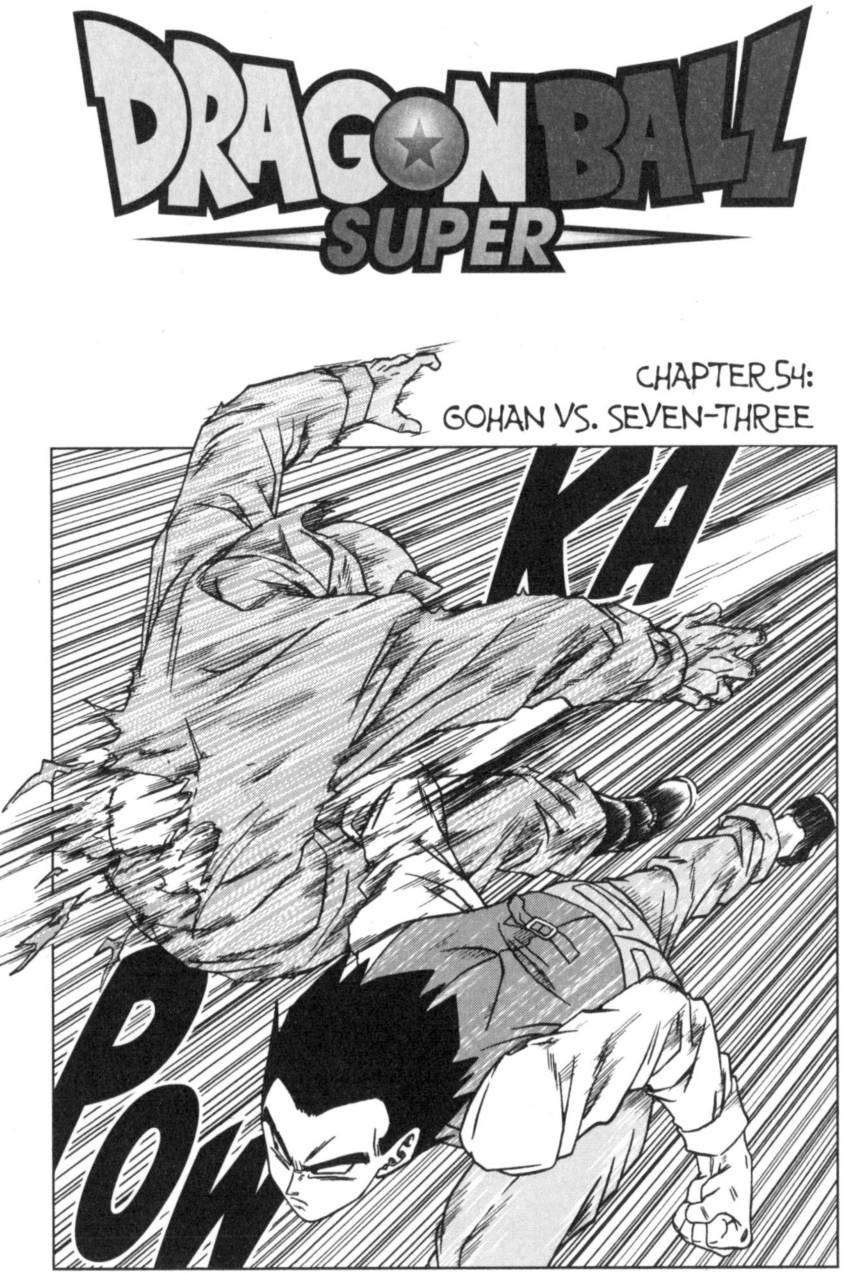
KA
DOH

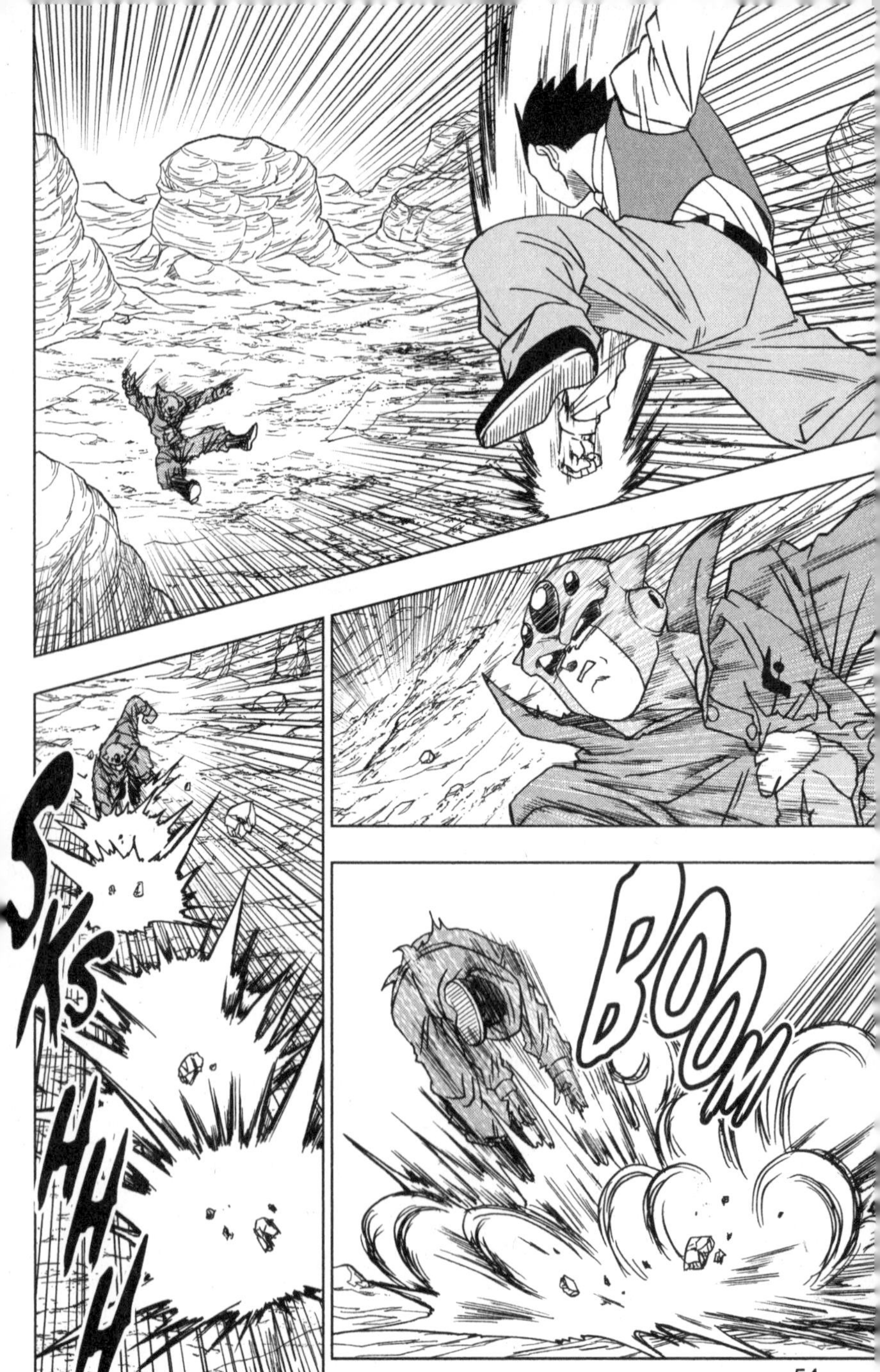
BOOM
SKSHHHH

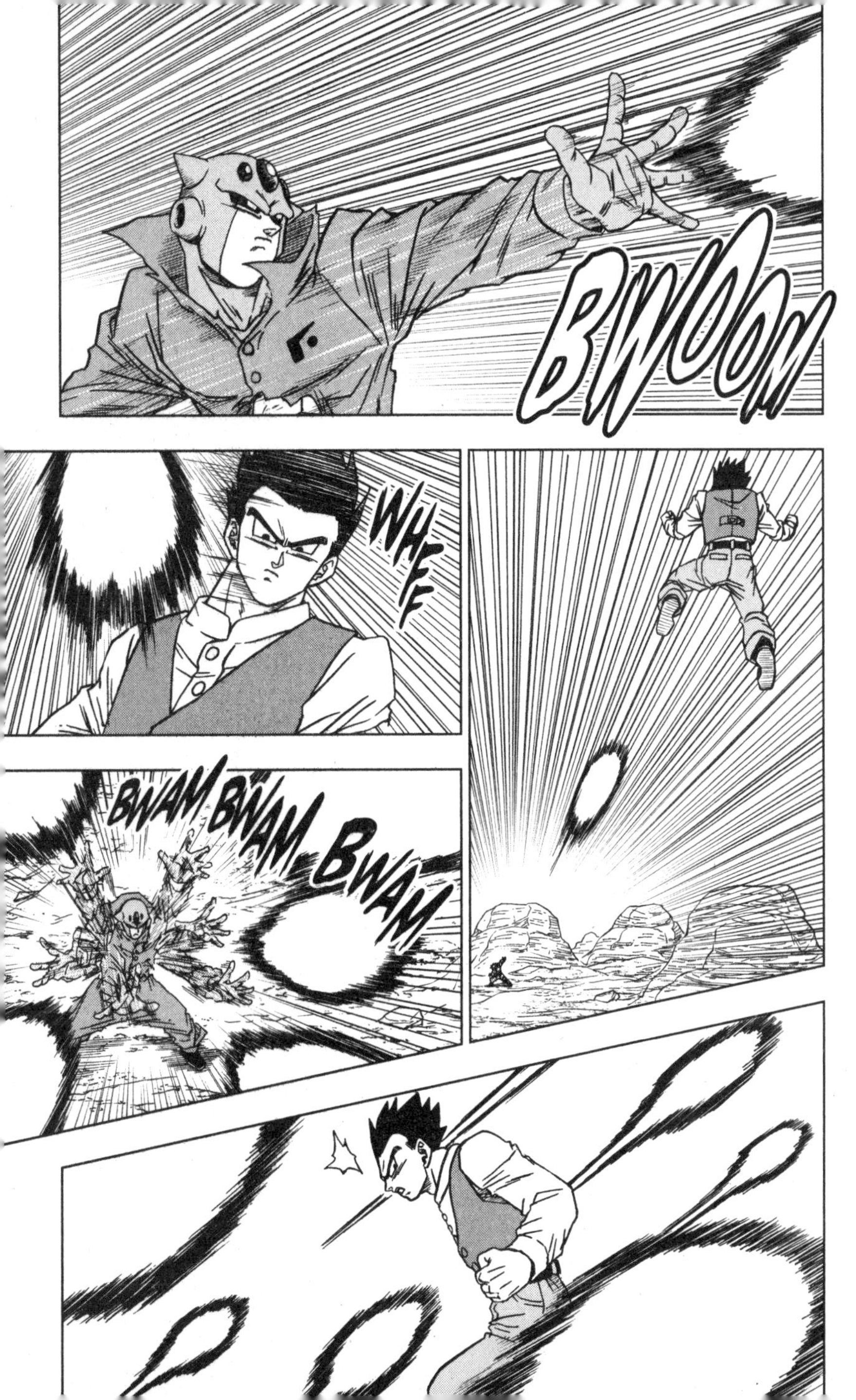
BWOOM
WHFF
BWAM BWAM BWAM

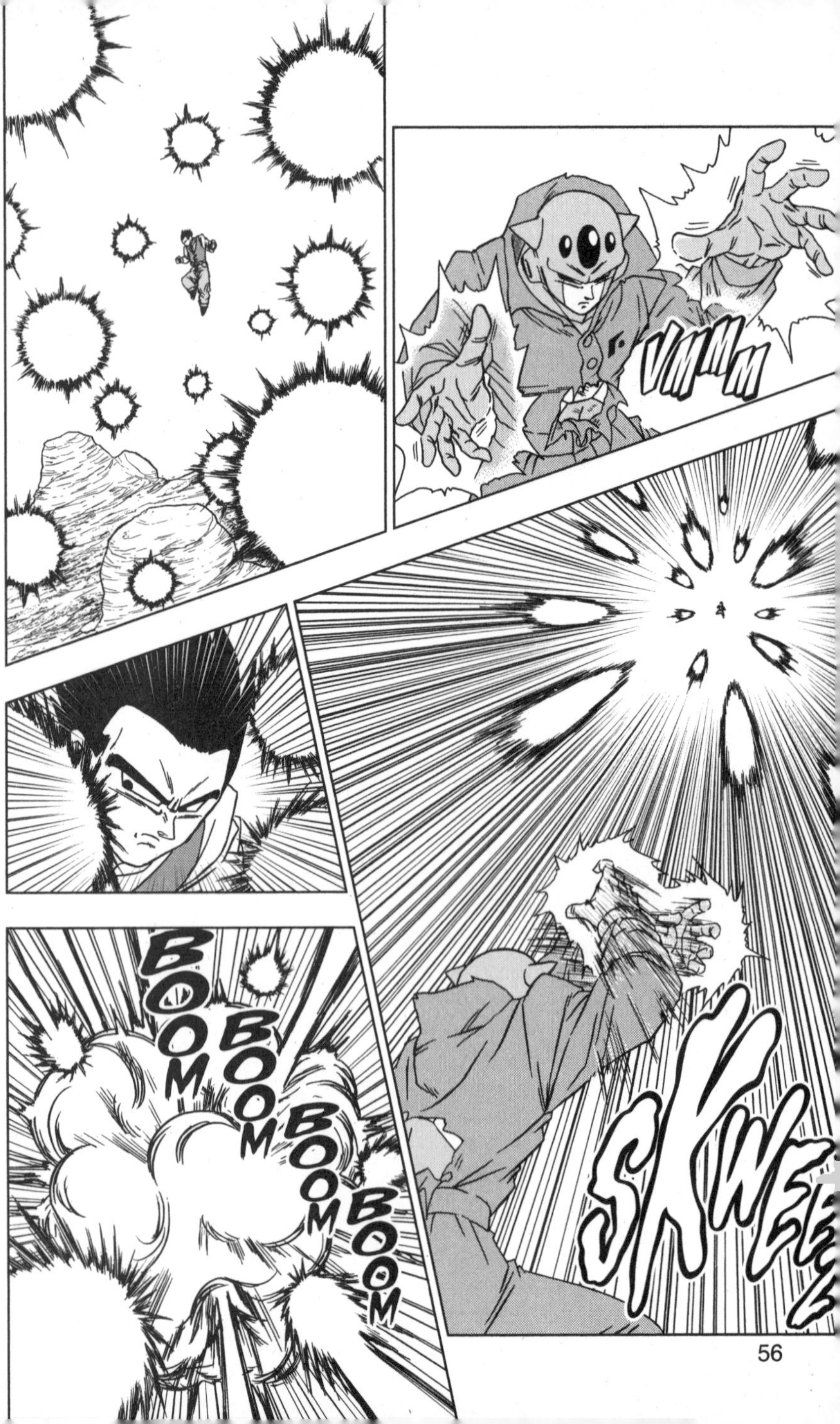
VMMMM
SKWEEE
BOOM
BOOM
BOOM
BOOM

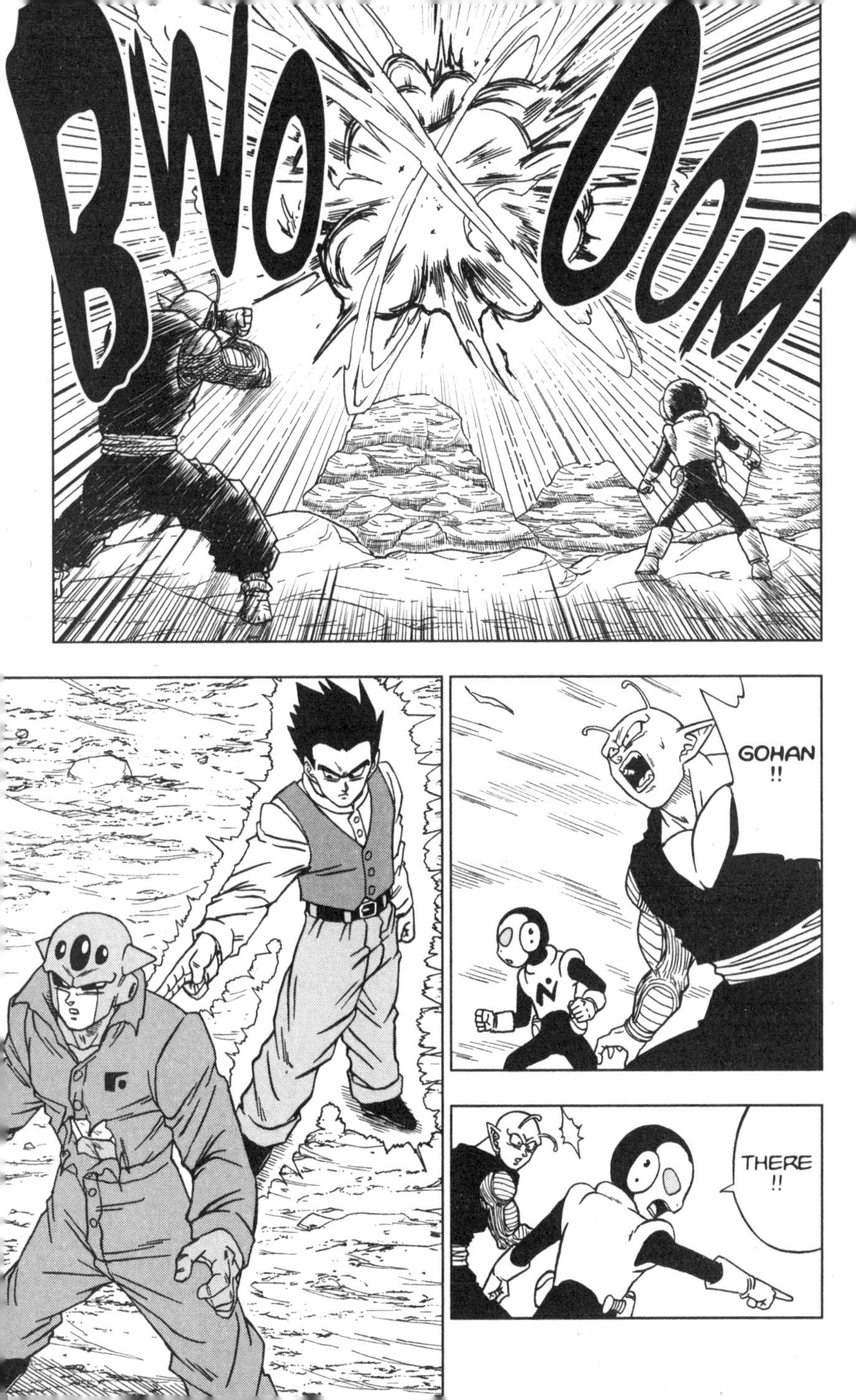
BWOOOM
GOHAN !!
THERE !!

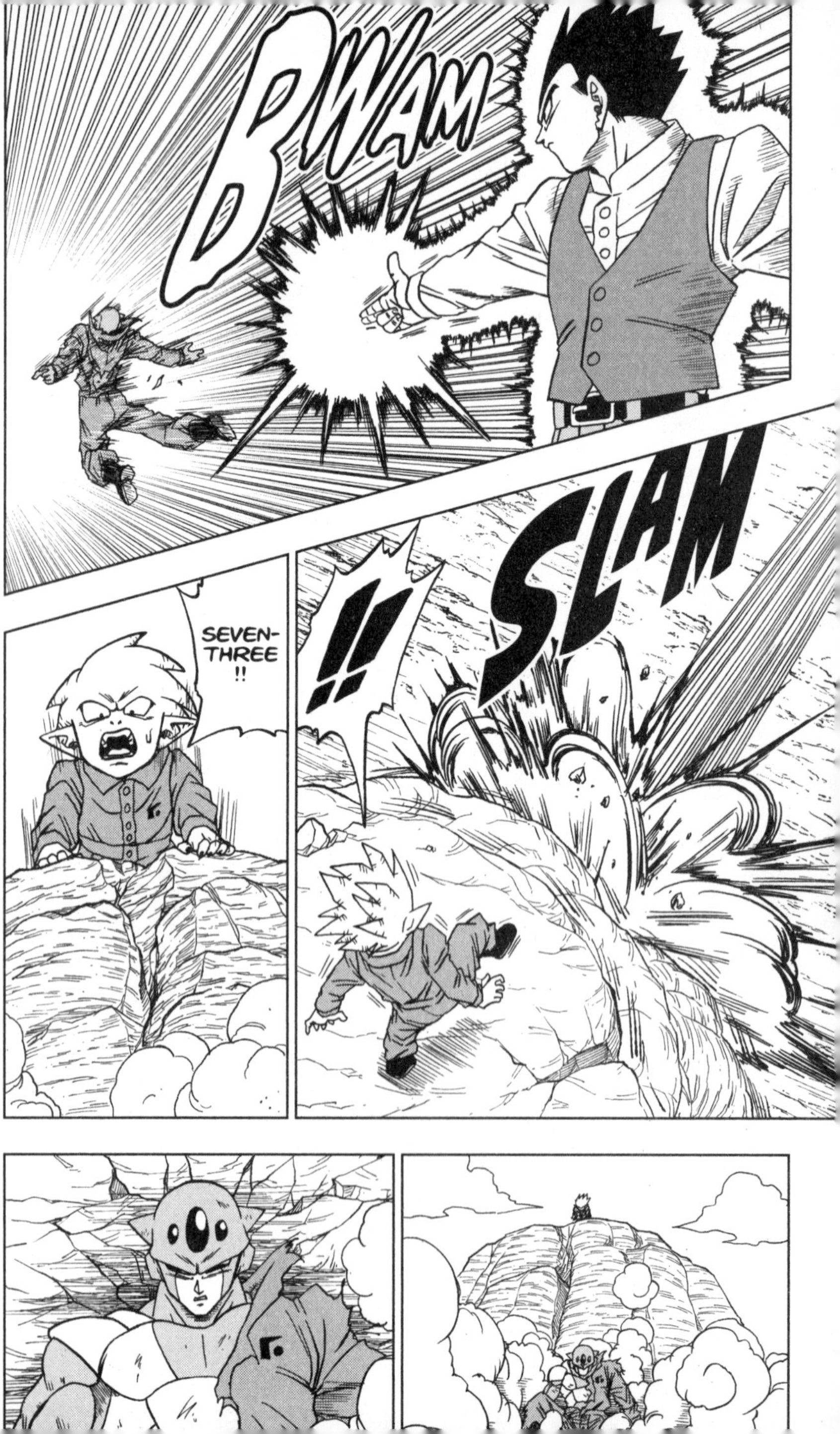
BWAM
SLAM
!!
SEVEN-THREE !!

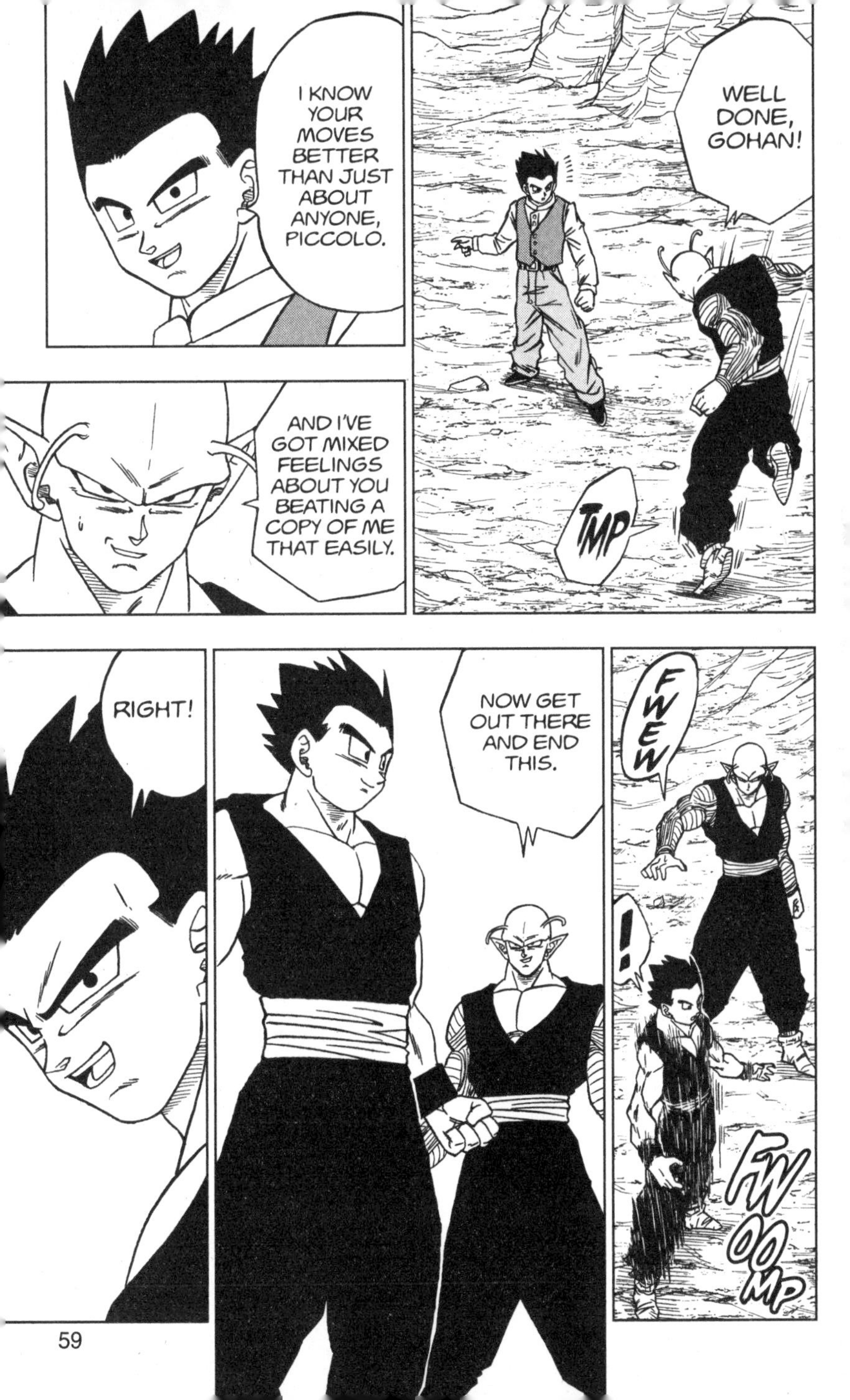
WELL DONE, GOHAN!
TMP
I KNOW YOUR MOVES BETTER THAN JUST ABOUT ANYONE, PICCOLO.
AND I'VE GOT MIXED FEELINGS ABOUT YOU BEATING A COPY OF ME THAT EASILY.
FWEW
!
FWOOMP
NOW GET OUT THERE AND END THIS.
RIGHT!

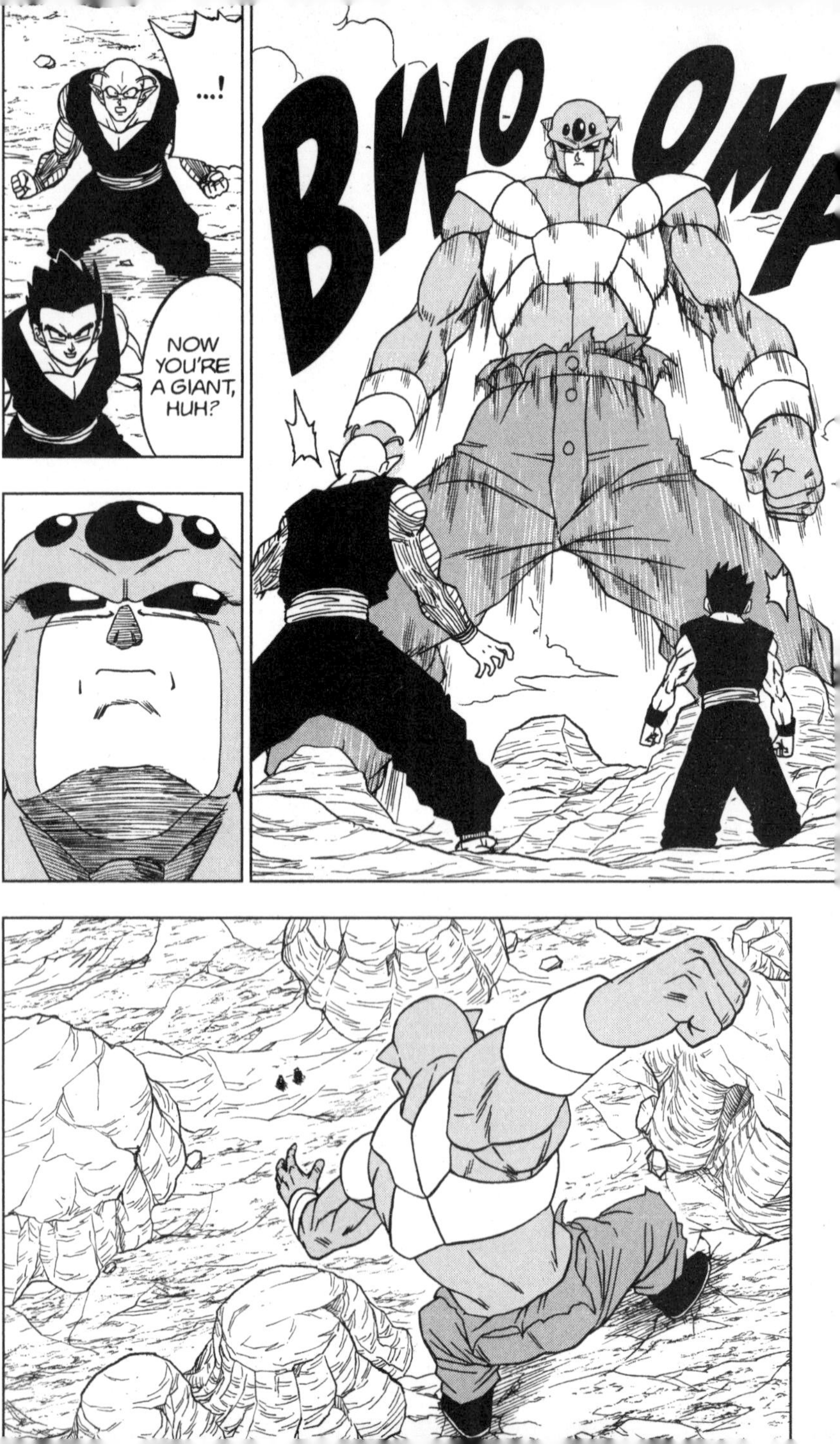
BWOOM
...!
NOW YOU'RE A GIANT, HUH?

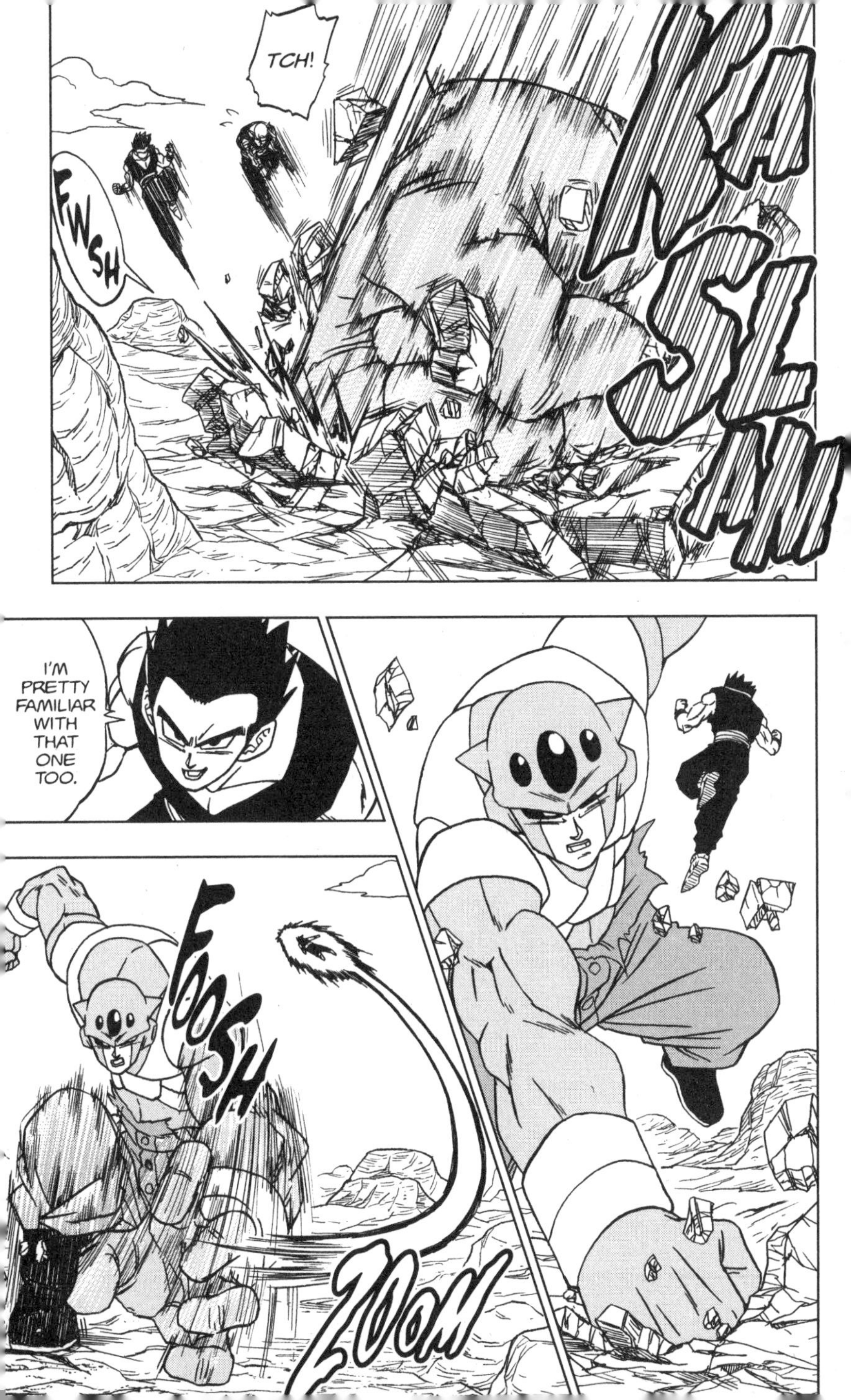
KASLAM
TCH!
FWSH
ZOOM
I'M PRETTY FAMILIAR WITH THAT ONE TOO.
FOOSH

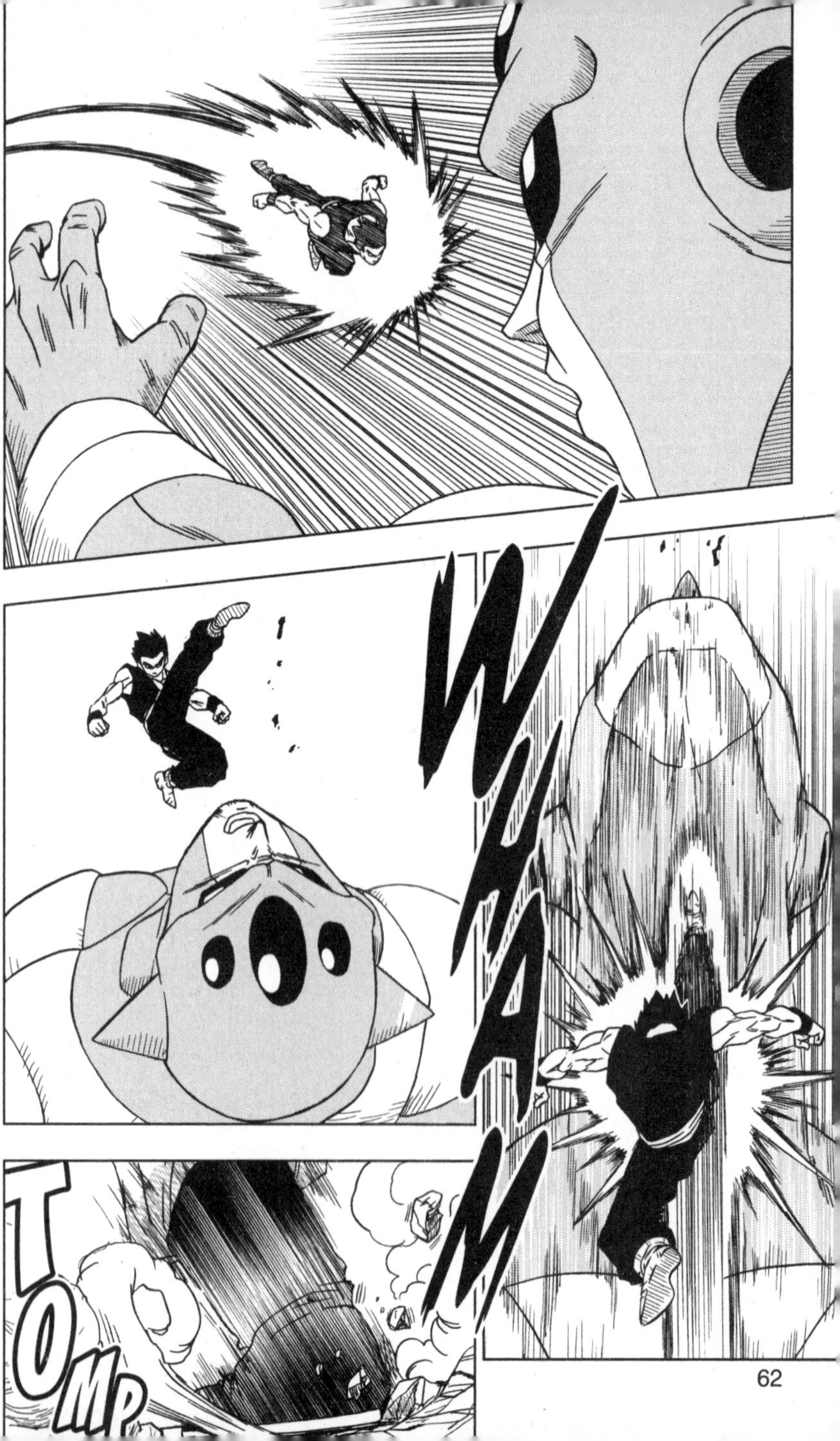
WHAM
TOMP

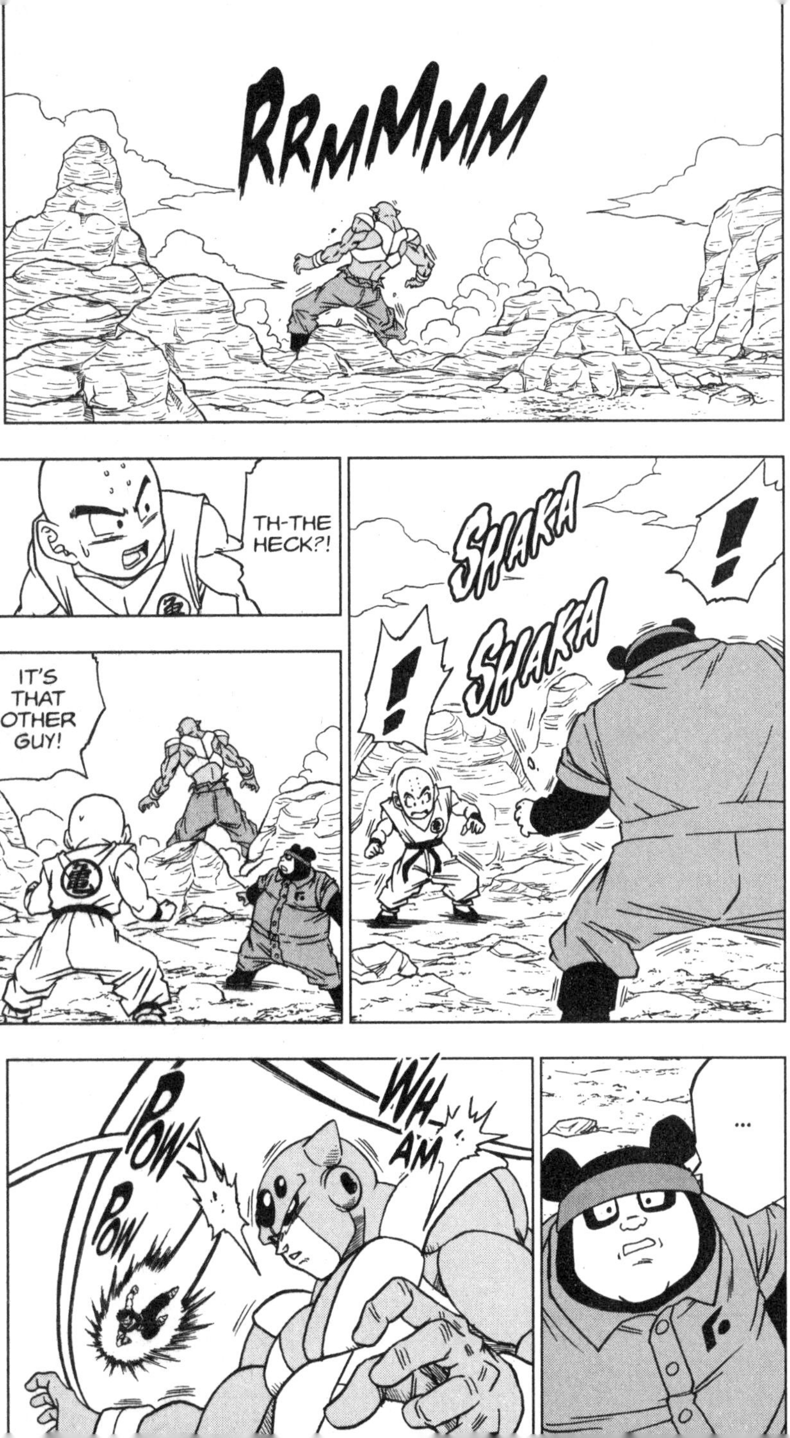
RRMMMM
SHAKA
SHAKA
!
!
TH-THE HECK?!
IT'S THAT OTHER GUY!
...
WH-AM
POW
POW

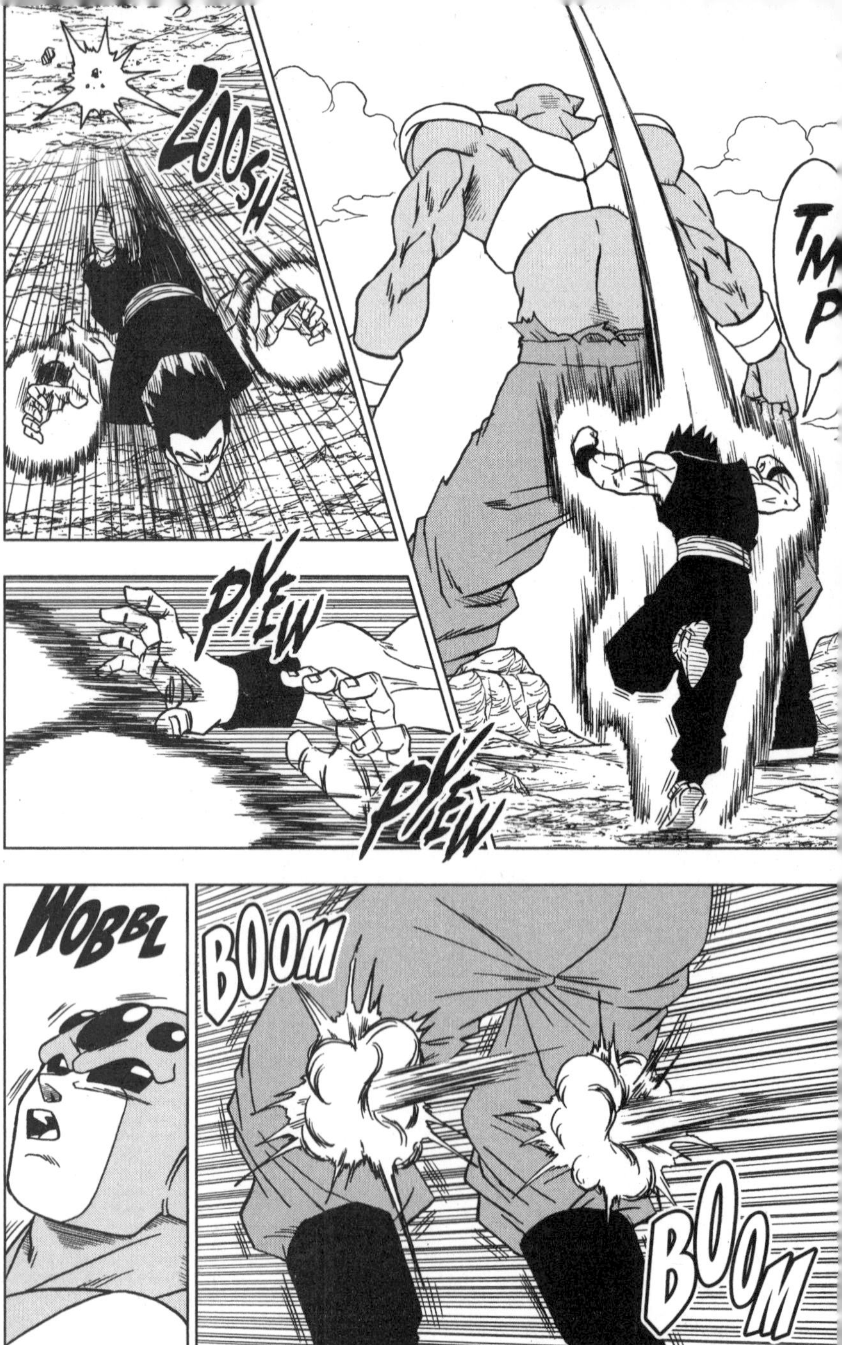
TMP
ZOOSH
PYEW
PYEW
BOOM
BOOM
WOBBL

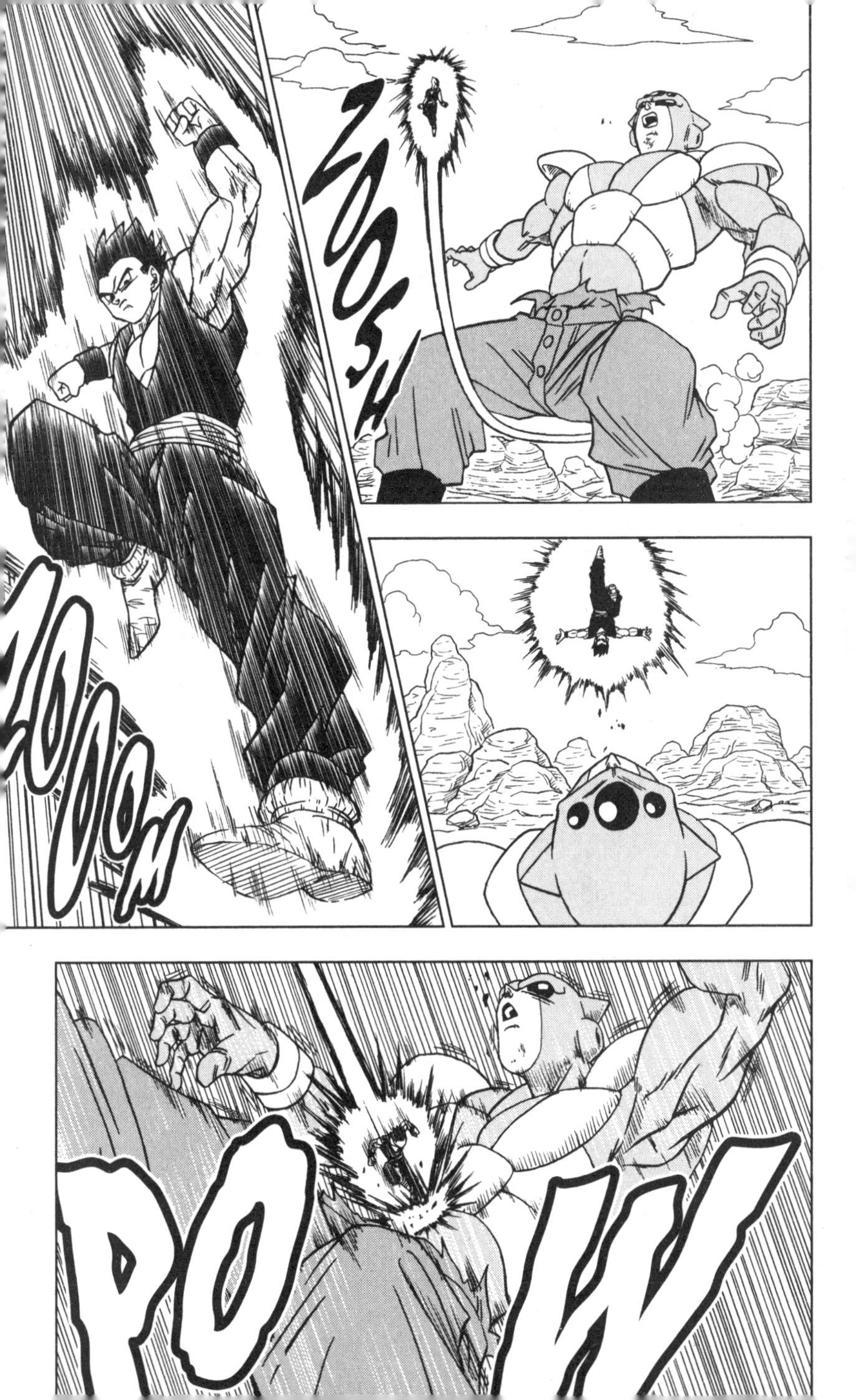
WOOSH
ZOOOOM
POW

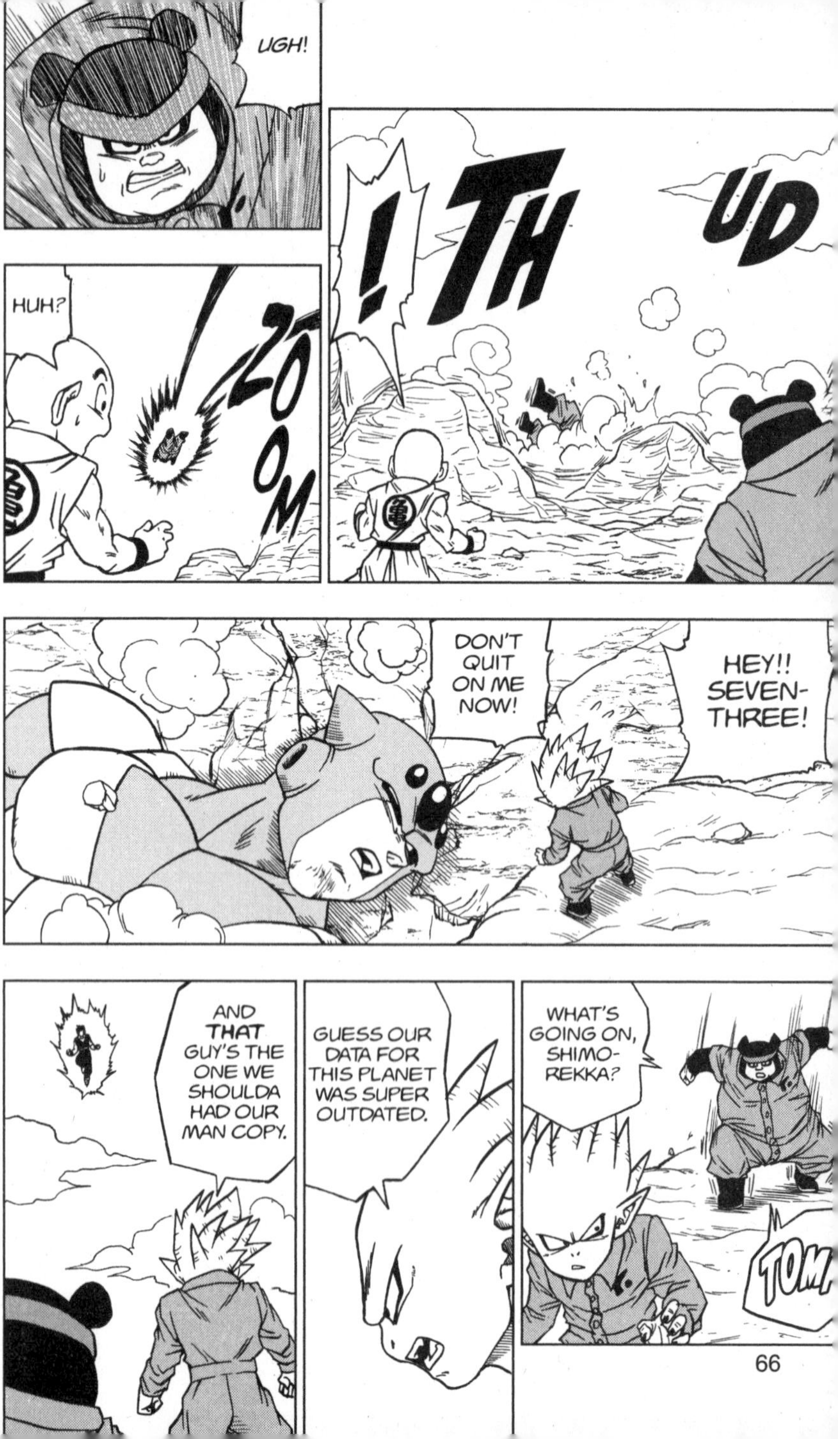
UGH!
HUH?
ZOOM
!
THUD
HEY!! SEVEN-THREE!
DON'T QUIT ON ME NOW!
WHAT'S GOING ON, SHIMO-REKKA?
TOM
GUESS OUR DATA FOR THIS PLANET WAS SUPER OUTDATED.
AND **THAT** GUY'S THE ONE WE SHOULDA HAD OUR MAN COPY.

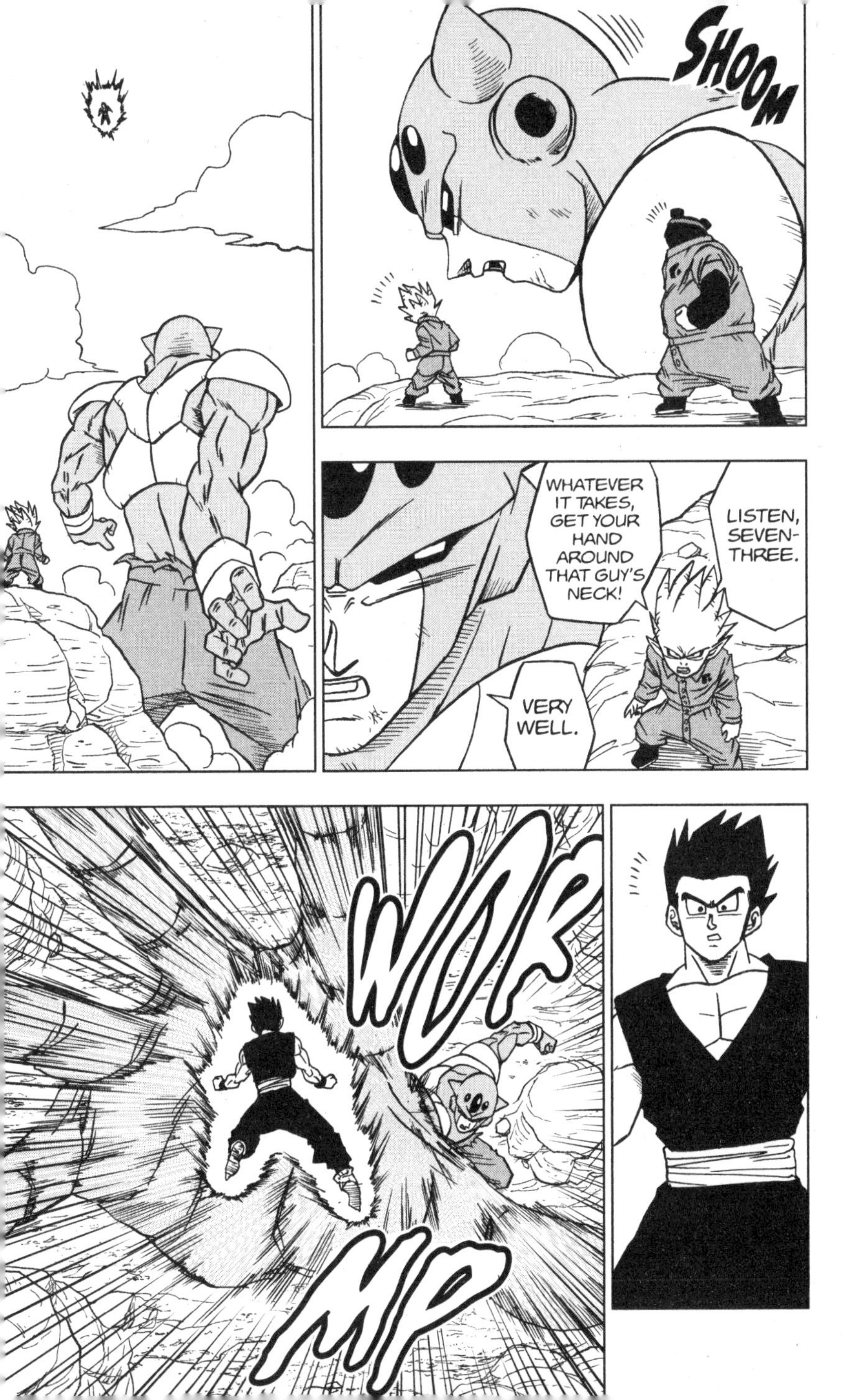
SHOOM
LISTEN, SEVEN-THREE.
WHATEVER IT TAKES, GET YOUR HAND AROUND THAT GUY'S NECK!
VERY WELL.
WOMP

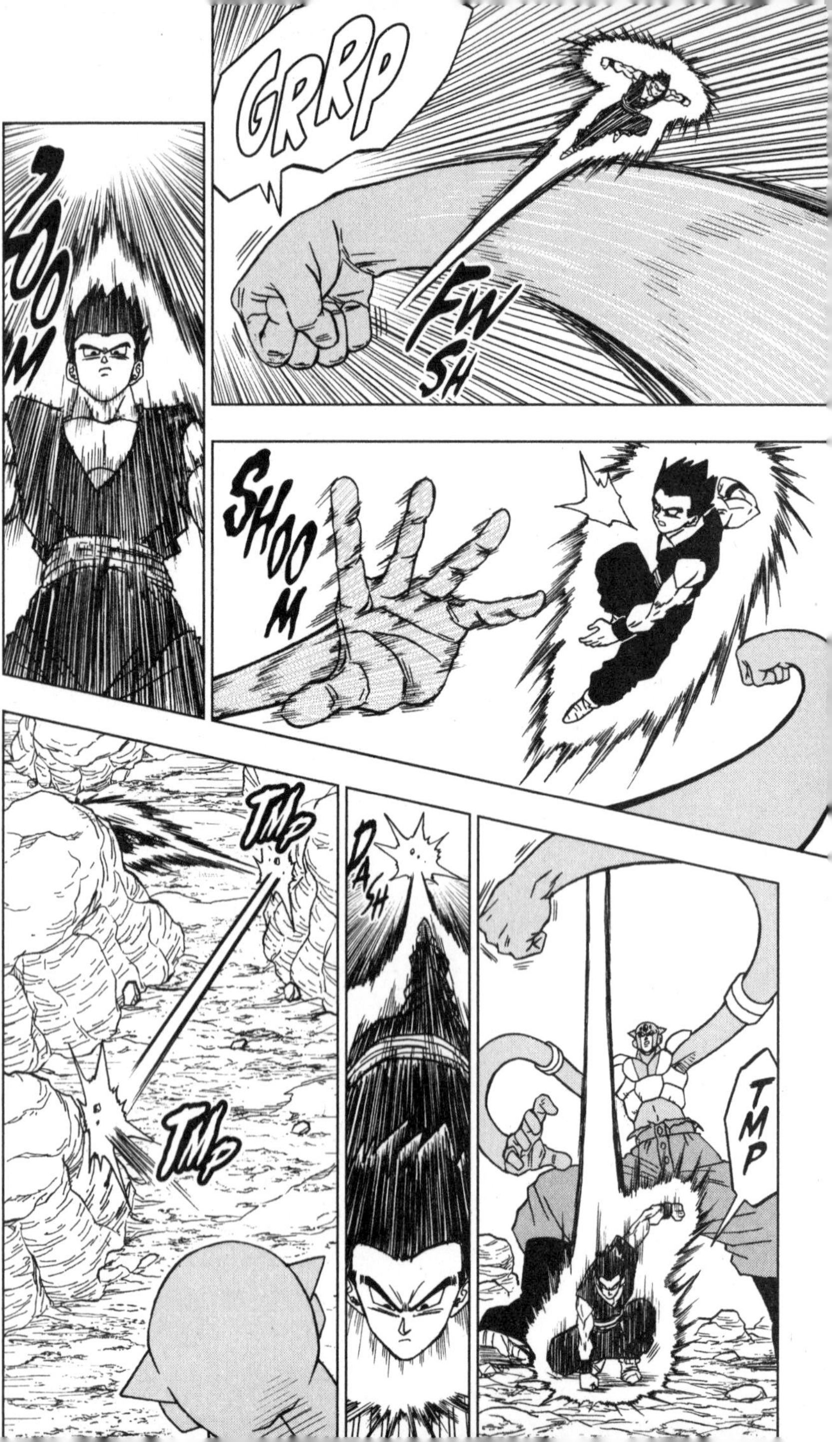
GRRP
FWSH
ZOOOM
SHOOOM
TMP
DASH
TMP
TMP

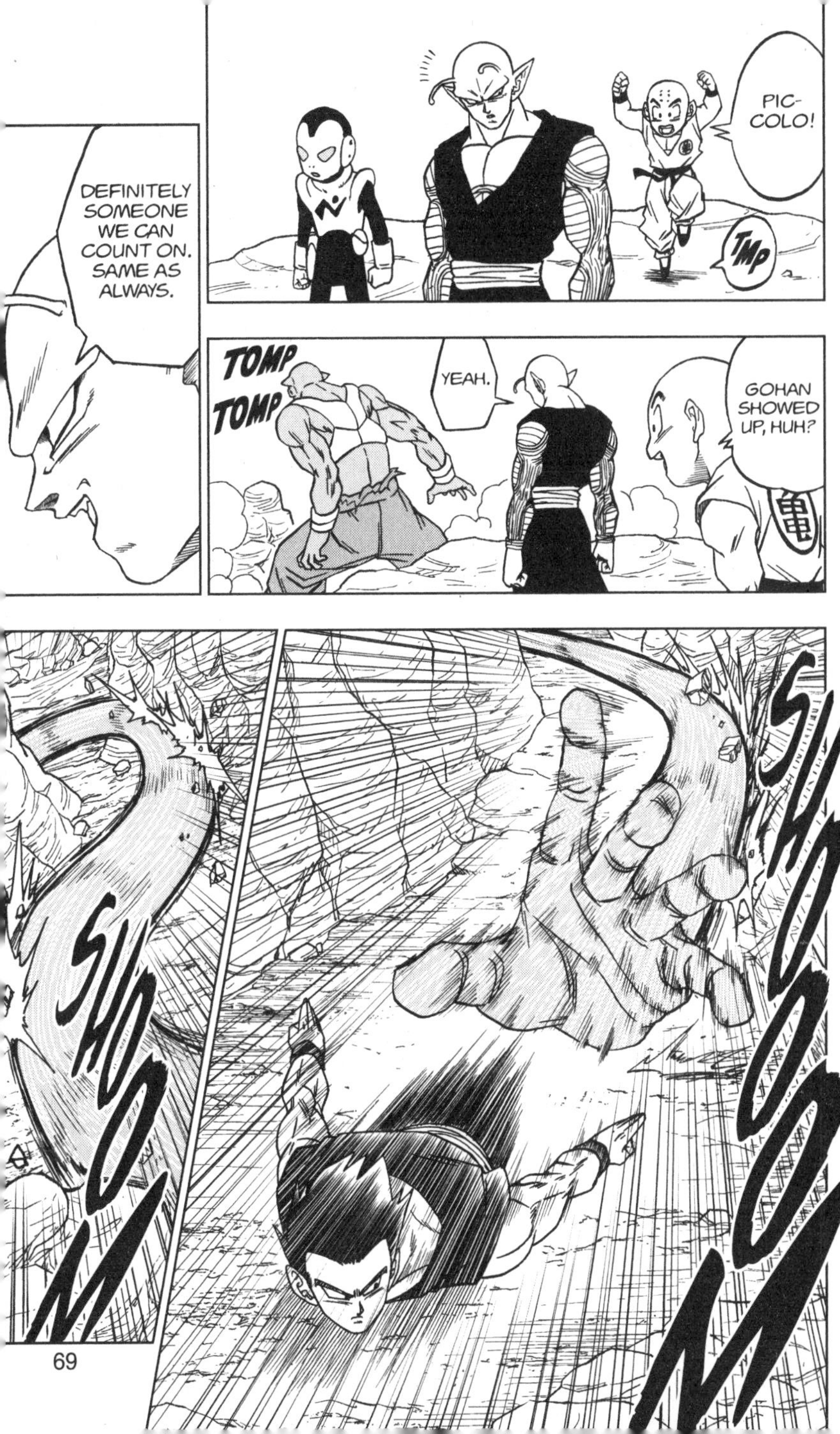
PIC-COLO!
TMP
GOHAN SHOWED UP, HUH?
YEAH.
TOMP TOMP
DEFINITELY SOMEONE WE CAN COUNT ON. SAME AS ALWAYS.
SHOOOOM
SHOOM

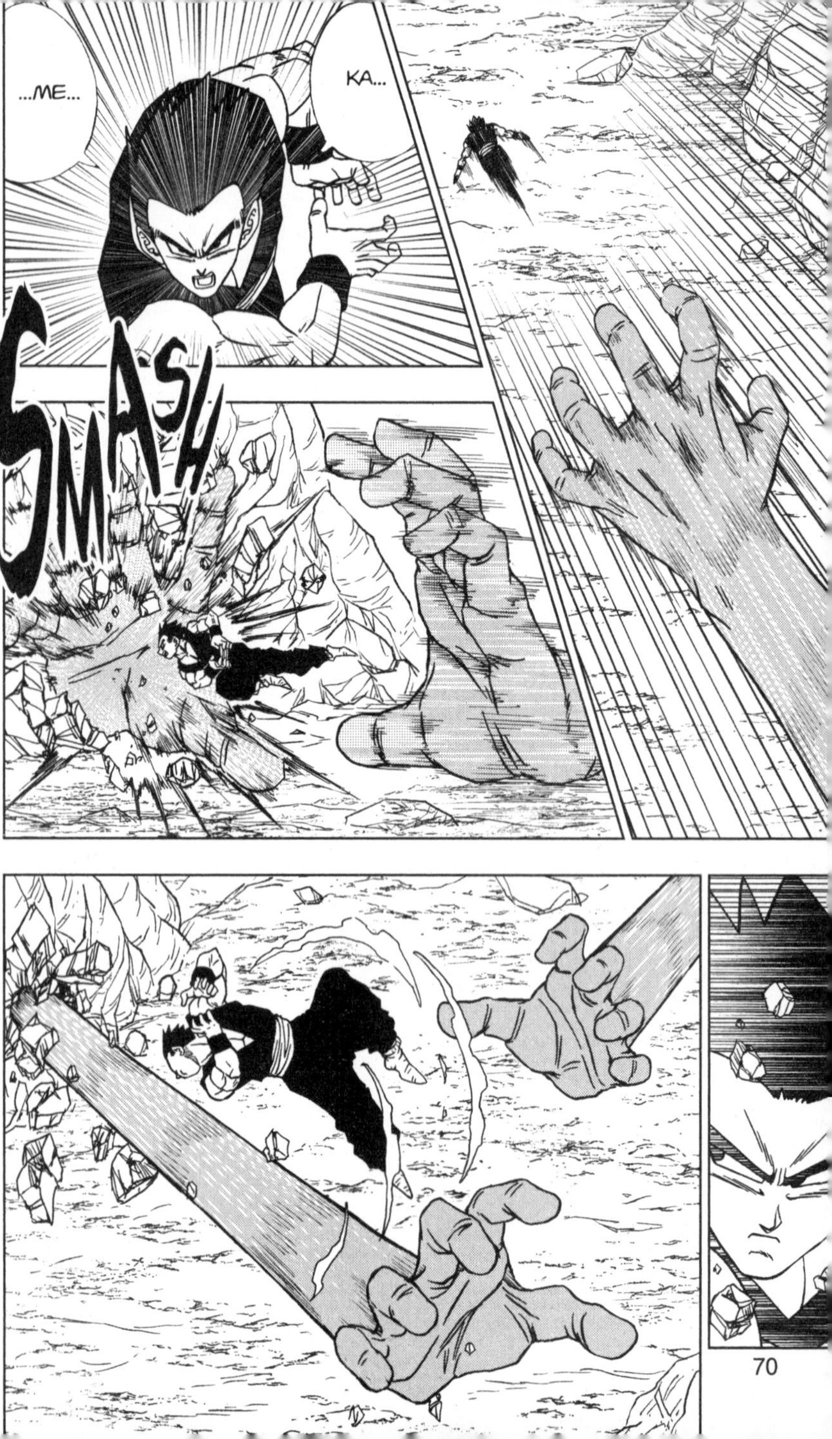
KA...
...ME...
SMASH

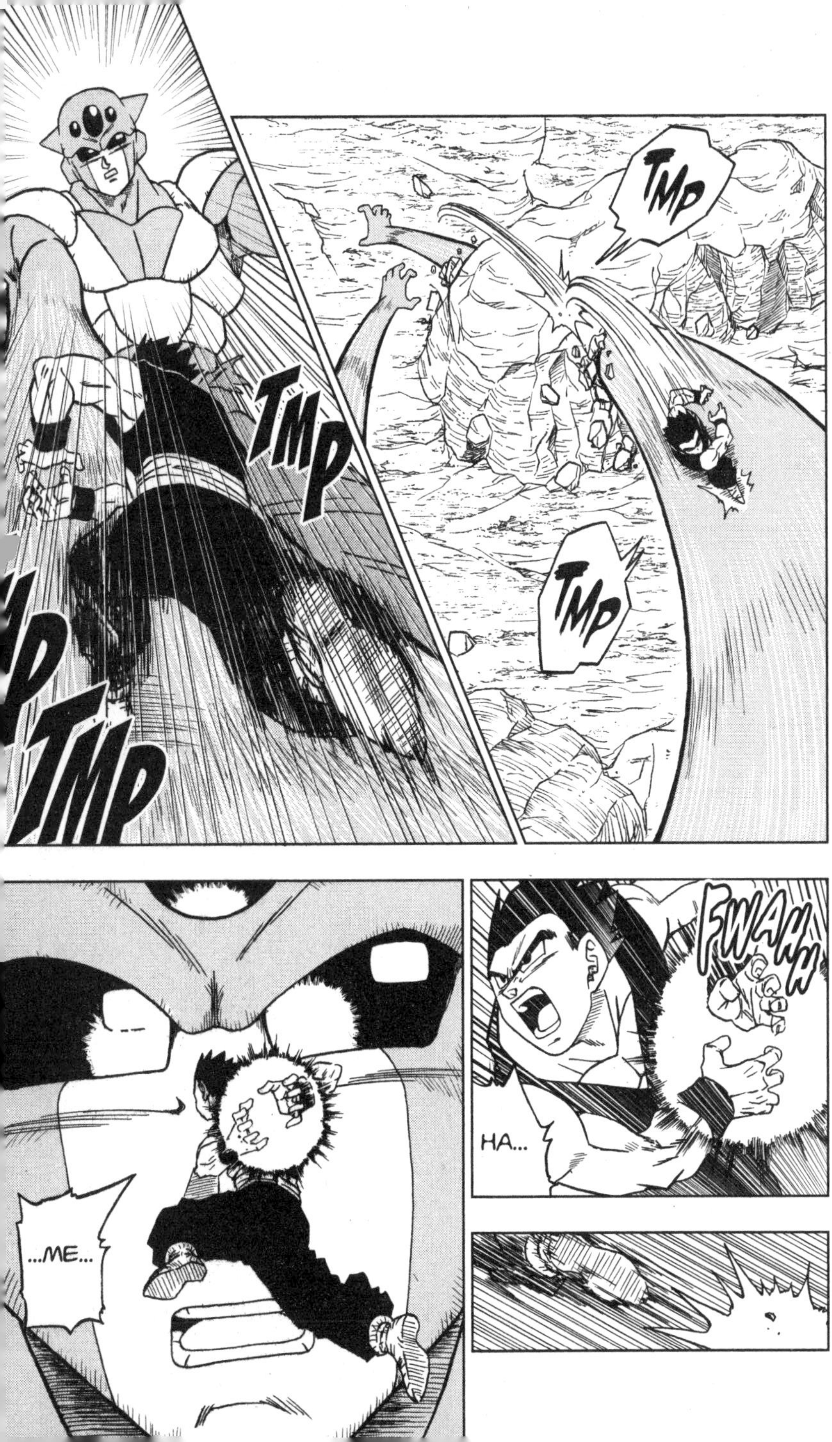
TMP
TMP
TMP
TMP
FWAHH
HA...
...ME...

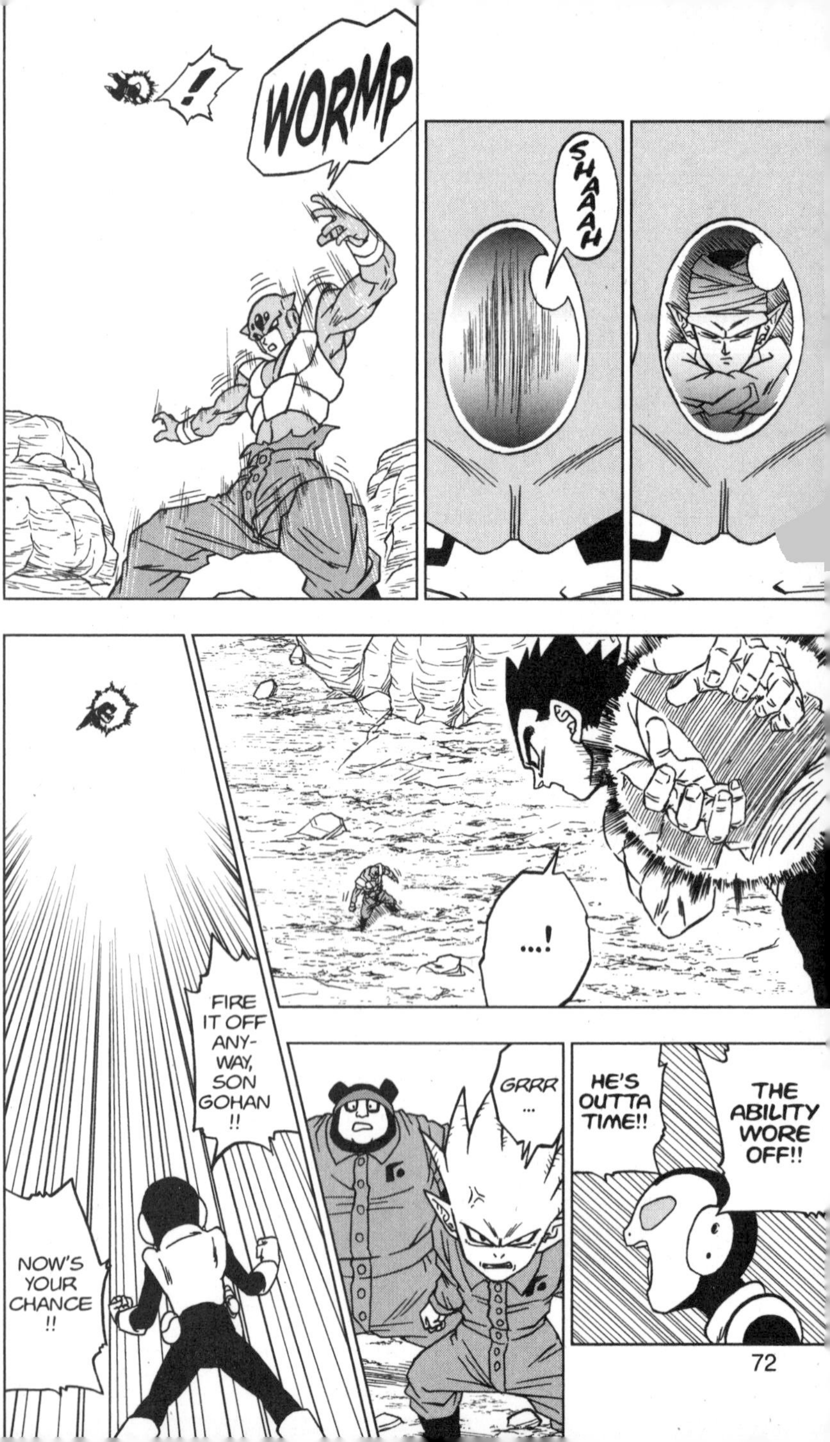
SHAAAH
WORMP
!
...!
THE ABILITY WORE OFF!!
HE'S OUTTA TIME!!
GRRR...
FIRE IT OFF ANY-WAY, SON GOHAN!!
NOW'S YOUR CHANCE!!

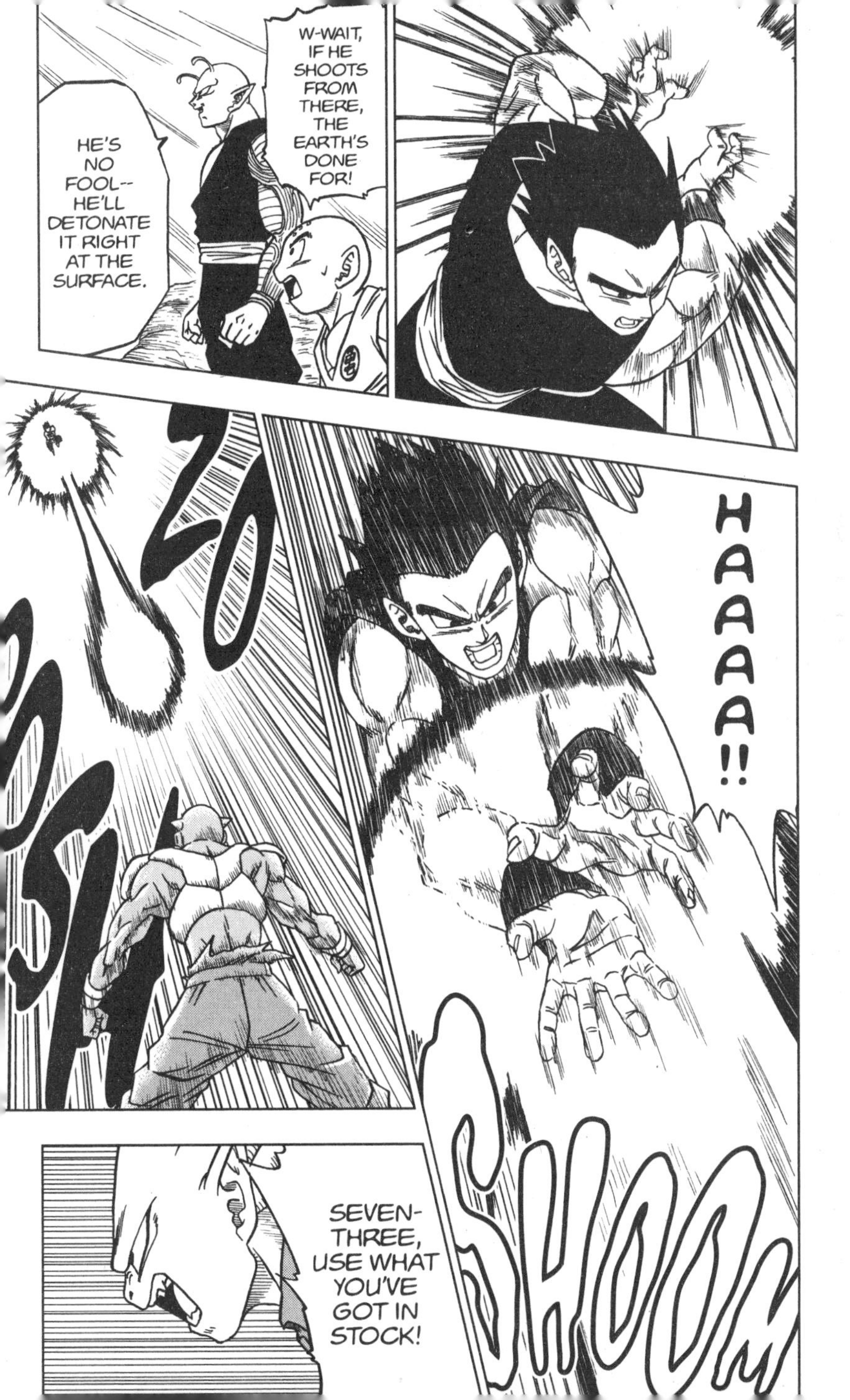
W-WAIT, IF HE SHOOTS FROM THERE, THE EARTH'S DONE FOR!
HE'S NO FOOL-- HE'LL DETONATE IT RIGHT AT THE SURFACE.
HAAAAA!!
SHOOM
SEVEN-THREE, USE WHAT YOU'VE GOT IN STOCK!

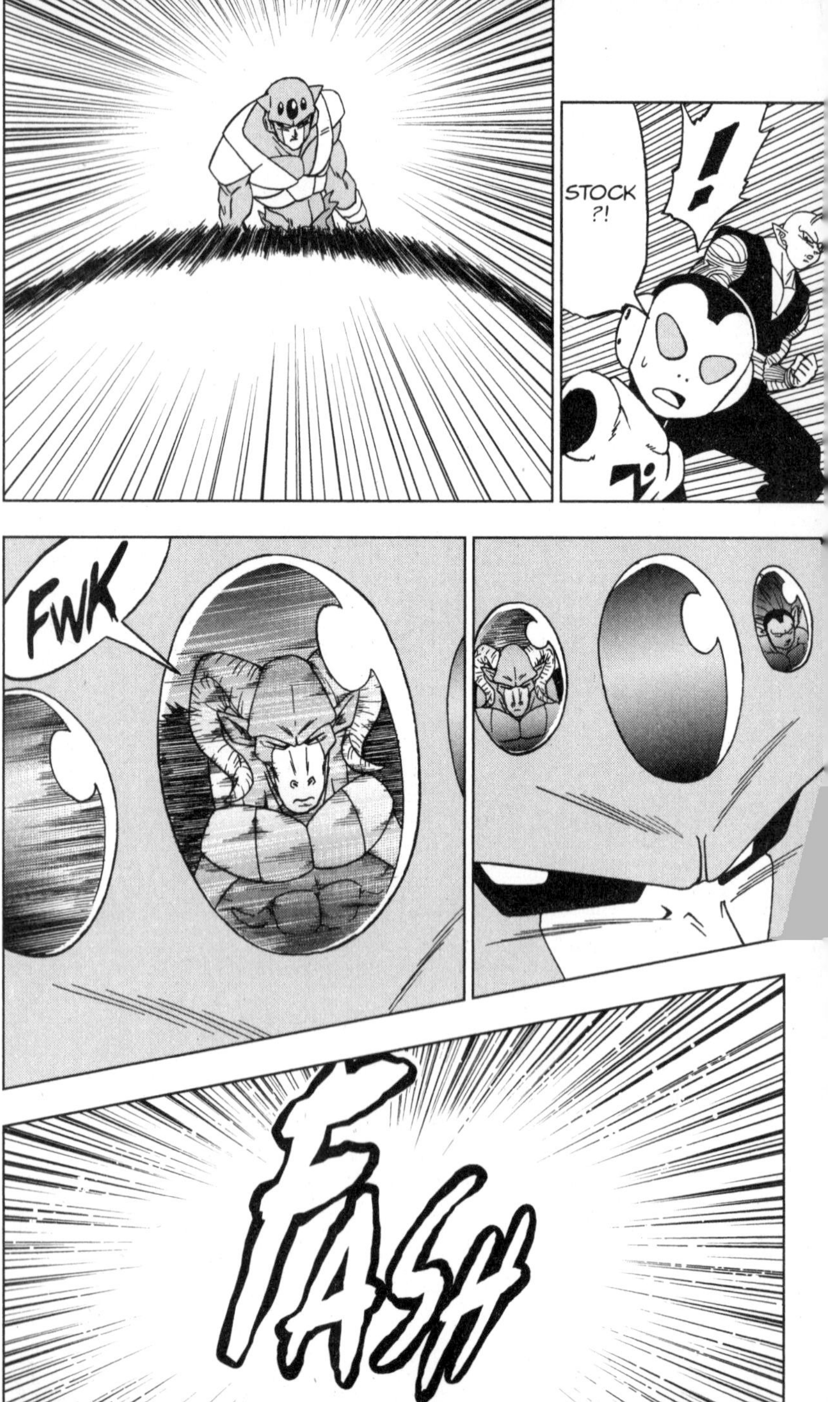
STOCK ?!
!
FWK
FASH

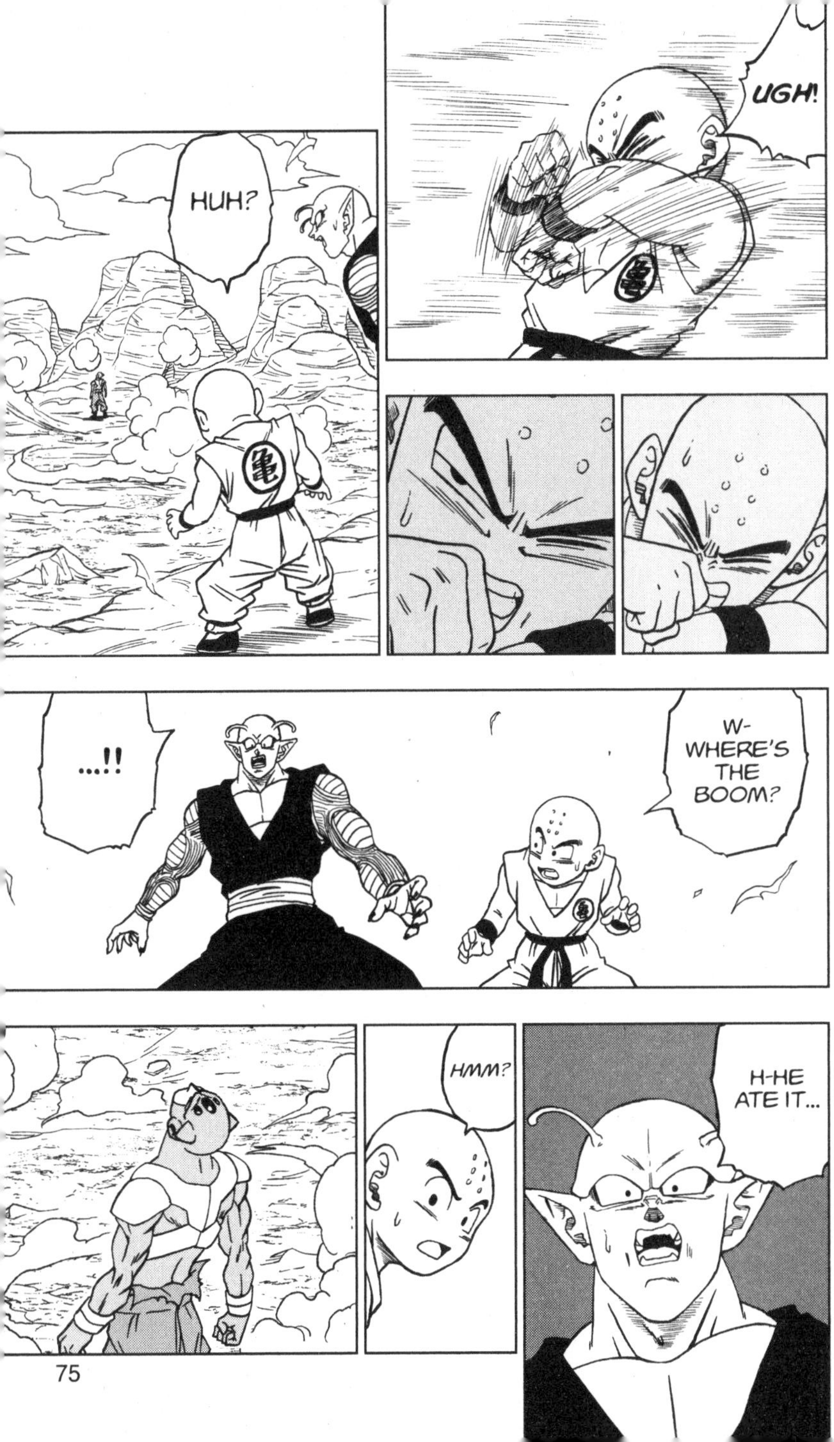
UGH!
HUH?
W-WHERE'S THE BOOM?
...!!
H-HE ATE IT...
HMM?

HE ATE THE CH! BLAST!

LOOK! MORO!!

HAAH!

GULP

HE HAD MORO'S POWERS IN STOCK!!

FWP

IN STOCK? YOU NEVER SAID ANYTHING ABOUT THAT!

YEAH, WELL, HE CAN SWITCH TO OTHER COPIED ABILITIES, STORING UP TO THREE IDENTITIES AT A TIME!!

WHAT'S THAT MEAN...?

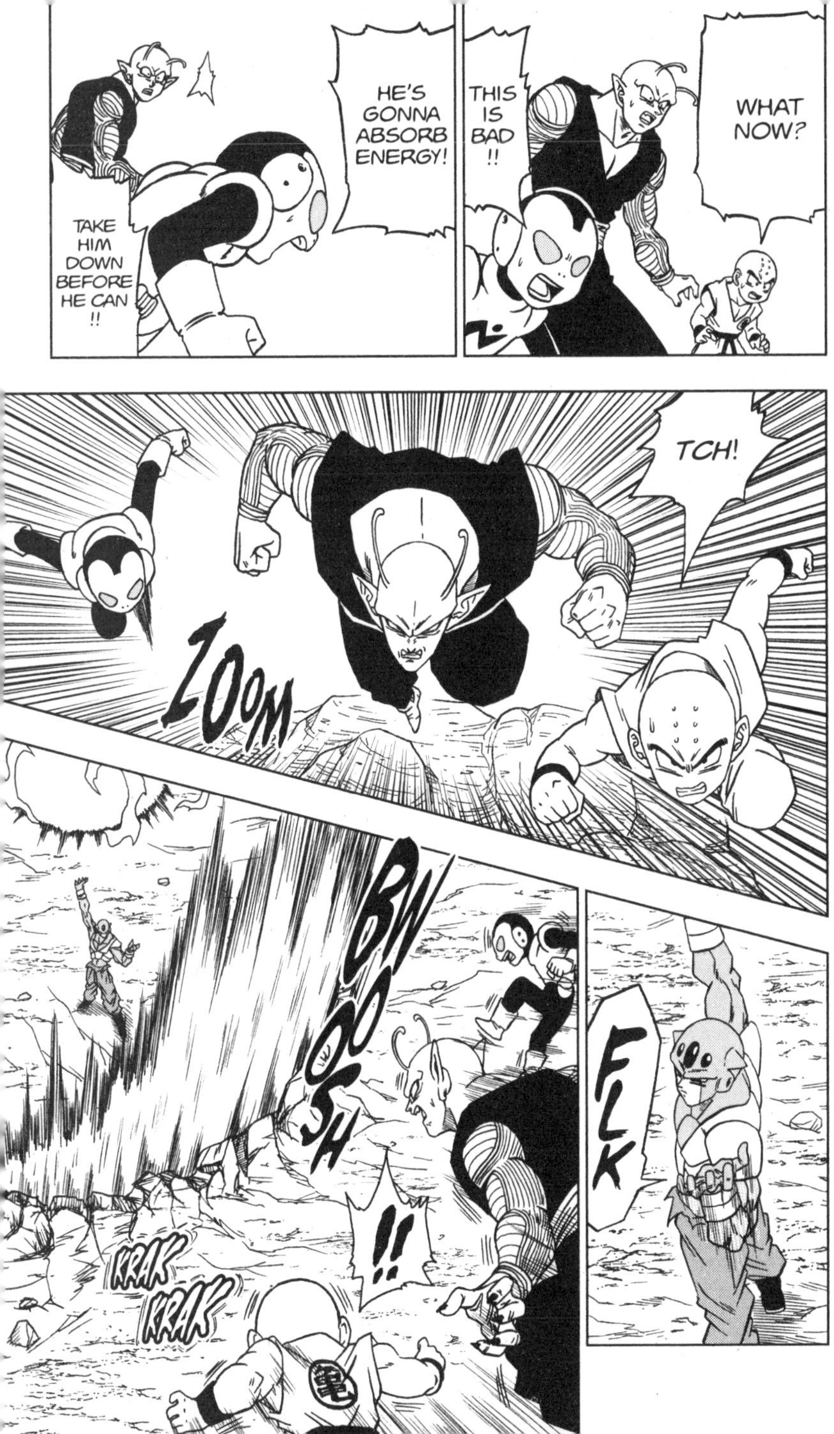
WHAT NOW?
THIS IS BAD !!
HE'S GONNA ABSORB ENERGY!
TAKE HIM DOWN BEFORE HE CAN !!
TCH!
ZOOM
FLK
BWOOOSH
!!
KRAK KRAK

FWSH

BWOOSH

GAHH!!

FWK

WHAT'S ALL THAT ABOUT?!

....!!

WE CAN'T GET CLOSE!!

SO Y'SEE, CAPTAIN, WE HAD TO RESORT TO THAT. SORRY.

HMPH... CLOSE ONE, HUH? NEVER THOUGHT WE'D NEED OUR SECRET WEAPON SO SOON.

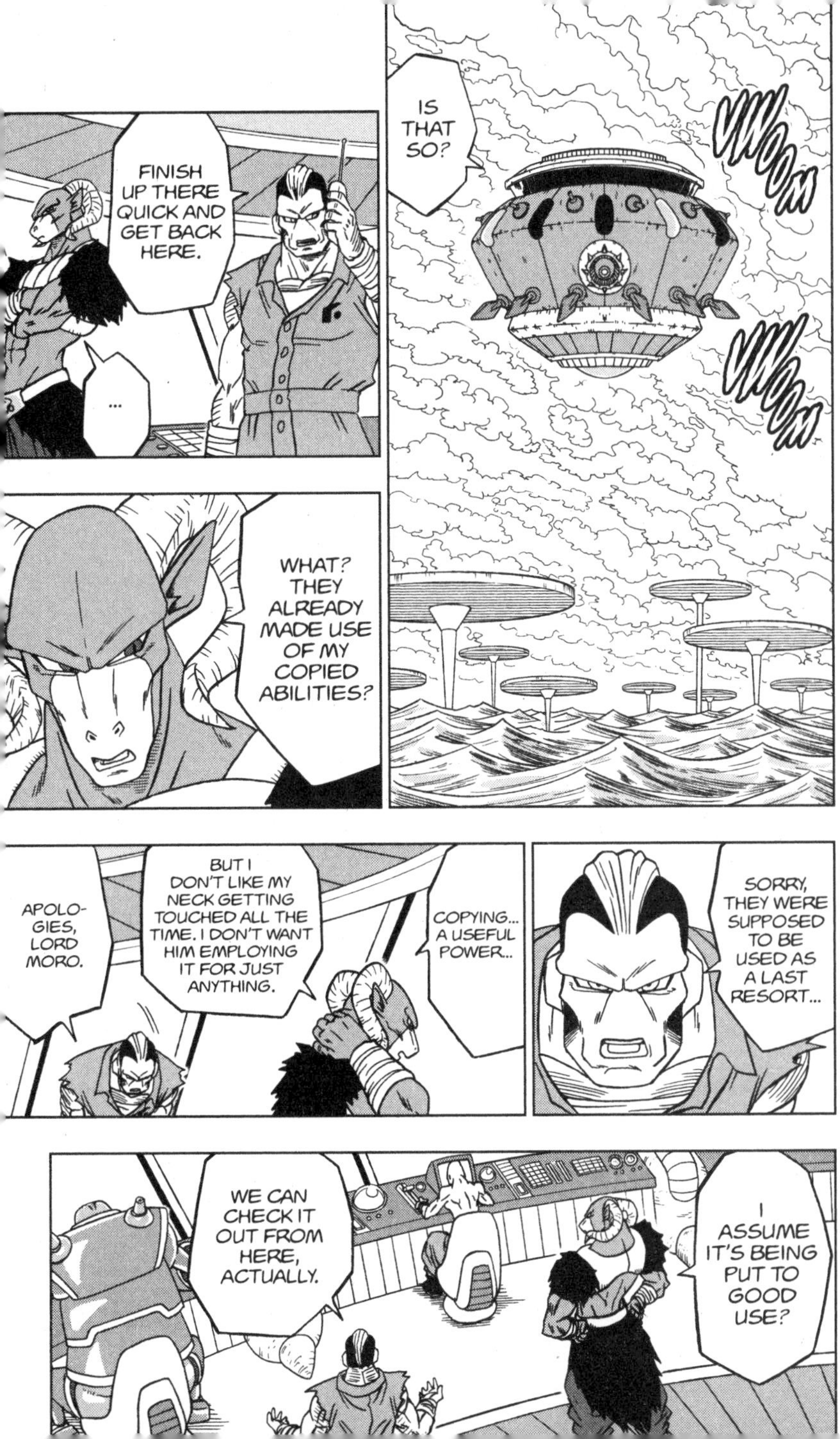
IS THAT SO?
VWOOM
VWOOM
FINISH UP THERE QUICK AND GET BACK HERE.
...
WHAT? THEY ALREADY MADE USE OF MY COPIED ABILITIES?
SORRY, THEY WERE SUPPOSED TO BE USED AS A LAST RESORT...
COPYING... A USEFUL POWER...
BUT I DON'T LIKE MY NECK GETTING TOUCHED ALL THE TIME. I DON'T WANT HIM EMPLOYING IT FOR JUST ANYTHING.
APOLOGIES, LORD MORO.
I ASSUME IT'S BEING PUT TO GOOD USE?
WE CAN CHECK IT OUT FROM HERE, ACTUALLY.

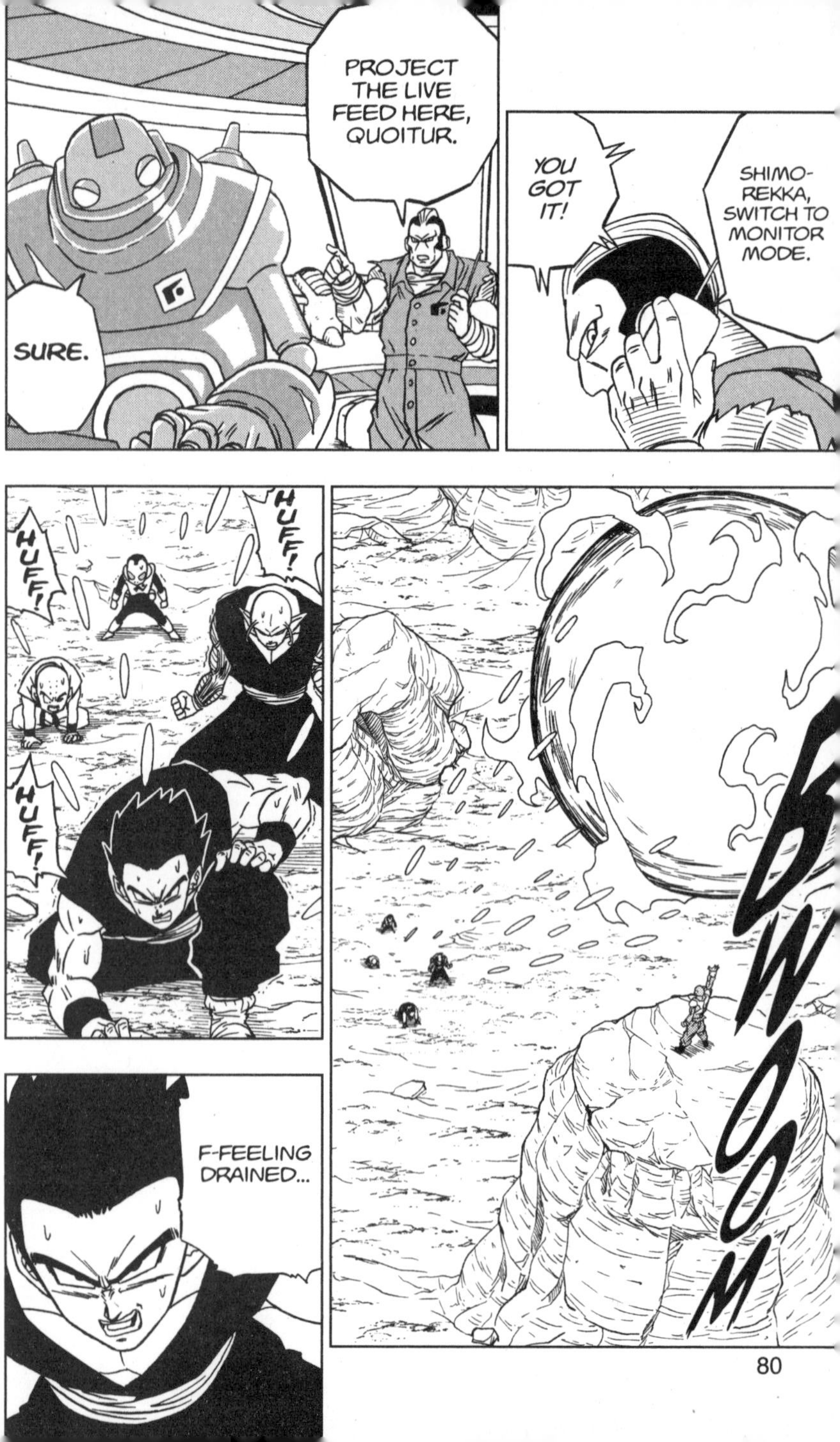
SHIMO-REKKA, SWITCH TO MONITOR MODE.
YOU GOT IT!
PROJECT THE LIVE FEED HERE, QUOITUR.
SURE.
BWOOOM
HUFF!
HUFF!
HUFF!
F-FEELING DRAINED...

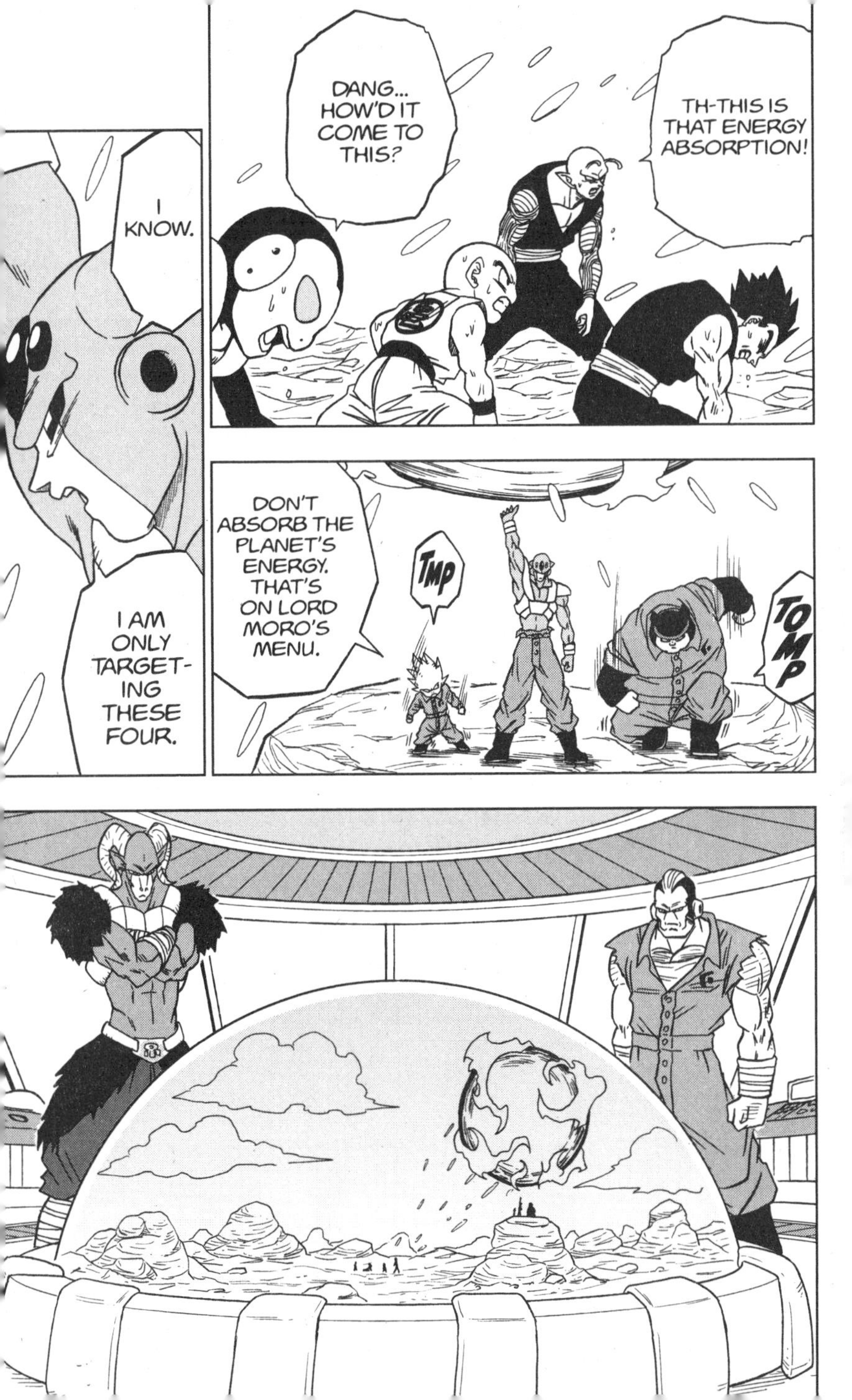
TH-THIS IS THAT ENERGY ABSORPTION!
DANG... HOW'D IT COME TO THIS?
TOMP
DON'T ABSORB THE PLANET'S ENERGY. THAT'S ON LORD MORO'S MENU.
TMP
I KNOW.
I AM ONLY TARGET-ING THESE FOUR.

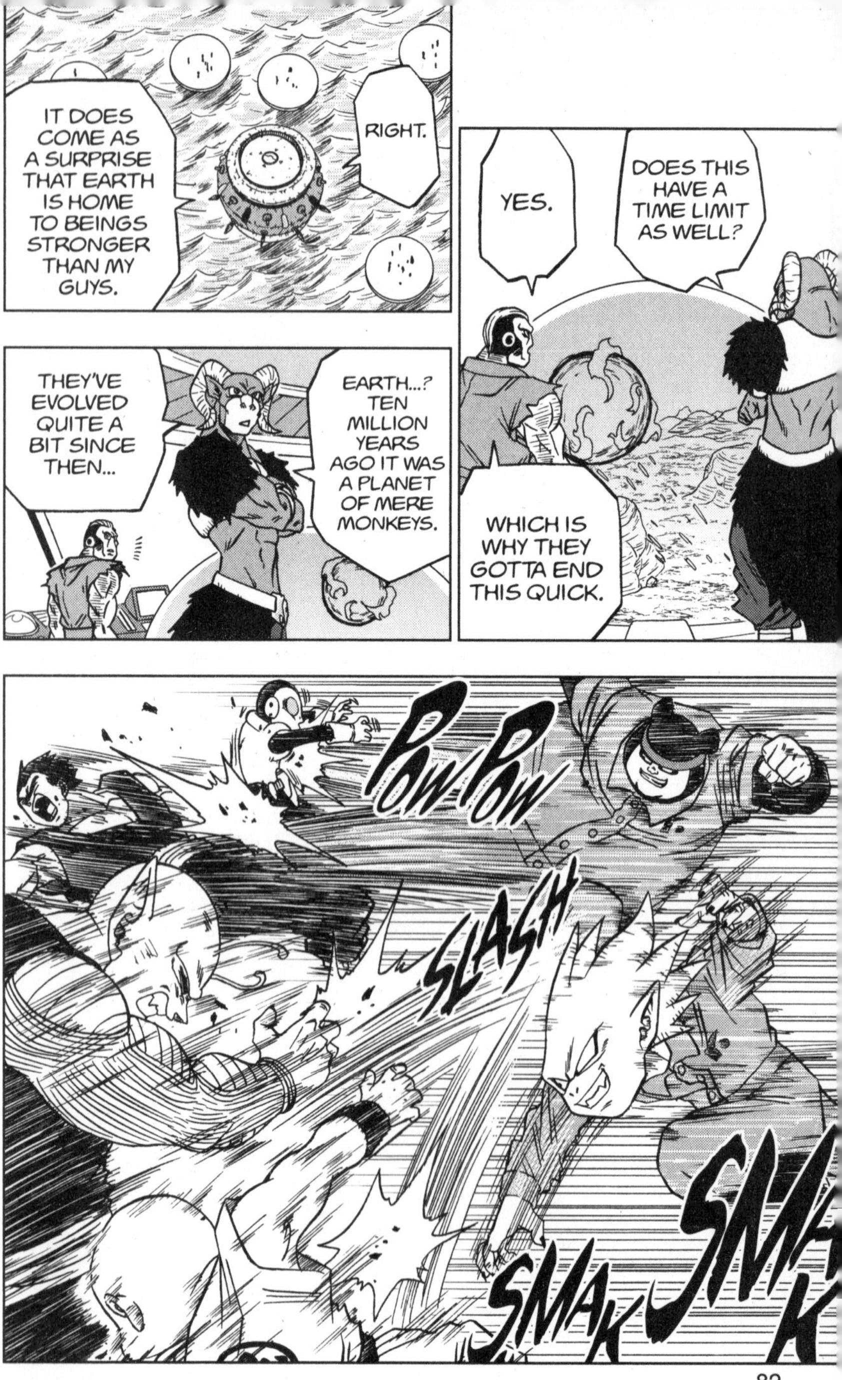
RIGHT.
IT DOES COME AS A SURPRISE THAT EARTH IS HOME TO BEINGS STRONGER THAN MY GUYS.
EARTH...? TEN MILLION YEARS AGO IT WAS A PLANET OF MERE MONKEYS.
THEY'VE EVOLVED QUITE A BIT SINCE THEN...
DOES THIS HAVE A TIME LIMIT AS WELL?
YES.
WHICH IS WHY THEY GOTTA END THIS QUICK.
POW POW
SLASH
SMAK SMAK

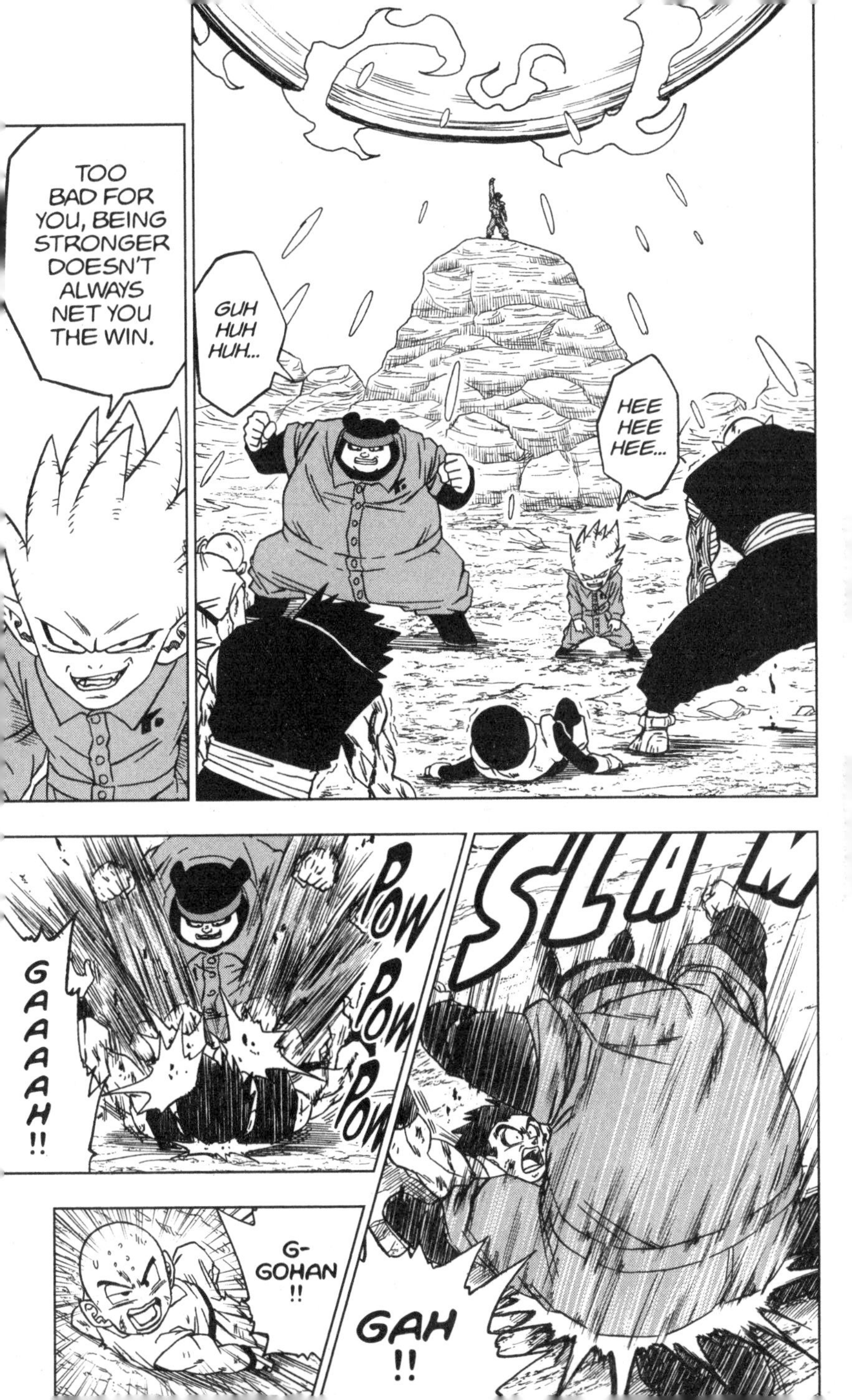
GUH HUH HUH...
HEE HEE HEE...
TOO BAD FOR YOU, BEING STRONGER DOESN'T ALWAYS NET YOU THE WIN.
SLAM
GAH!!
POW POW POW POW
GAAAAAH!!
G-GOHAN!!

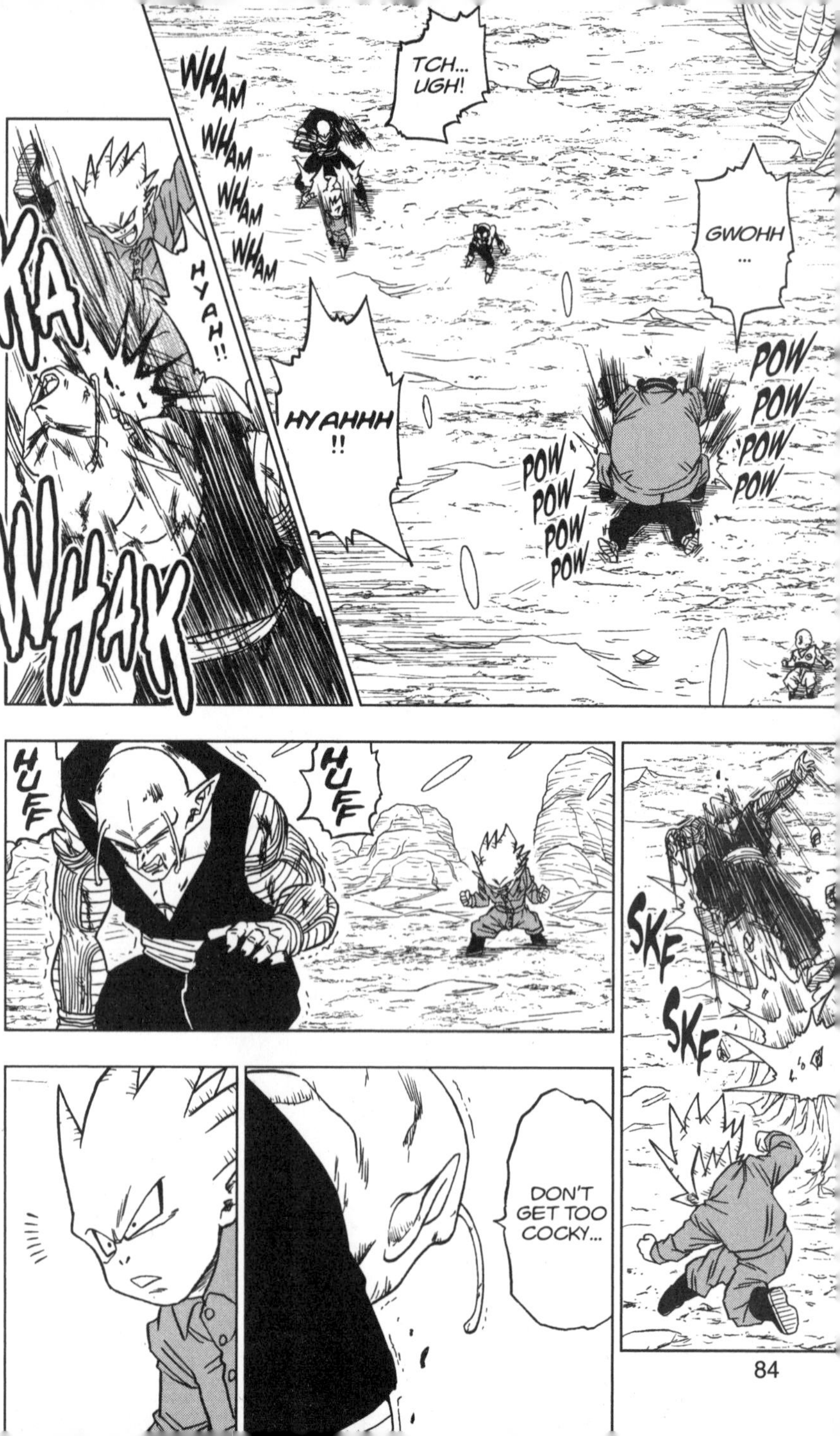
TCH... UGH!
GWOHH ...
POW POW POW POW
POW POW POW POW
HYAHHH !!
WHAM WHAM WHAM WHAM WHAM
HYAH!!
KA
WHAK
SKF
SKF
HUFF
HUFF
DON'T GET TOO COCKY...

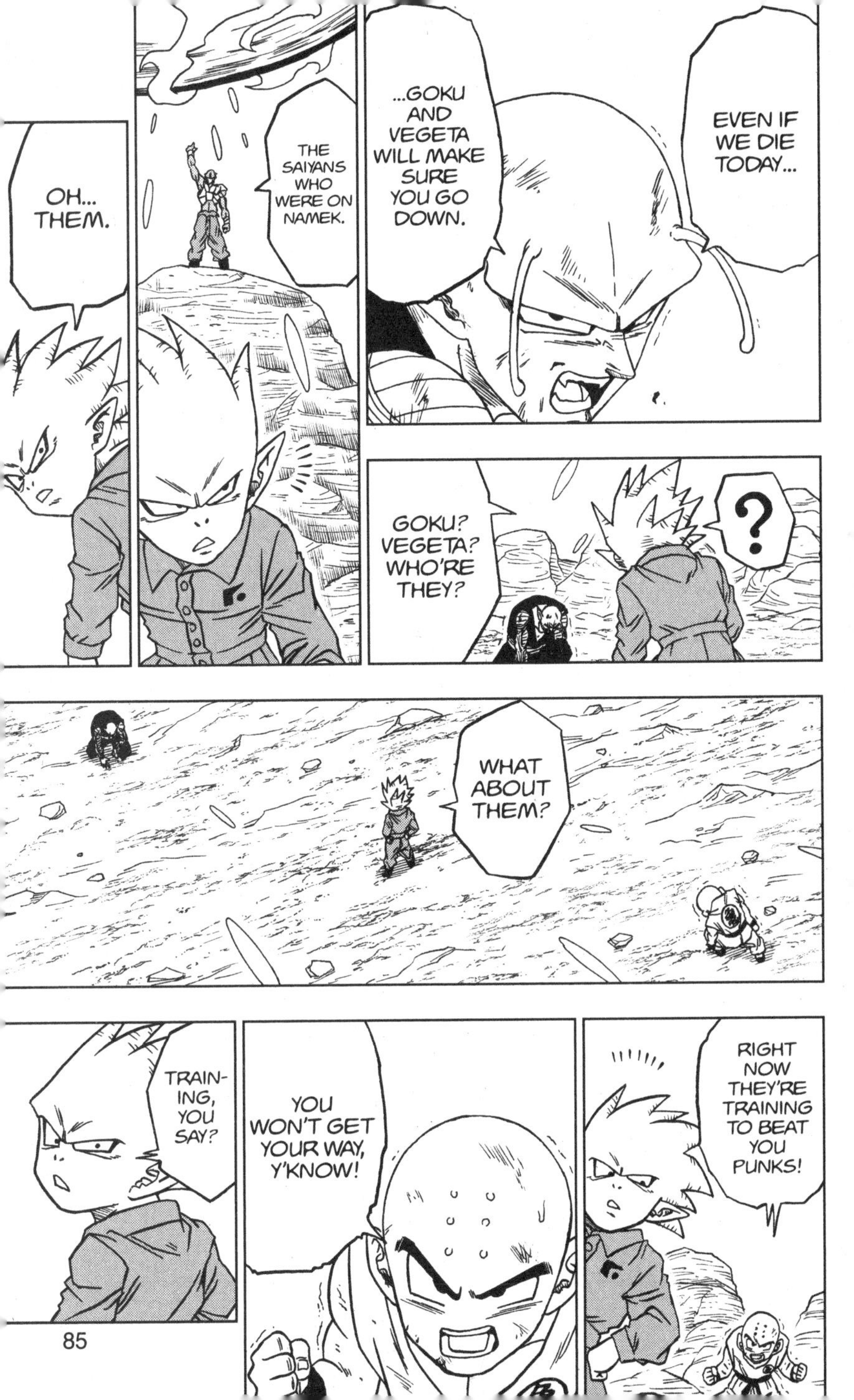
EVEN IF WE DIE TODAY...
...GOKU AND VEGETA WILL MAKE SURE YOU GO DOWN.
?
GOKU? VEGETA? WHO'RE THEY?
THE SAIYANS WHO WERE ON NAMEK.
OH... THEM.
WHAT ABOUT THEM?
RIGHT NOW THEY'RE TRAINING TO BEAT YOU PUNKS!
YOU WON'T GET YOUR WAY, Y'KNOW!
TRAIN-ING, YOU SAY?

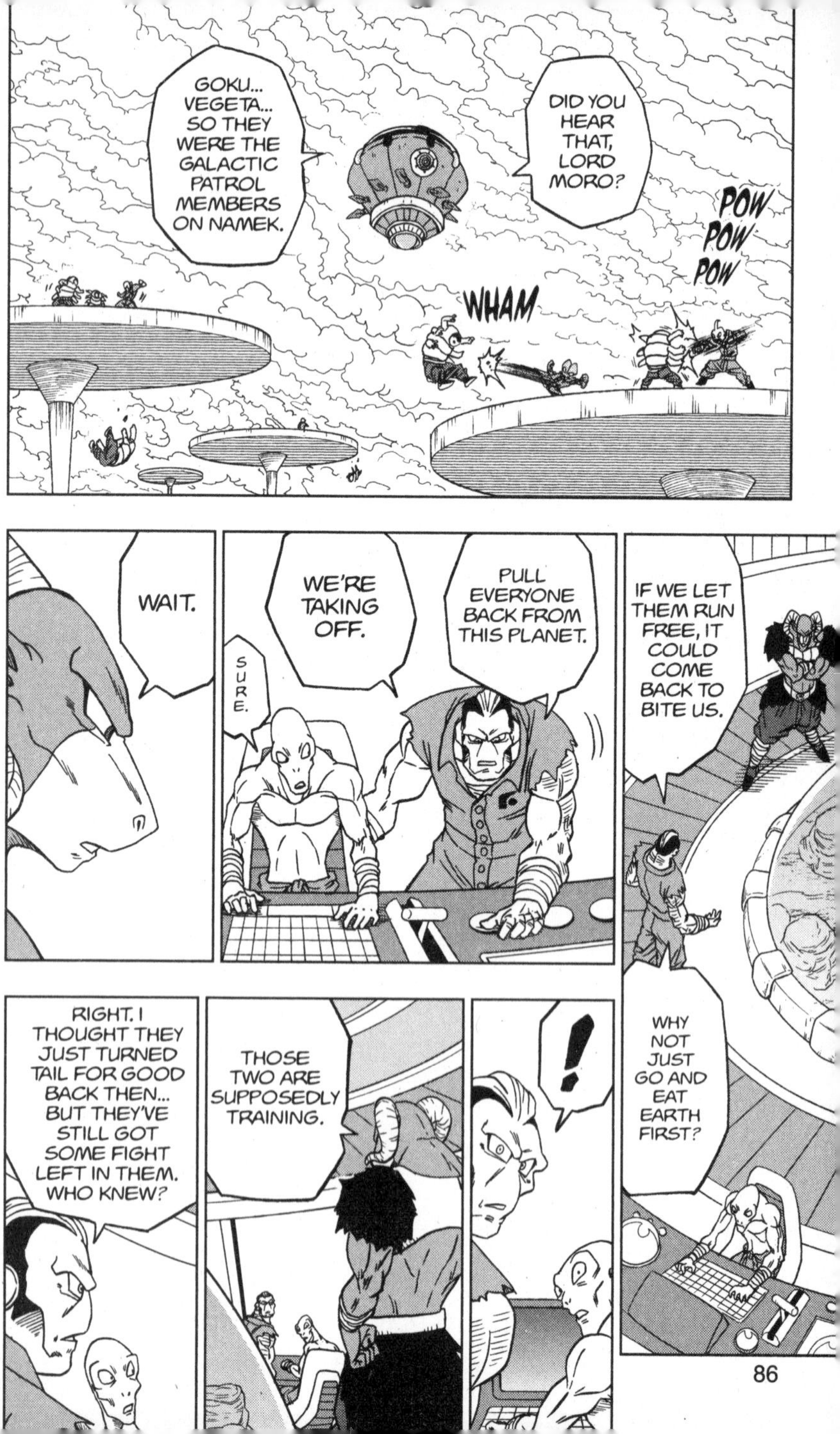
DID YOU HEAR THAT, LORD MORO?
GOKU... VEGETA... SO THEY WERE THE GALACTIC PATROL MEMBERS ON NAMEK.
POW POW POW
WHAM
IF WE LET THEM RUN FREE, IT COULD COME BACK TO BITE US.
PULL EVERYONE BACK FROM THIS PLANET.
WE'RE TAKING OFF.
SURE.
WAIT.
WHY NOT JUST GO AND EAT EARTH FIRST?
!
THOSE TWO ARE SUPPOSEDLY TRAINING.
RIGHT. I THOUGHT THEY JUST TURNED TAIL FOR GOOD BACK THEN... BUT THEY'VE STILL GOT SOME FIGHT LEFT IN THEM. WHO KNEW?

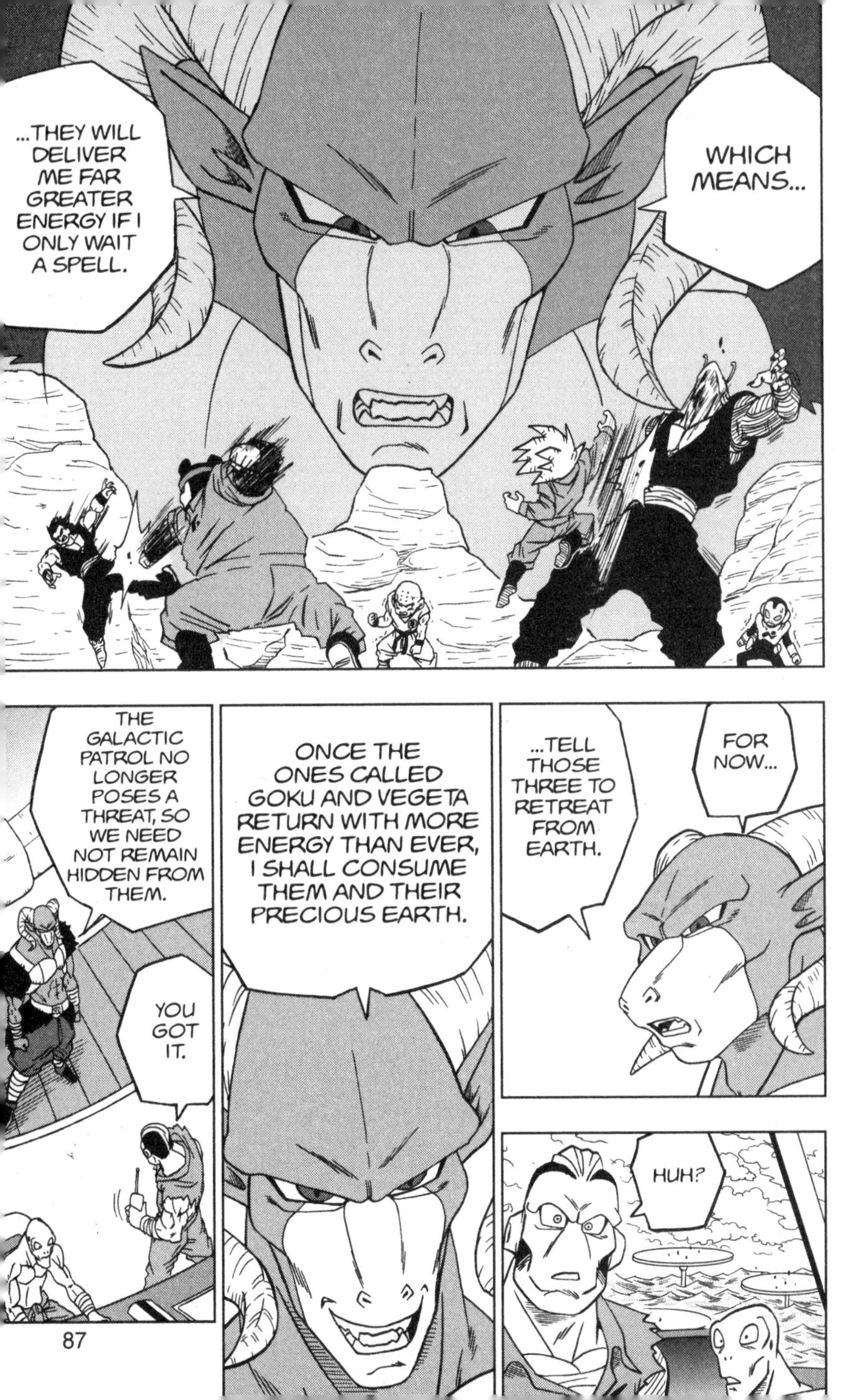
WHICH MEANS...
...THEY WILL DELIVER ME FAR GREATER ENERGY IF I ONLY WAIT A SPELL.
FOR NOW...
...TELL THOSE THREE TO RETREAT FROM EARTH.
HUH?
ONCE THE ONES CALLED GOKU AND VEGETA RETURN WITH MORE ENERGY THAN EVER, I SHALL CONSUME THEM AND THEIR PRECIOUS EARTH.
THE GALACTIC PATROL NO LONGER POSES A THREAT, SO WE NEED NOT REMAIN HIDDEN FROM THEM.
YOU GOT IT.

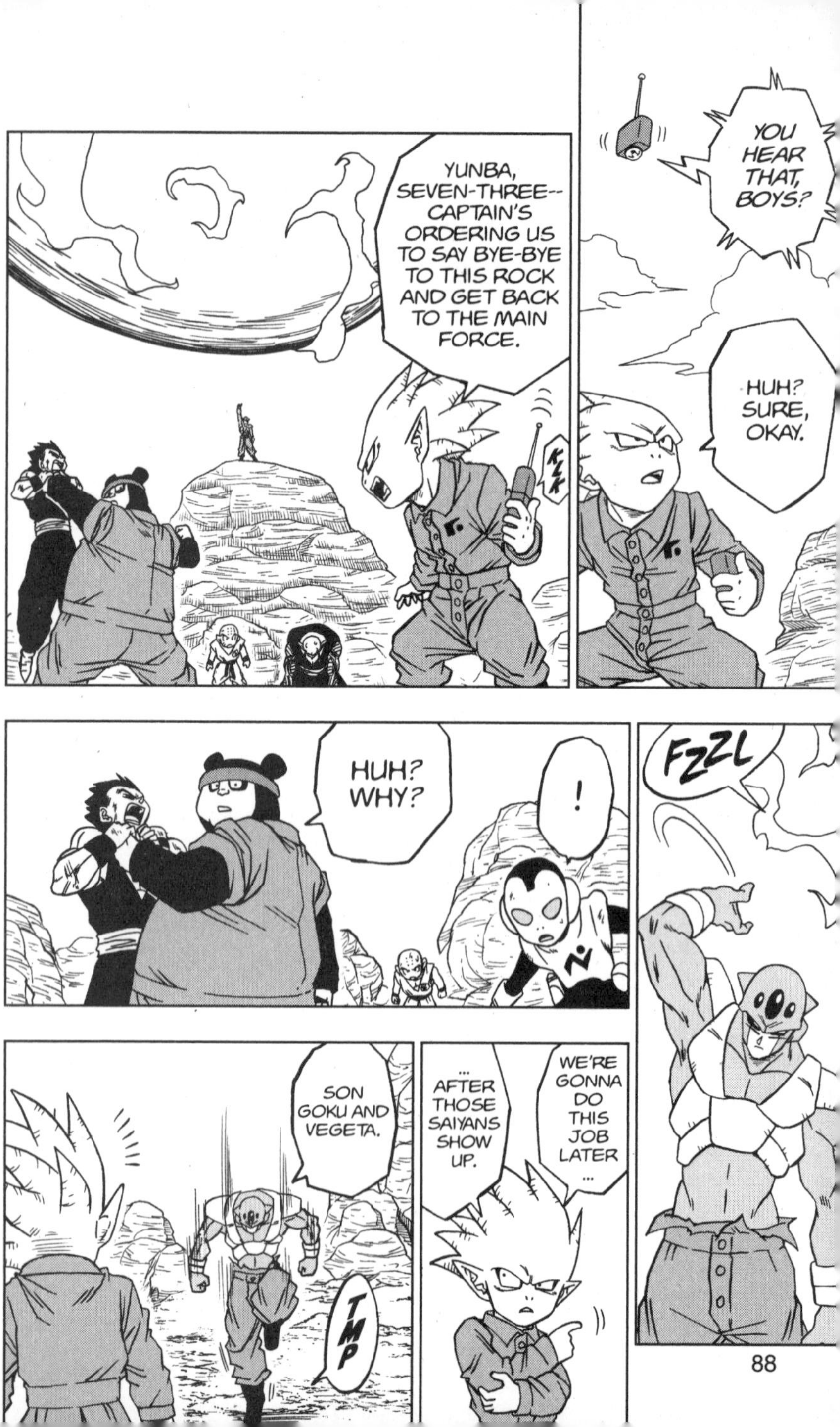
YOU HEAR THAT, BOYS?
HUH? SURE, OKAY.
YUNBA, SEVEN-THREE-- CAPTAIN'S ORDERING US TO SAY BYE-BYE TO THIS ROCK AND GET BACK TO THE MAIN FORCE.
KLIK
FZZL
HUH? WHY?
!
WE'RE GONNA DO THIS JOB LATER ...
... AFTER THOSE SAIYANS SHOW UP.
SON GOKU AND VEGETA.
TMP

BAH!

YEAH. THOSE TWO.

HUFF!

HUFF!

HUFF!

HUFF!

...!

YOU PEOPLE GOT OFF EASY.

BORING...

SO THE BIG BOSS IS COMING HERE?

LORD MORO'S GONNA COME AND GOBBLE UP THOSE SAIYANS HIMSELF.

BUT WHY...? WHAT'S GOING ON?

BETTER TELL YOUR SAIYAN PALS TO GET BACK HERE, 'KAY?

YEP. THEN YOU FOOLS AND THIS PLANET ARE DONE FOR.

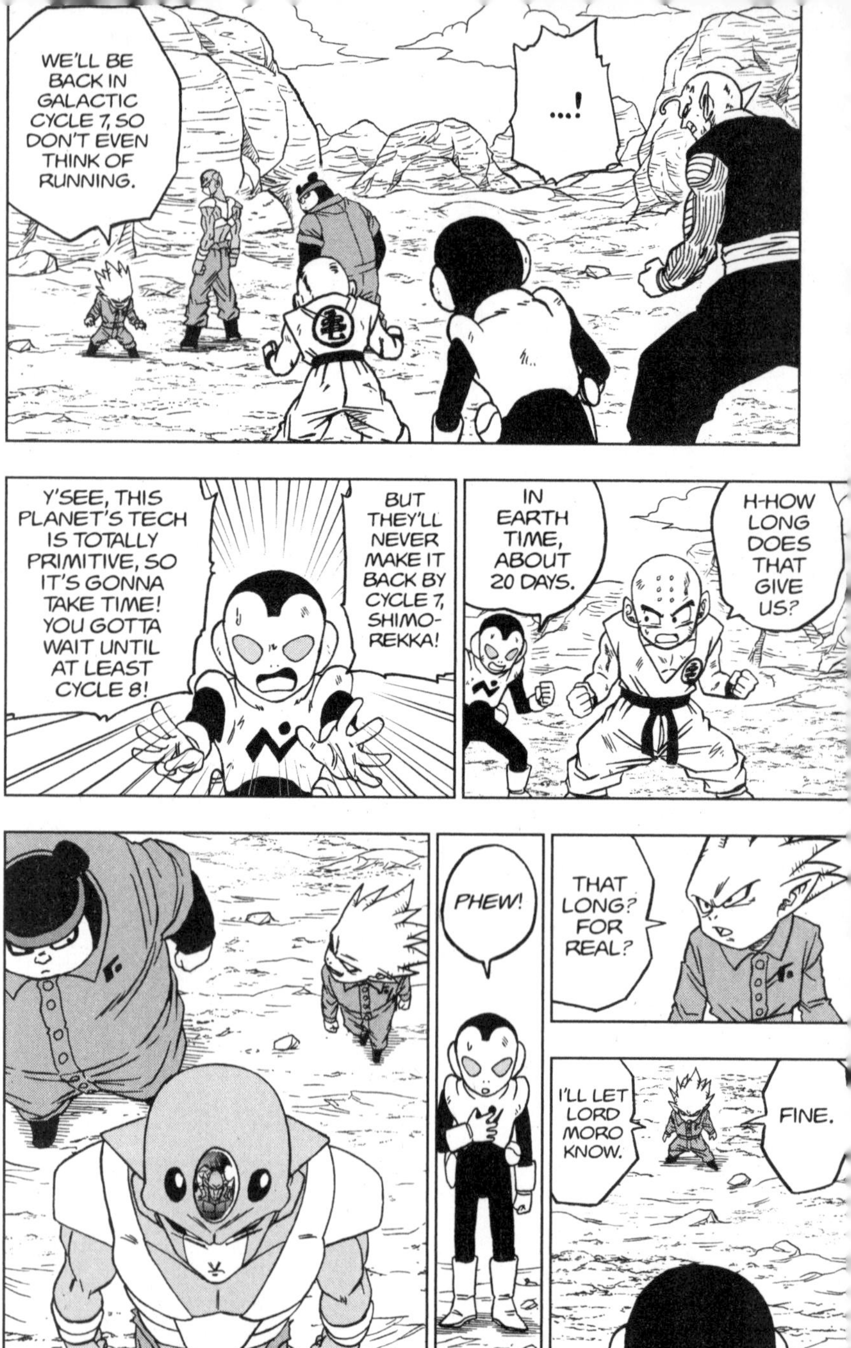
WE'LL BE BACK IN GALACTIC CYCLE 7, SO DON'T EVEN THINK OF RUNNING.
...!
H-HOW LONG DOES THAT GIVE US?
IN EARTH TIME, ABOUT 20 DAYS.
BUT THEY'LL NEVER MAKE IT BACK BY CYCLE 7, SHIMO-REKKA!
Y'SEE, THIS PLANET'S TECH IS TOTALLY PRIMITIVE, SO IT'S GONNA TAKE TIME! YOU GOTTA WAIT UNTIL AT LEAST CYCLE 8!
THAT LONG? FOR REAL?
FINE.
I'LL LET LORD MORO KNOW.
PHEW!

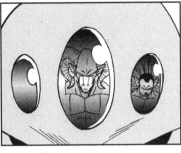

ZWOOM

KACHK

SKWEEZ

POP

SHOOP

TMP

LATER.

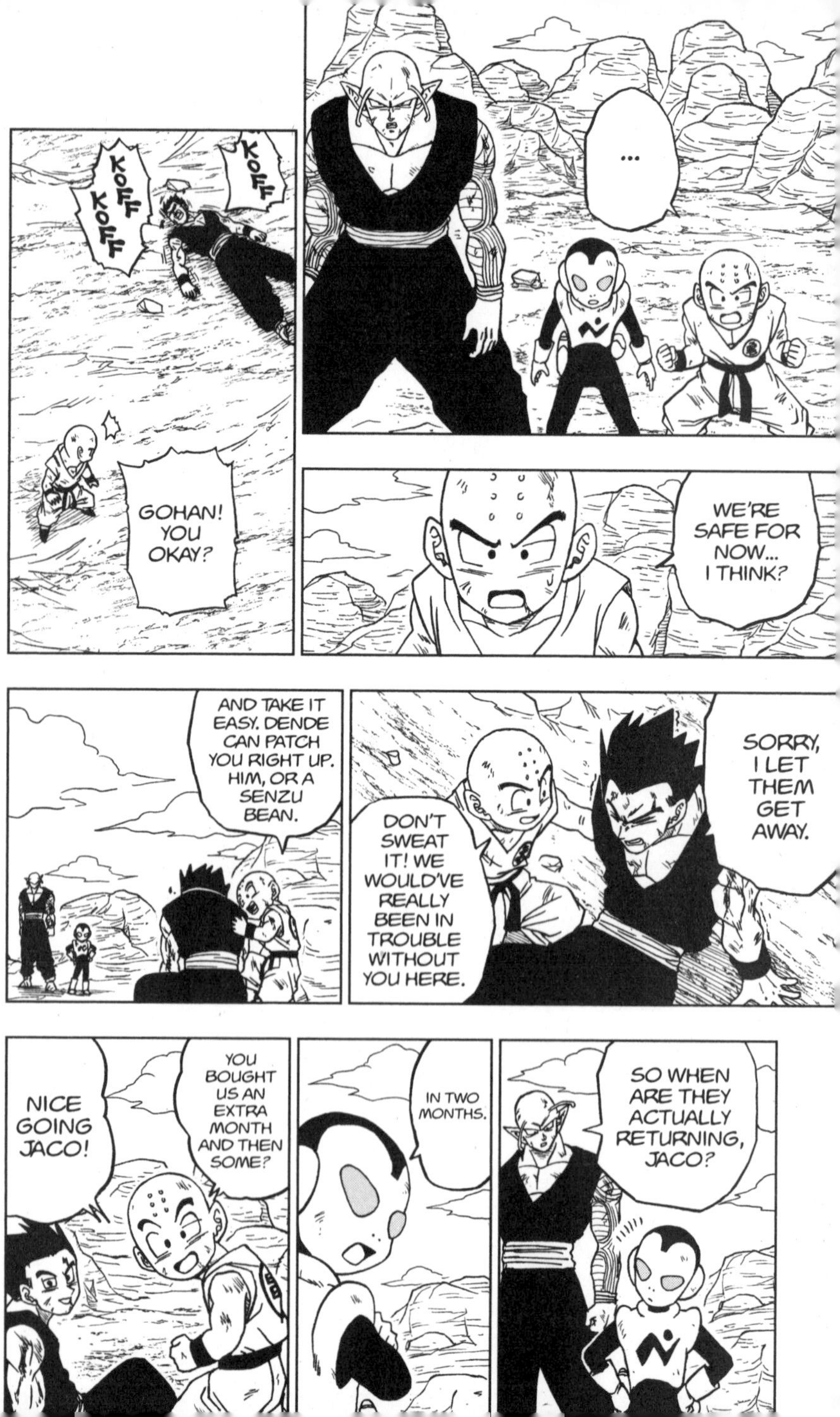
...
WE'RE SAFE FOR NOW... I THINK?
KOFF
KOFF KOFF
GOHAN! YOU OKAY?
SORRY, I LET THEM GET AWAY.
DON'T SWEAT IT! WE WOULD'VE REALLY BEEN IN TROUBLE WITHOUT YOU HERE.
AND TAKE IT EASY. DENDE CAN PATCH YOU RIGHT UP. HIM, OR A SENZU BEAN.
SO WHEN ARE THEY ACTUALLY RETURNING, JACO?
IN TWO MONTHS.
YOU BOUGHT US AN EXTRA MONTH AND THEN SOME?
NICE GOING JACO!

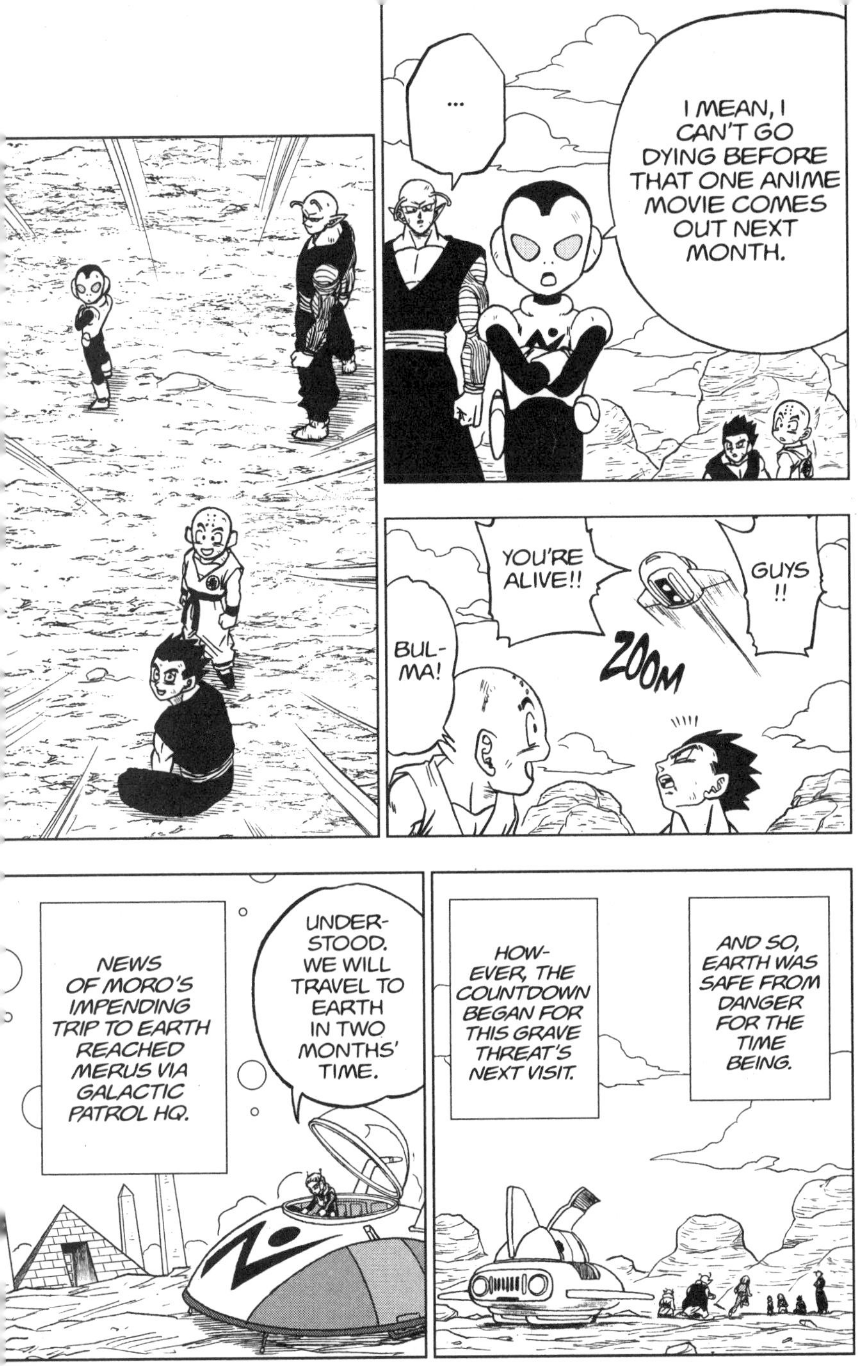
I MEAN, I CAN'T GO DYING BEFORE THAT ONE ANIME MOVIE COMES OUT NEXT MONTH.
...
GUYS !!
YOU'RE ALIVE!!
ZOOM
BUL- MA!
AND SO, EARTH WAS SAFE FROM DANGER FOR THE TIME BEING.
HOW- EVER, THE COUNTDOWN BEGAN FOR THIS GRAVE THREAT'S NEXT VISIT.
NEWS OF MORO'S IMPENDING TRIP TO EARTH REACHED MERUS VIA GALACTIC PATROL HQ.
UNDER- STOOD. WE WILL TRAVEL TO EARTH IN TWO MONTHS' TIME.

IT SEEMS ALL IS WELL, THOUGH. THANK GOODNESS AGENT JACO WAS THERE FOR THEM.

MORO'S PALS SHOWED UP ON EARTH?!

HUH ?!

GOTCHA! BUT THEY SAID THE BAD GUYS ARE GONNA COME BACK?

YES.

IT GIVES US SIX MONTHS IN HERE. I FEEL SORRY FOR THE PLANETS THAT WILL BE SACRIFICED IN THE MEANTIME, BUT ASSURING MORO'S CAPTURE WHEN THE TIME COMES IS OUR TOP PRIORITY.

TWO MONTHS... THAT'S MORE TIME THAN WE THOUGHT, HUH?

YES.

MY BELLY'S FULL, SO LET'S GET RIGHT BACK TO IT!

WELL, FINE!

THAT MEANS MY TRAINING'S GOTTA PAY OFF, OR ELSE.

94

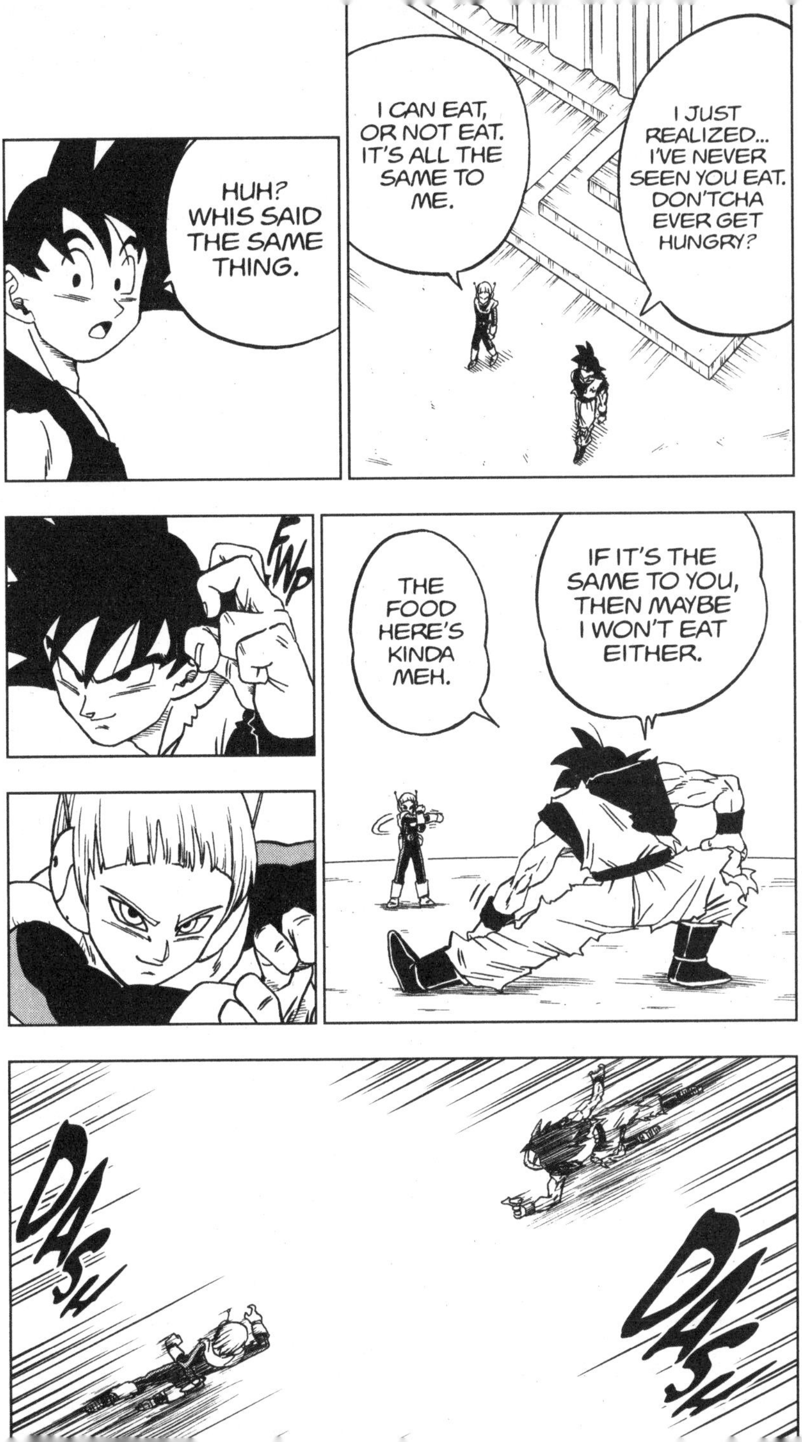
I JUST REALIZED... I'VE NEVER SEEN YOU EAT. DON'TCHA EVER GET HUNGRY?
I CAN EAT, OR NOT EAT. IT'S ALL THE SAME TO ME.
HUH? WHIS SAID THE SAME THING.
IF IT'S THE SAME TO YOU, THEN MAYBE I WON'T EAT EITHER.
THE FOOD HERE'S KINDA MEH.
FWP
DASH
DASH

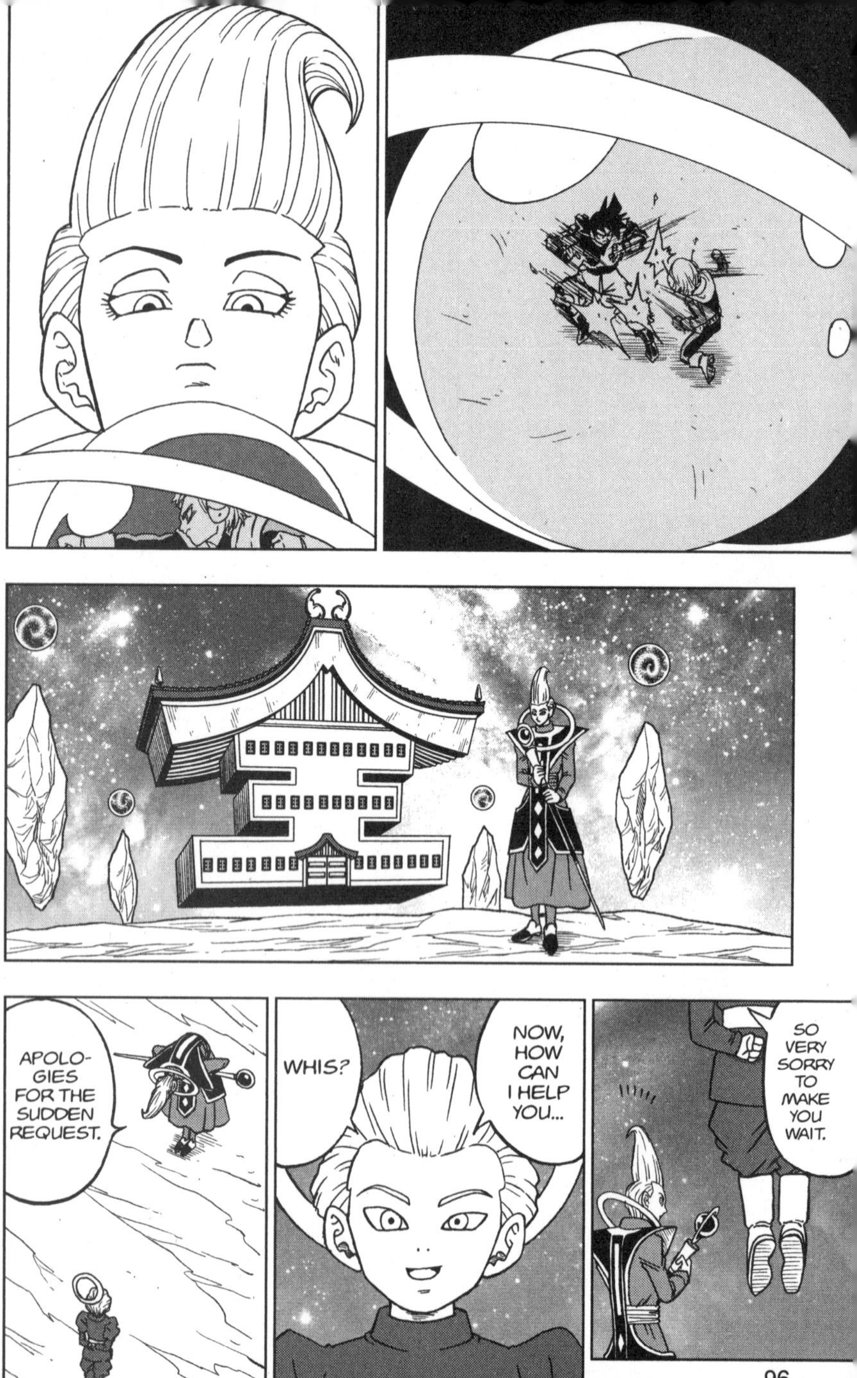
SO VERY SORRY TO MAKE YOU WAIT.
NOW, HOW CAN I HELP YOU...
WHIS?
APOLOGIES FOR THE SUDDEN REQUEST.

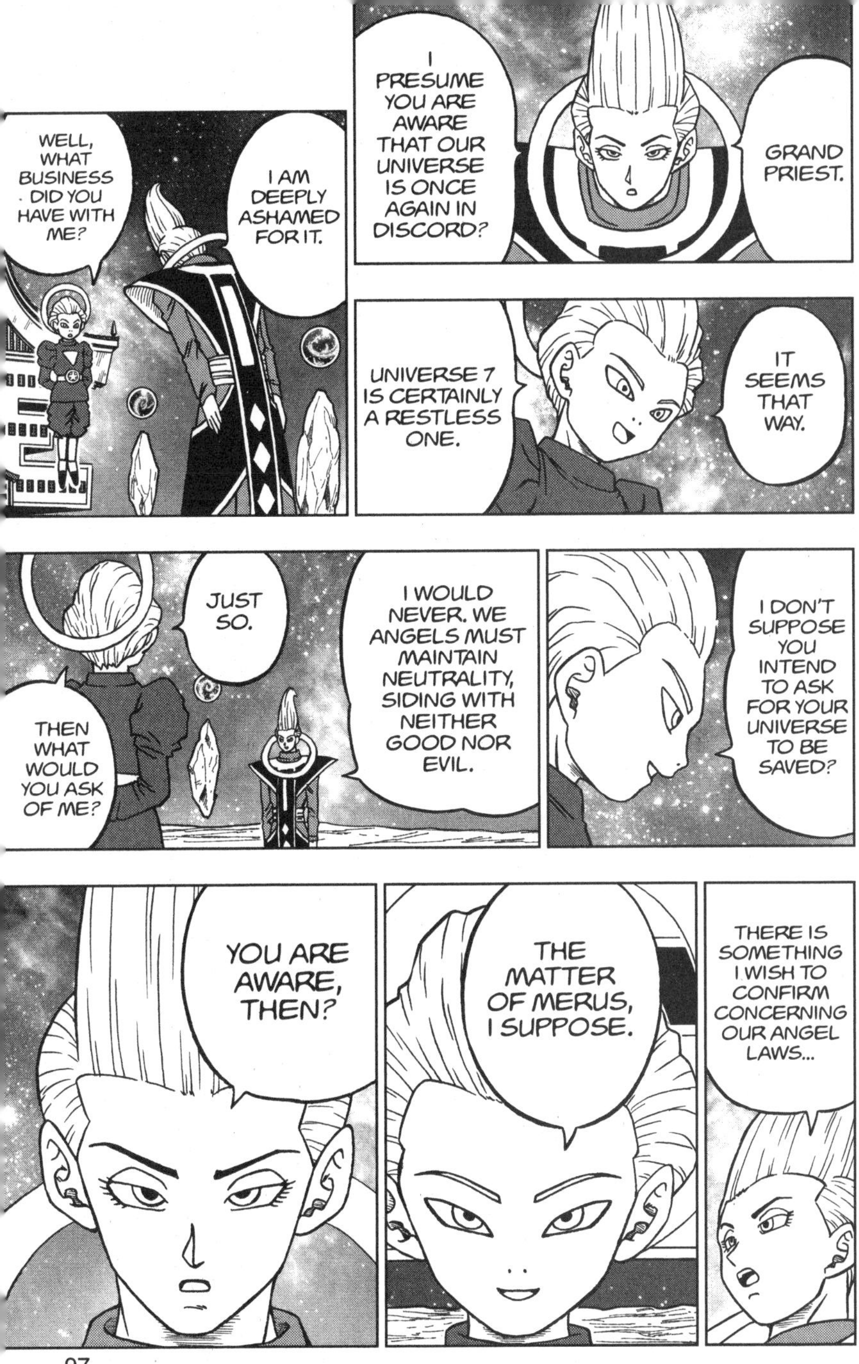
GRAND PRIEST.
I PRESUME YOU ARE AWARE THAT OUR UNIVERSE IS ONCE AGAIN IN DISCORD?
IT SEEMS THAT WAY.
UNIVERSE 7 IS CERTAINLY A RESTLESS ONE.
I AM DEEPLY ASHAMED FOR IT.
WELL, WHAT BUSINESS DID YOU HAVE WITH ME?
I DON'T SUPPOSE YOU INTEND TO ASK FOR YOUR UNIVERSE TO BE SAVED?
I WOULD NEVER. WE ANGELS MUST MAINTAIN NEUTRALITY, SIDING WITH NEITHER GOOD NOR EVIL.
JUST SO.
THEN WHAT WOULD YOU ASK OF ME?
THERE IS SOMETHING I WISH TO CONFIRM CONCERNING OUR ANGEL LAWS...
THE MATTER OF MERUS, I SUPPOSE.
YOU ARE AWARE, THEN?

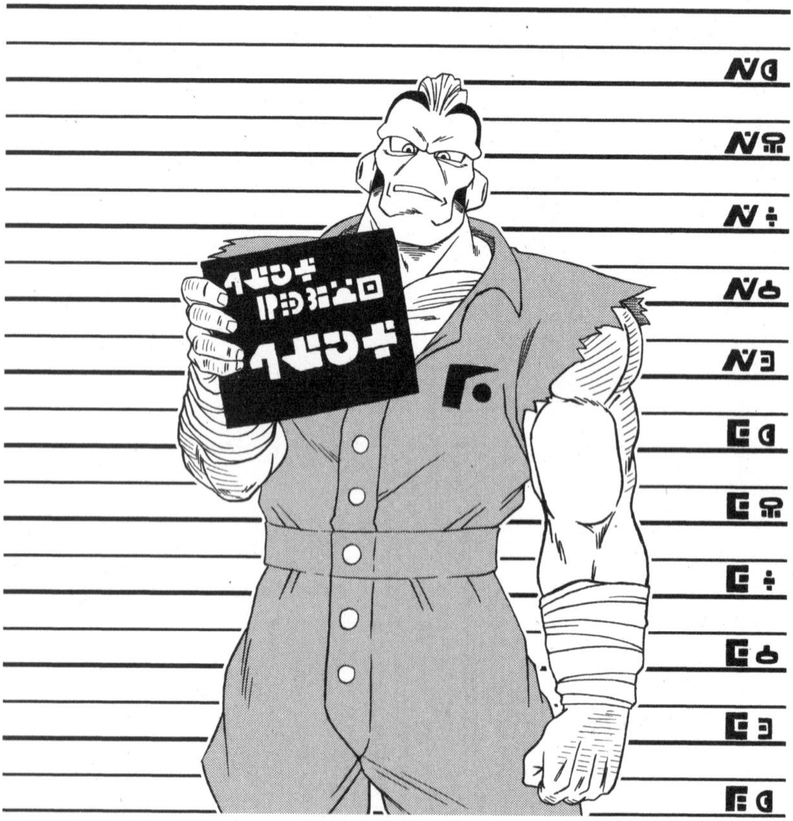

SAGANBO'S
GALACTIC BANDIT
BRIGADE LEADER:
SAGANBO

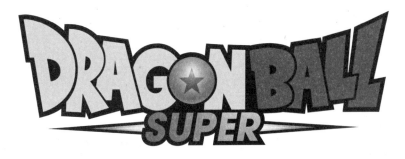

DRAGON BALL SUPER

CHAPTER 55: MERUS'S TRUE IDENTITY

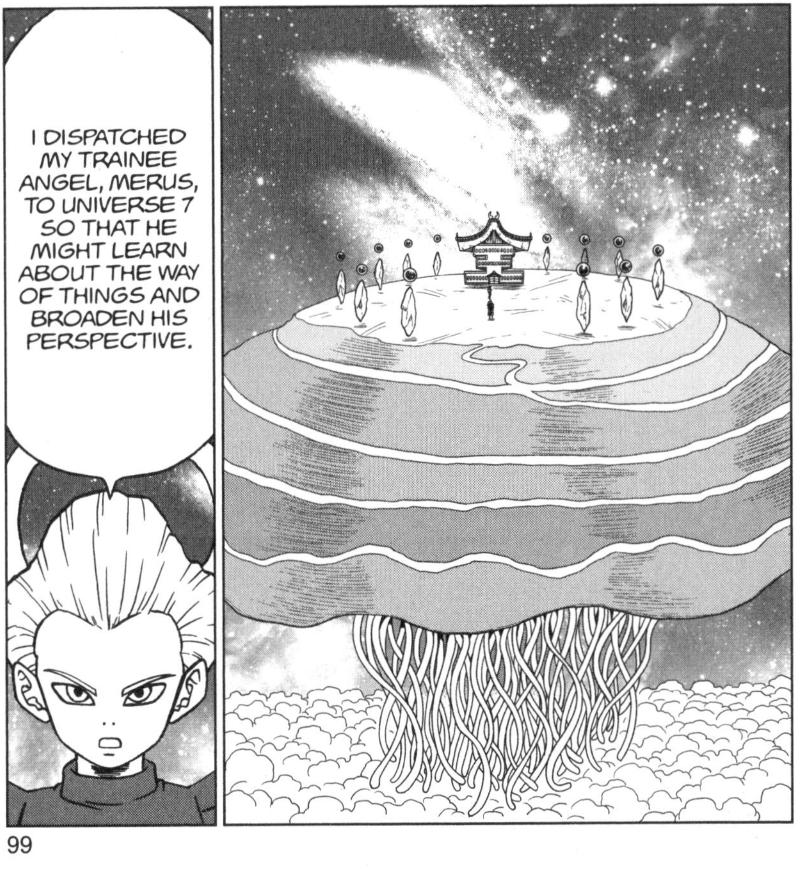
I DISPATCHED MY TRAINEE ANGEL, MERUS, TO UNIVERSE 7 SO THAT HE MIGHT LEARN ABOUT THE WAY OF THINGS AND BROADEN HIS PERSPECTIVE.

HIS ENLISTING IN THE GALACTIC PATROL SEEMED A DECENT CHOICE, AS IT WOULD ALLOW HIM TO OBSERVE THE SIDE OF GOOD AND VIRTUE, BUT, ALAS...

BEYOND THAT SINGLE LAW, THERE ARE NO RESTRICTIONS ON WHAT WE CAN OR CANNOT DO.

WE ANGELS MUST ALWAYS ACT IM-PARTIALLY.

INDEED.

ANY FURTHER INVOLVE-MENT WOULD MAKE HIM IN VIOLATION OF OUR CODE.

JUST SO.

HE SEEMS TO HAVE GAINED A BIAS?

MEAN-ING?

...

MIGHT YOU ALLOW ME TO COLLECT MERUS AND DEAL WITH HIM ON MY OWN?

GRAND PRIEST.

...I SHALL HAVE TO END MERUS'S TENURE IN THE MORTAL REALM.

AS HE IS PUSH-ING THE LIMIT...

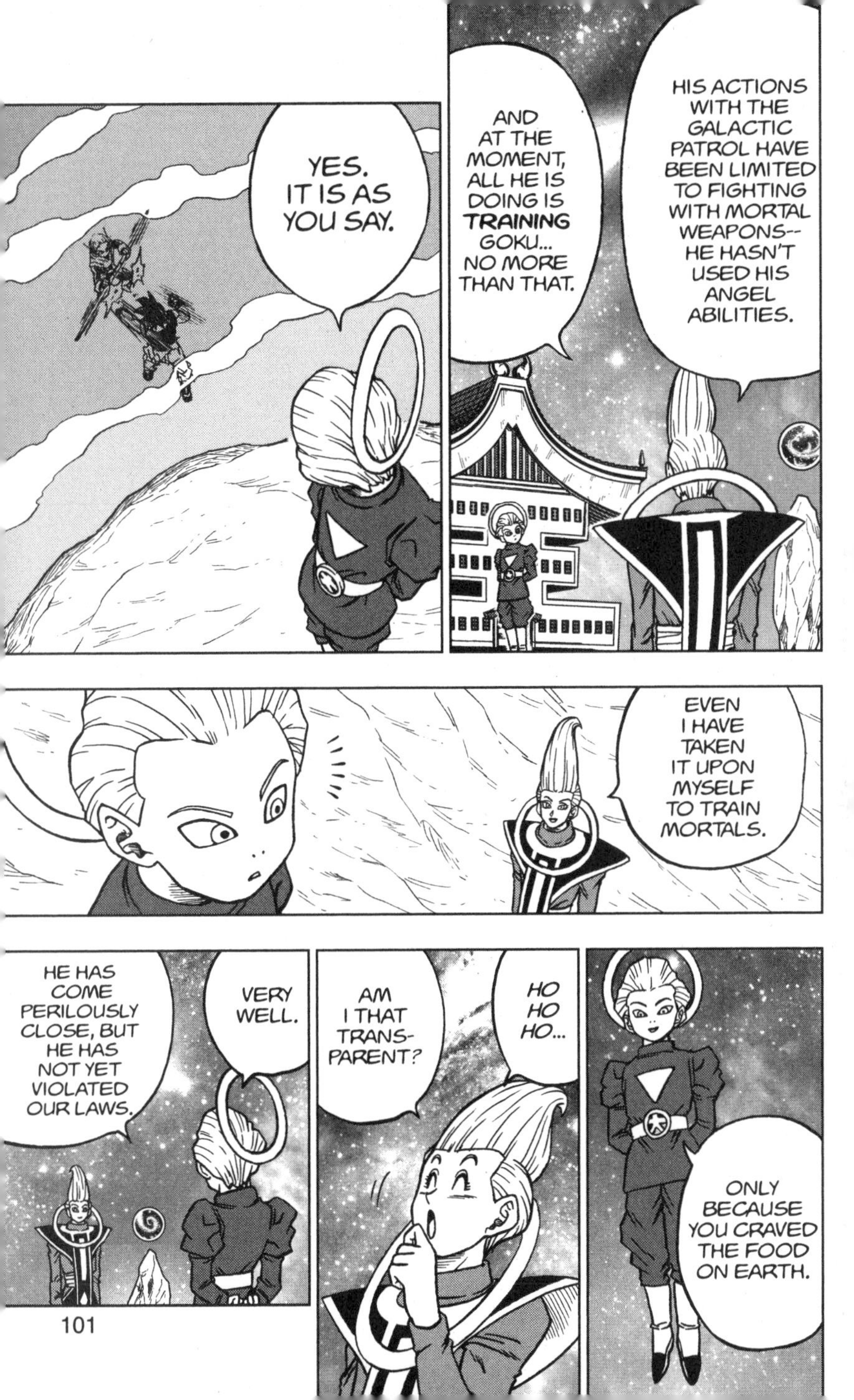
HIS ACTIONS WITH THE GALACTIC PATROL HAVE BEEN LIMITED TO FIGHTING WITH MORTAL WEAPONS-- HE HASN'T USED HIS ANGEL ABILITIES.
AND AT THE MOMENT, ALL HE IS DOING IS **TRAINING** GOKU... NO MORE THAN THAT.
YES. IT IS AS YOU SAY.
EVEN I HAVE TAKEN IT UPON MYSELF TO TRAIN MORTALS.
ONLY BECAUSE YOU CRAVED THE FOOD ON EARTH.
HO HO HO...
AM I THAT TRANSPARENT?
VERY WELL.
HE HAS COME PERILOUSLY CLOSE, BUT HE HAS NOT YET VIOLATED OUR LAWS.

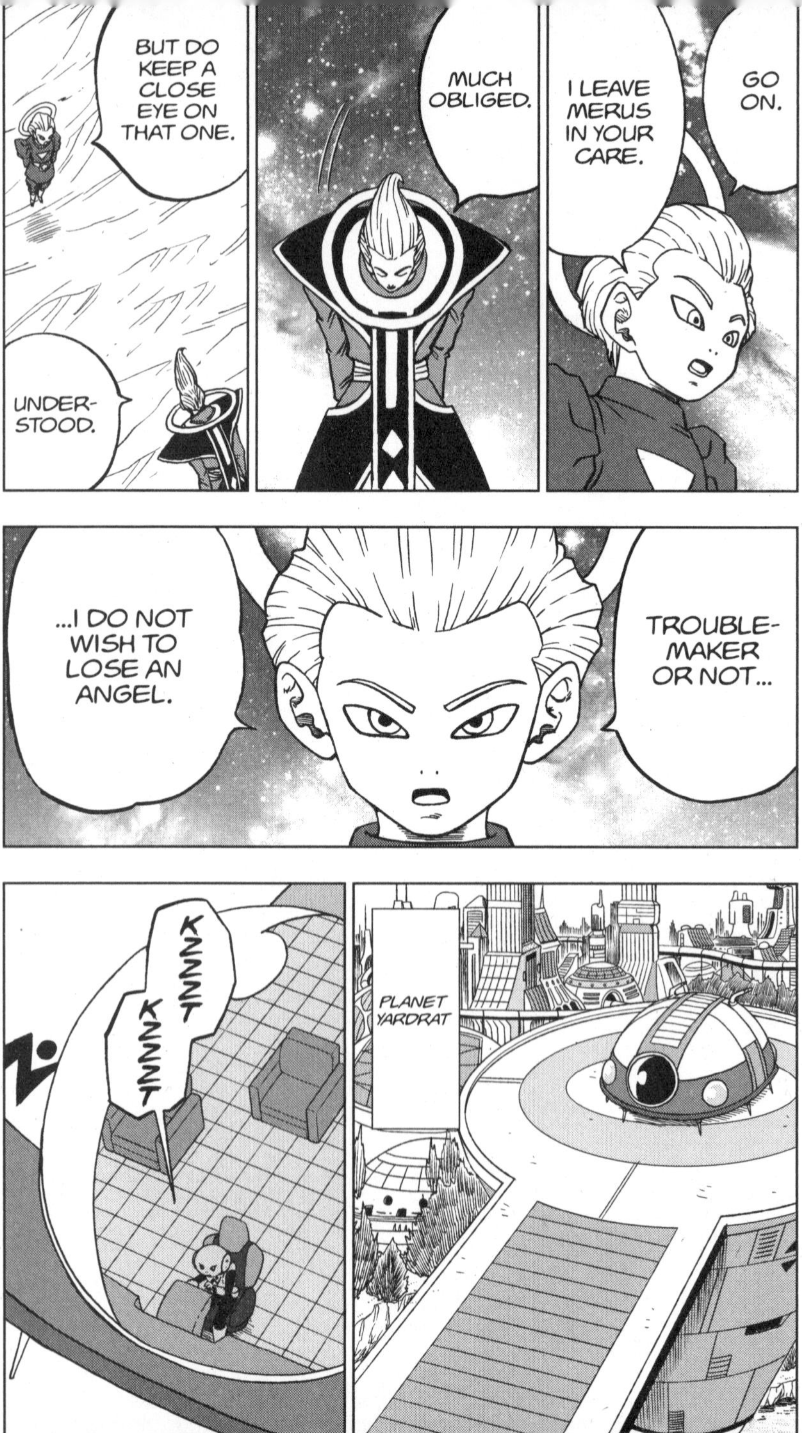
GO ON.
I LEAVE MERUS IN YOUR CARE.
MUCH OBLIGED.
BUT DO KEEP A CLOSE EYE ON THAT ONE.
UNDER-STOOD.
TROUBLE-MAKER OR NOT...
...I DO NOT WISH TO LOSE AN ANGEL.
PLANET YARDRAT
KZZZT KZZZT

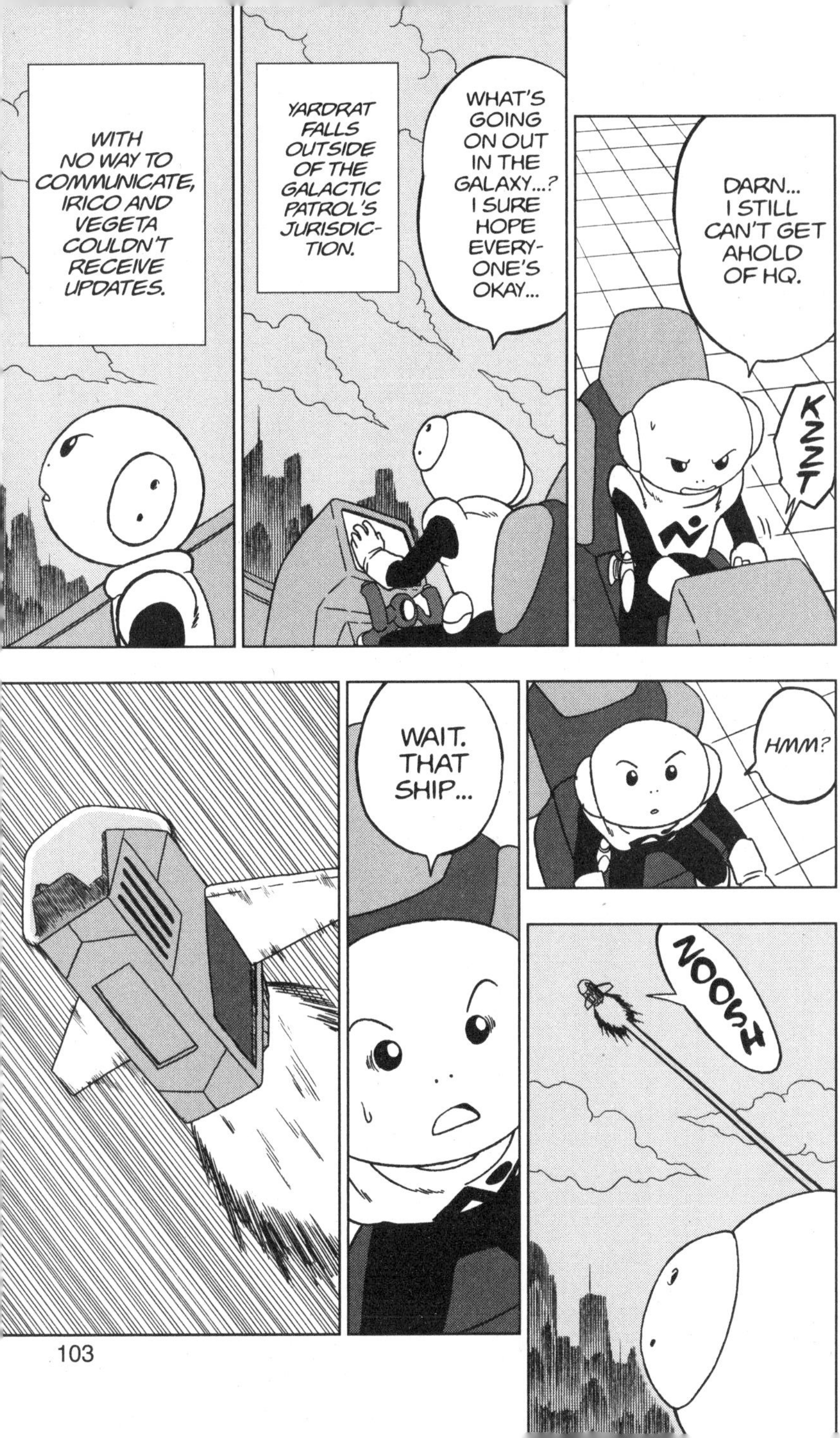
DARN... I STILL CAN'T GET AHOLD OF HQ.
KZZT
WHAT'S GOING ON OUT IN THE GALAXY...? I SURE HOPE EVERY-ONE'S OKAY...
YARDRAT FALLS OUTSIDE OF THE GALACTIC PATROL'S JURISDIC-TION.
WITH NO WAY TO COMMUNICATE, IRICO AND VEGETA COULDN'T RECEIVE UPDATES.
HMM?
NOOSH
WAIT. THAT SHIP...

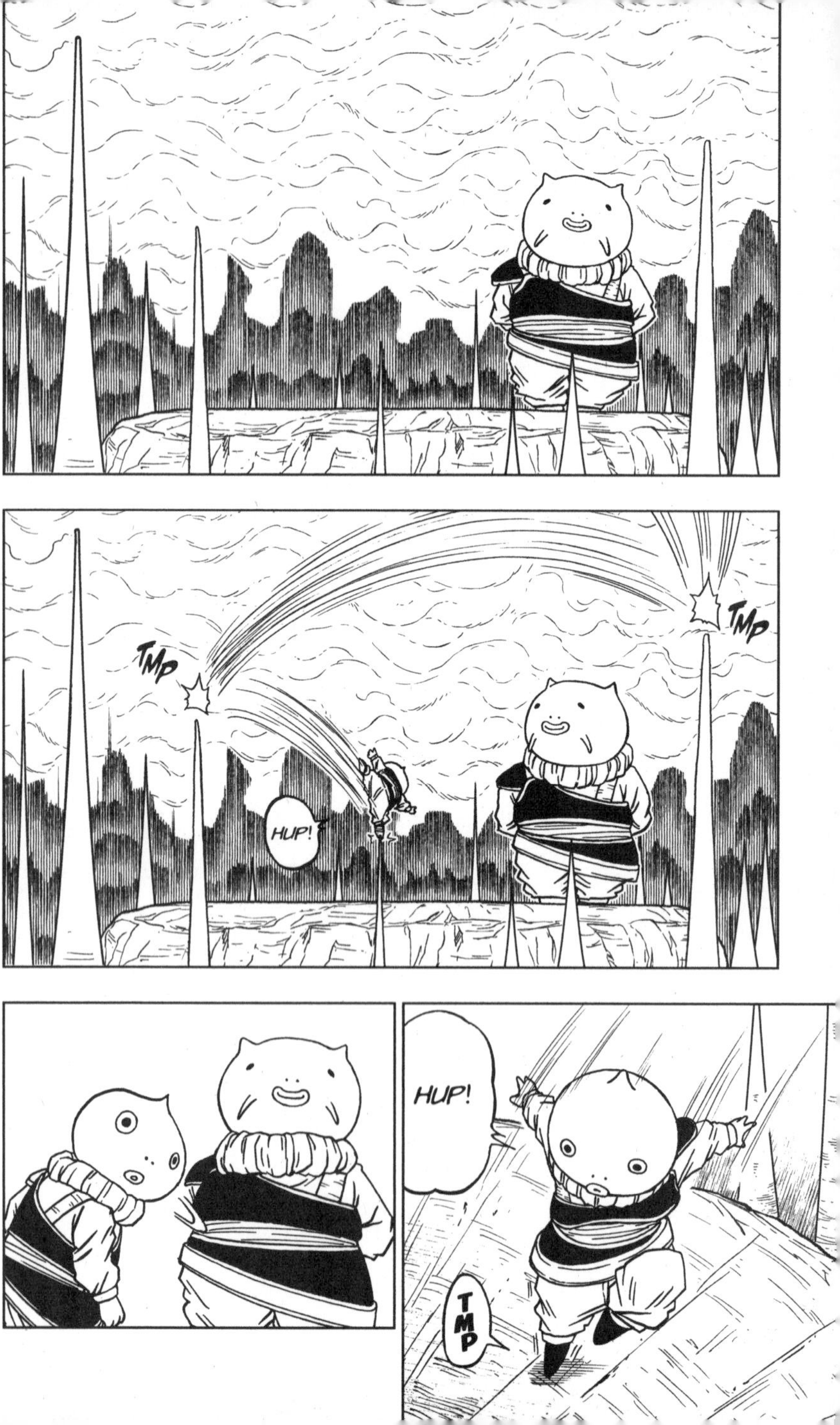
TMP
TMP
HUP!
HUP!
TMP

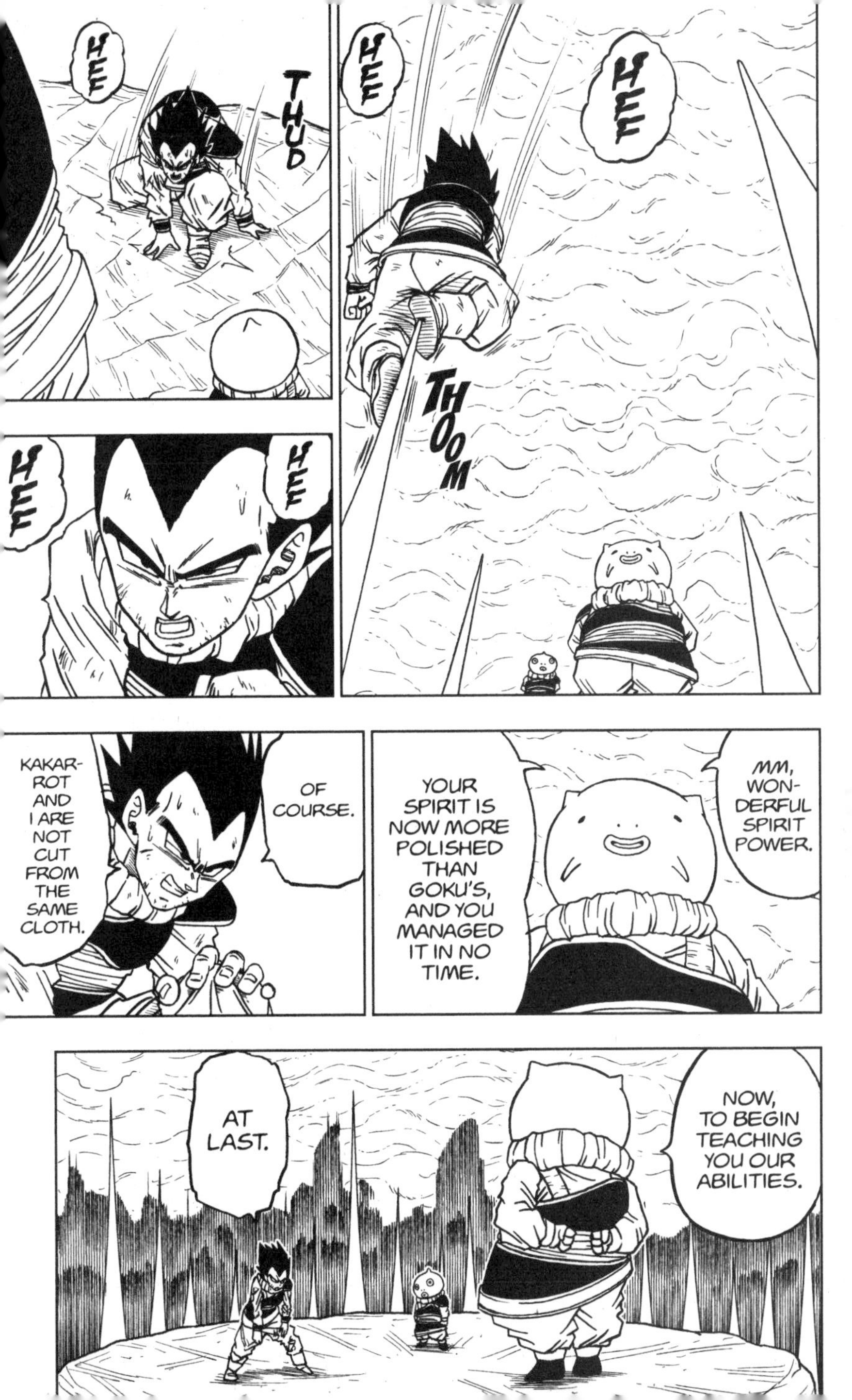
HEF
HEF
THOOOM
THUD
HEF
HEF
HEF
MM, WONDERFUL SPIRIT POWER.
YOUR SPIRIT IS NOW MORE POLISHED THAN GOKU'S, AND YOU MANAGED IT IN NO TIME.
OF COURSE.
KAKARROT AND I ARE NOT CUT FROM THE SAME CLOTH.
NOW, TO BEGIN TEACHING YOU OUR ABILITIES.
AT LAST.

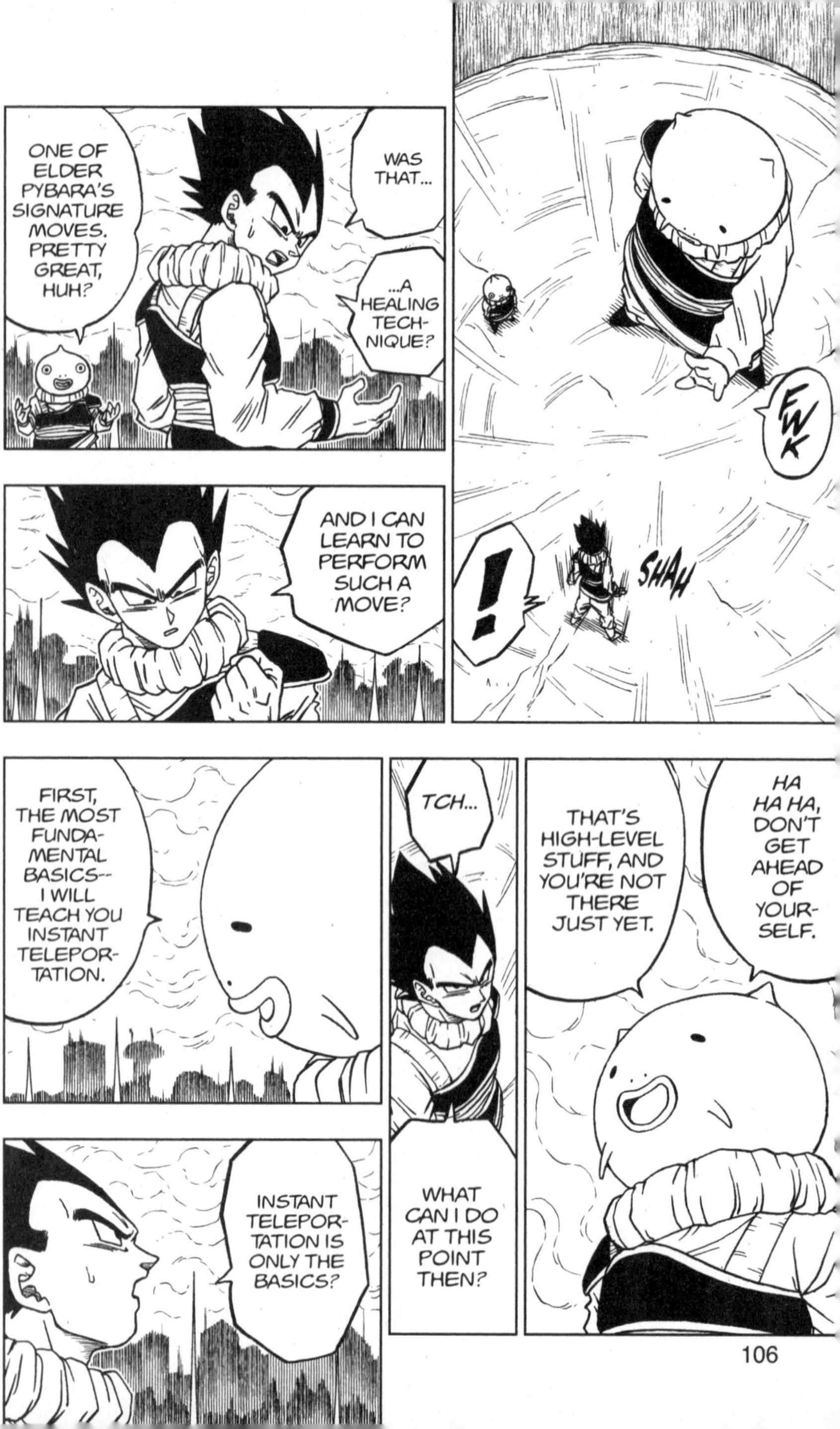
FWK
!
SHAH
WAS THAT...
...A HEALING TECHNIQUE?
ONE OF ELDER PYBARA'S SIGNATURE MOVES. PRETTY GREAT, HUH?
AND I CAN LEARN TO PERFORM SUCH A MOVE?
HA HA HA, DON'T GET AHEAD OF YOURSELF.
THAT'S HIGH-LEVEL STUFF, AND YOU'RE NOT THERE JUST YET.
TCH...
WHAT CAN I DO AT THIS POINT THEN?
FIRST, THE MOST FUNDAMENTAL BASICS-- I WILL TEACH YOU INSTANT TELEPORTATION.
INSTANT TELEPORTATION IS ONLY THE BASICS?

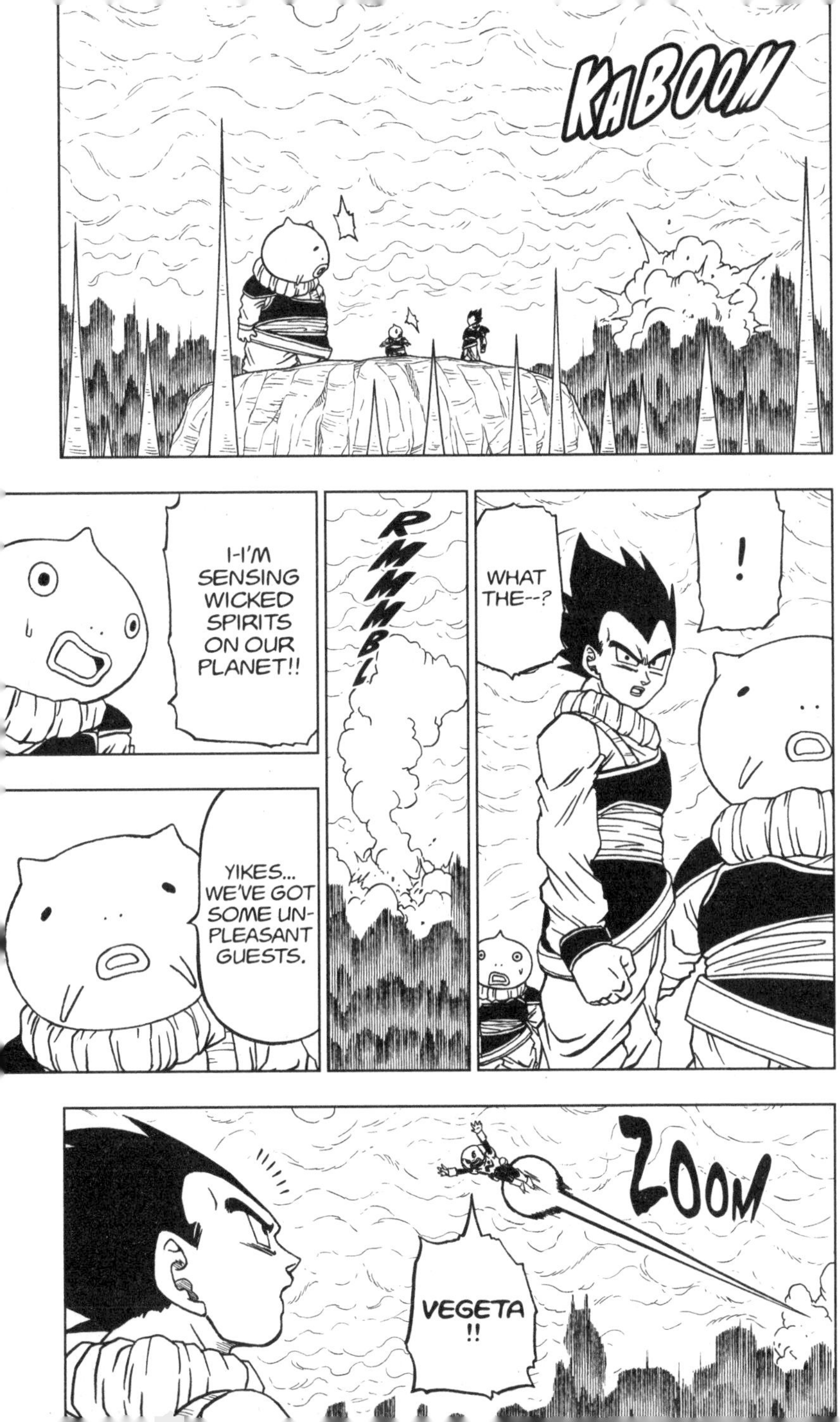
KABOOM
!
WHAT THE--?
RMMMMBL
I-I'M SENSING WICKED SPIRITS ON OUR PLANET!!
YIKES... WE'VE GOT SOME UN-PLEASANT GUESTS.
ZOOM
VEGETA!!

HEH
HEH
HEH
...

BWOOM

GAH!

KRAK

ONE
THAT IS
SURE TO
PLEASE
LORD
MORO.

A LOVELY
PLANET,
BRIMMING
WITH
ENERGY...

TMP

WHO
MIGHT
THIS
BE?

LORD MORO OUGHT TO KNOW ABOUT THIS...

THAT'S YUZUN-- ONE OF SAGANBO'S MINIONS.

MORO WON'T BE MAKING A MEAL OF THIS PLANET.

HO HO HO! SO YOU'VE FLED ALL THE WAY TO THIS ROCK?

OH, YOU ARE... YES, THE GALACTIC PATROL MEMBER FROM NAMEK!

NOT ON MY WATCH.

BWOOOM

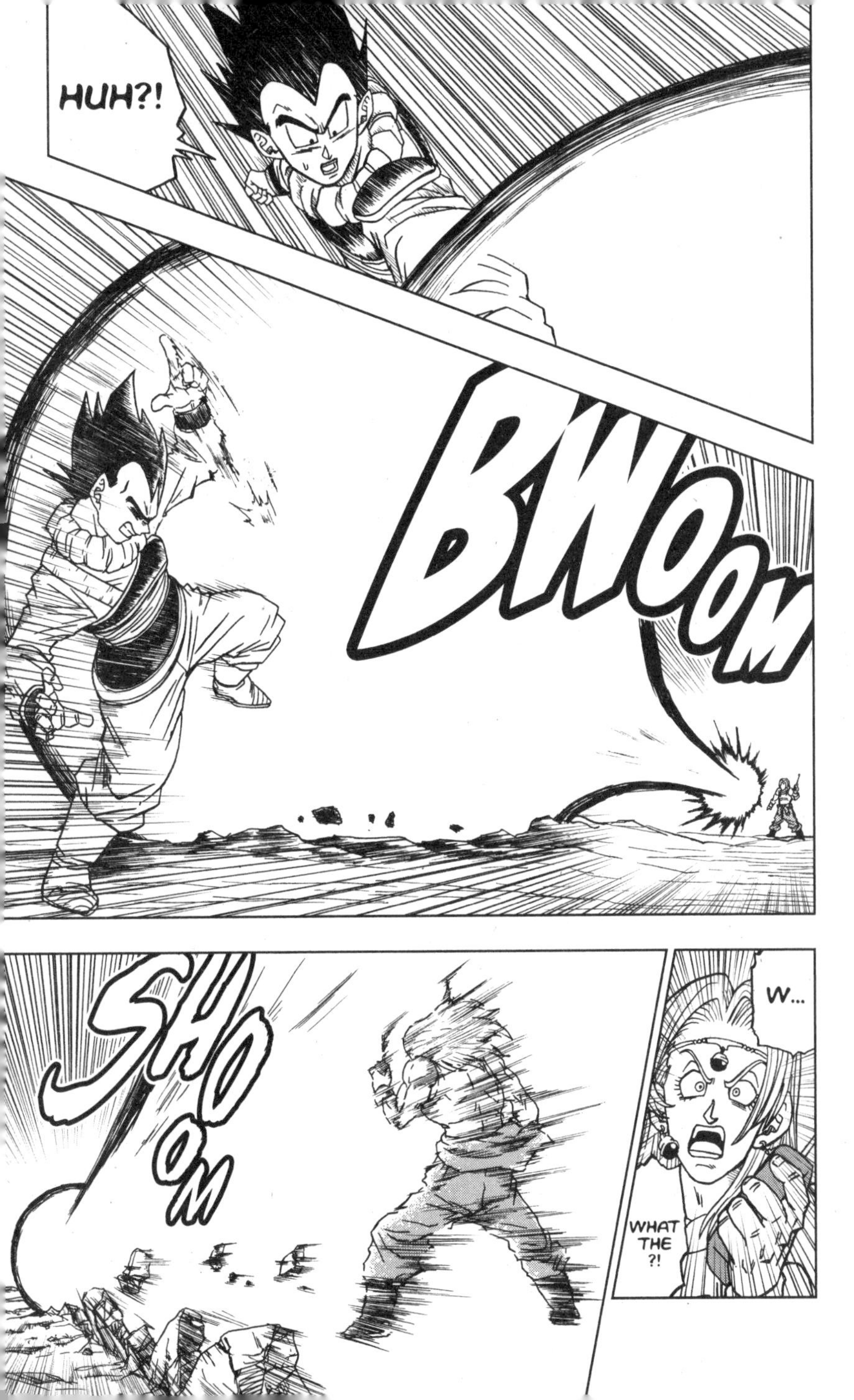
HUH?!
BWOOM
W...
WHAT THE ?!
SHOOM

KNOCK THAT OFF! DON'T GO WRECKING OUR PLANET!

FWK

FWK

WHAT WAS THAT ...?

W...

WHAT?

CARE TO EX- PLAIN?

GOOD THING NOBODY ACTUALLY LIVES IN THIS CITY, BUT STILL.

BEFORE YOUR TRAINING HERE, YOUR BODY AND SPIRIT WERE SO OFF- BALANCE THAT YOU COULDN'T PROJECT YOUR OWN POWER VERY WELL.

YOU JUST WIT- NESSED YOUR OWN NASCENT POWER.

BY LEAPS AND BOUNDS.

SURE HAVE.

MEANING I'VE ALREADY GROWN STRONGER SINCE I ARRIVED ...?

THUD

THUD

WHAM

UGH...

!

TWITCH

TWITCH

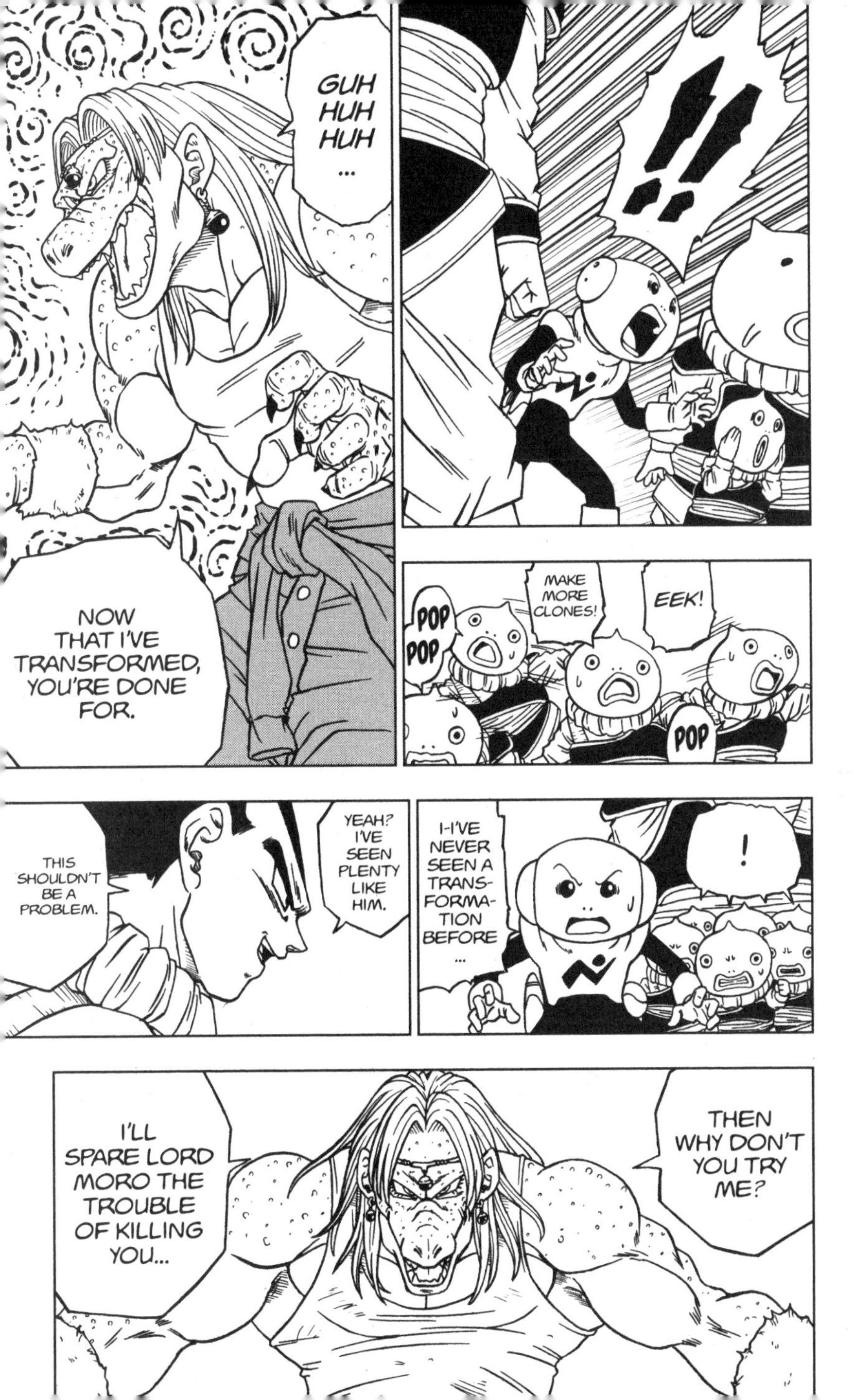
GUH HUH HUH ...
NOW THAT I'VE TRANSFORMED, YOU'RE DONE FOR.
!!
POP POP
MAKE MORE CLONES!
EEK!
POP
THIS SHOULDN'T BE A PROBLEM.
YEAH? I'VE SEEN PLENTY LIKE HIM.
I-I'VE NEVER SEEN A TRANSFORMATION BEFORE ...
!
I'LL SPARE LORD MORO THE TROUBLE OF KILLING YOU...
THEN WHY DON'T YOU TRY ME?

TRY YOU?
I BELIEVE
I JUST DID.

...WILL
YOU BE
KILLING
...?

SORRY,
I DIDN'T
QUITE
CATCH
THAT. WHO
EXACTLY
...

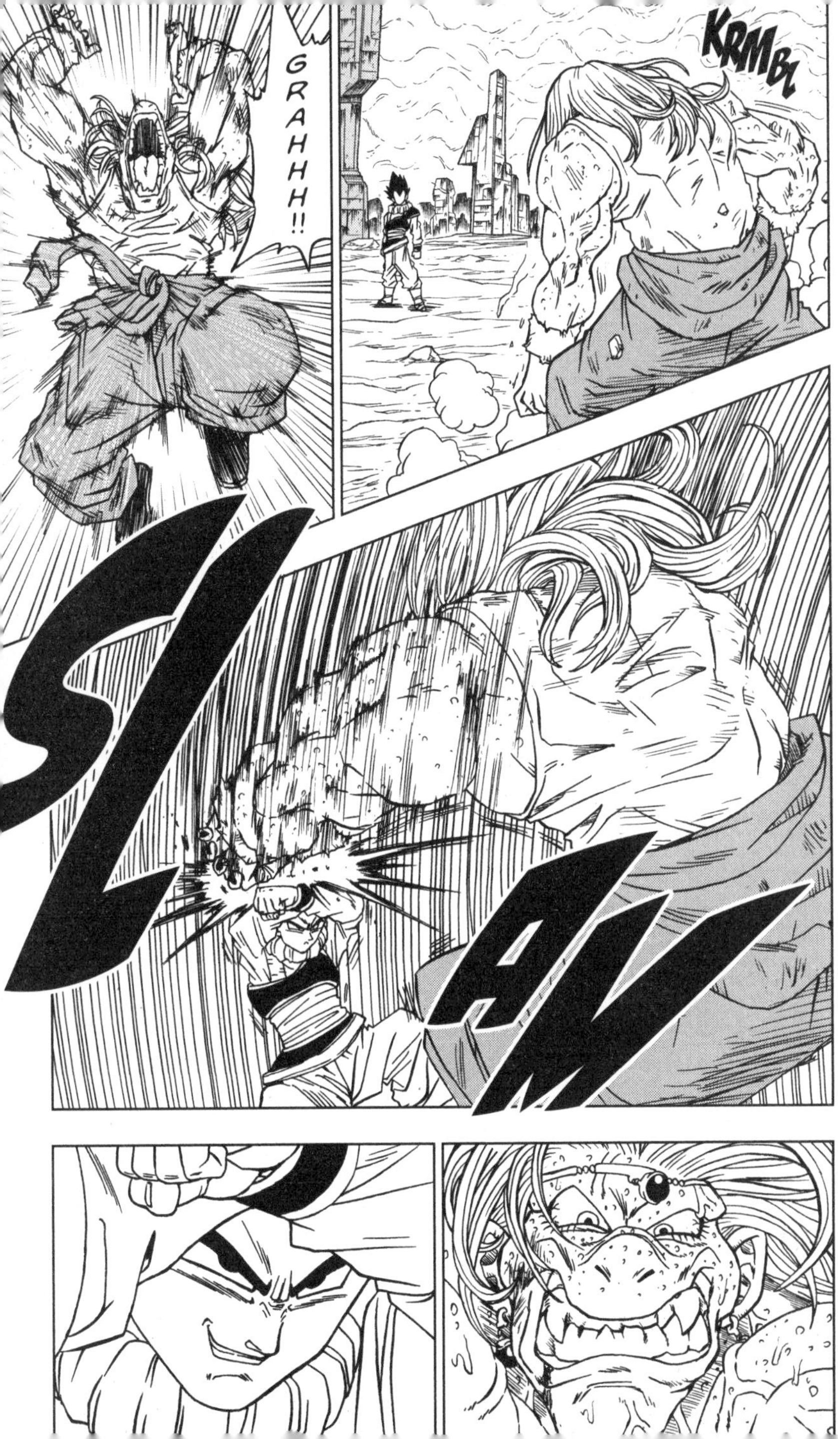
KRMBL
GRAHHHH!!
SLAM

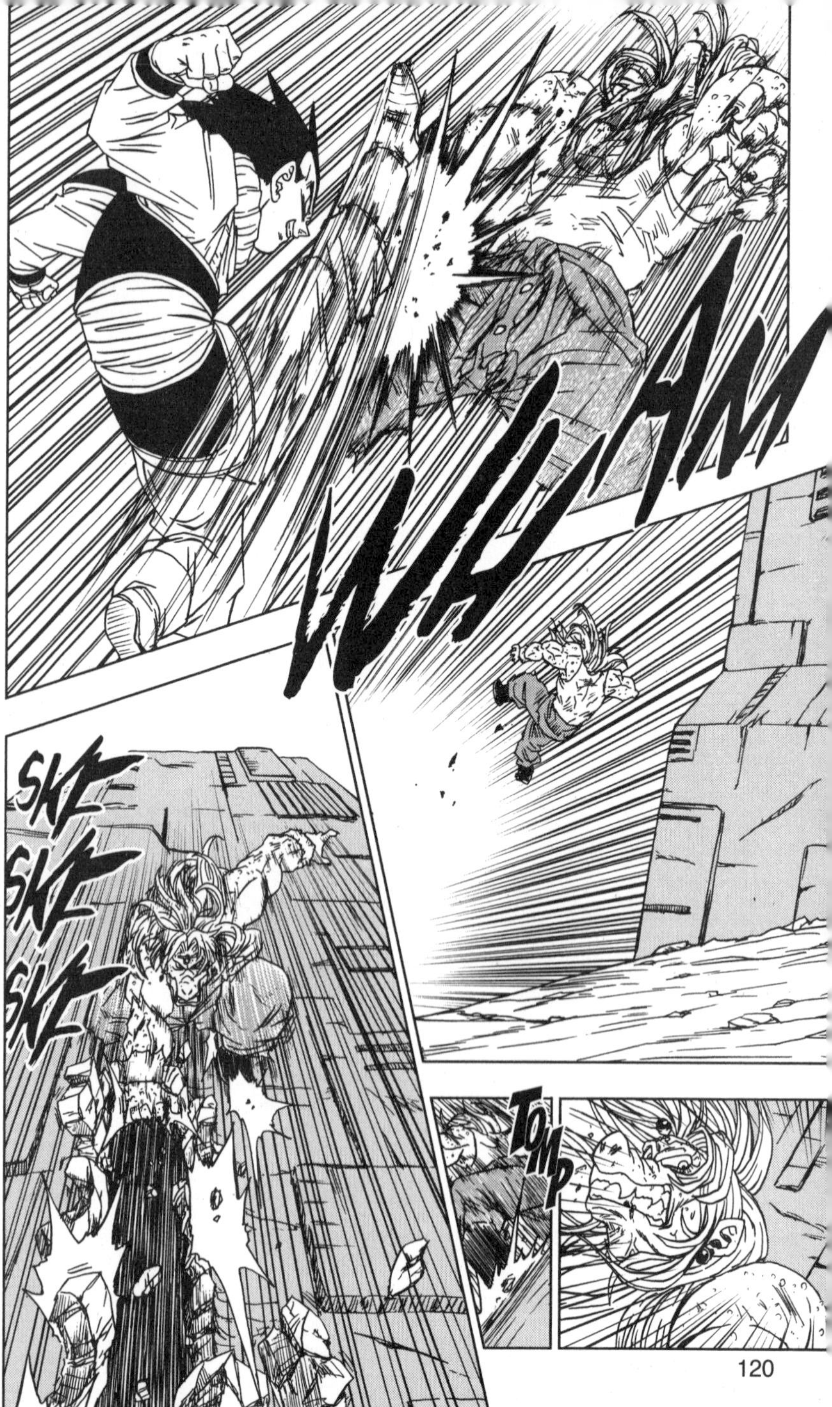
WHAM
TOMP

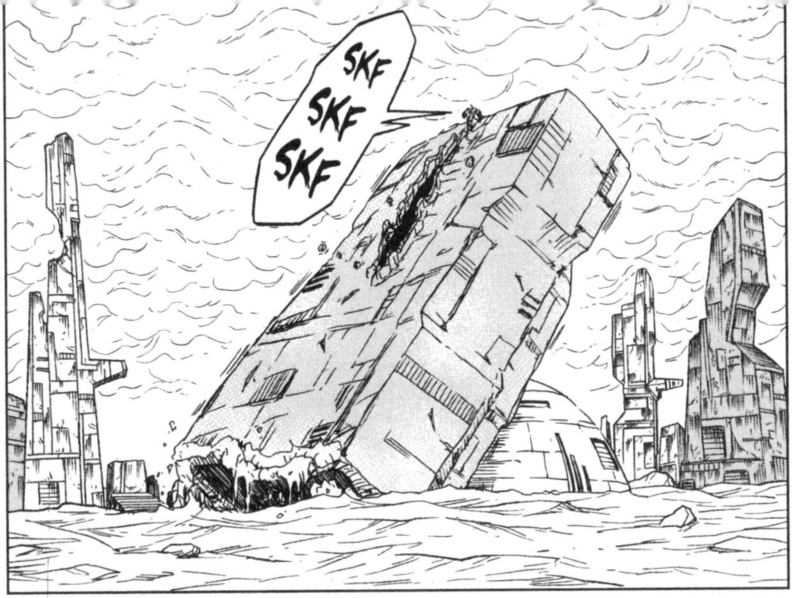
SKF
SKF
SKF
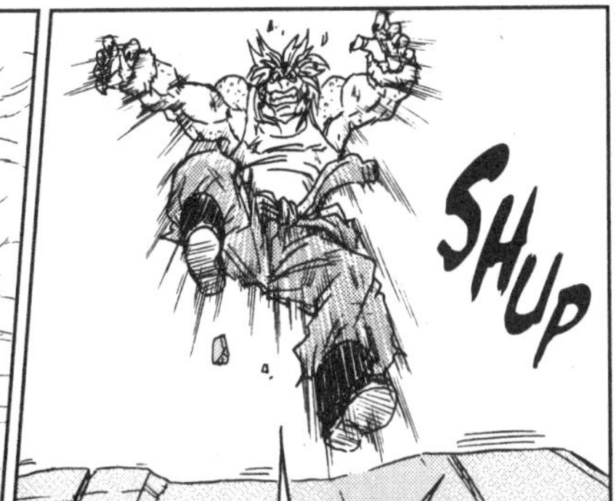
SHUP
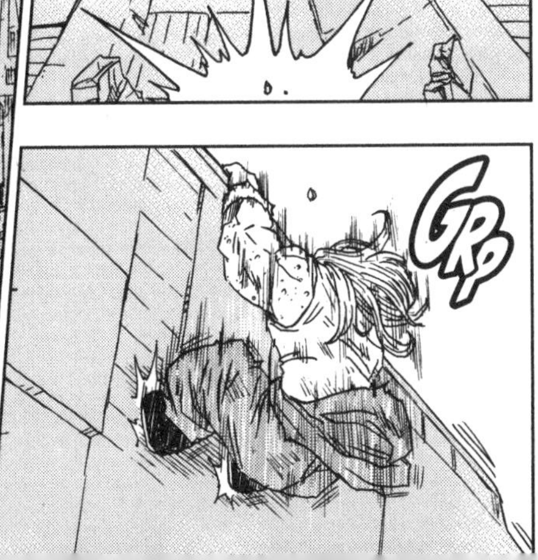
GRP
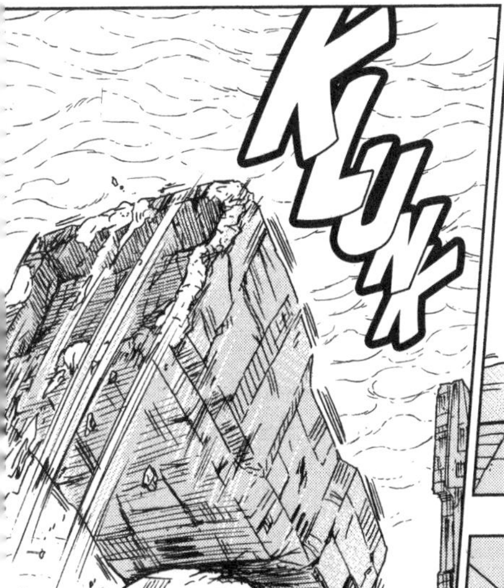
KLUNK

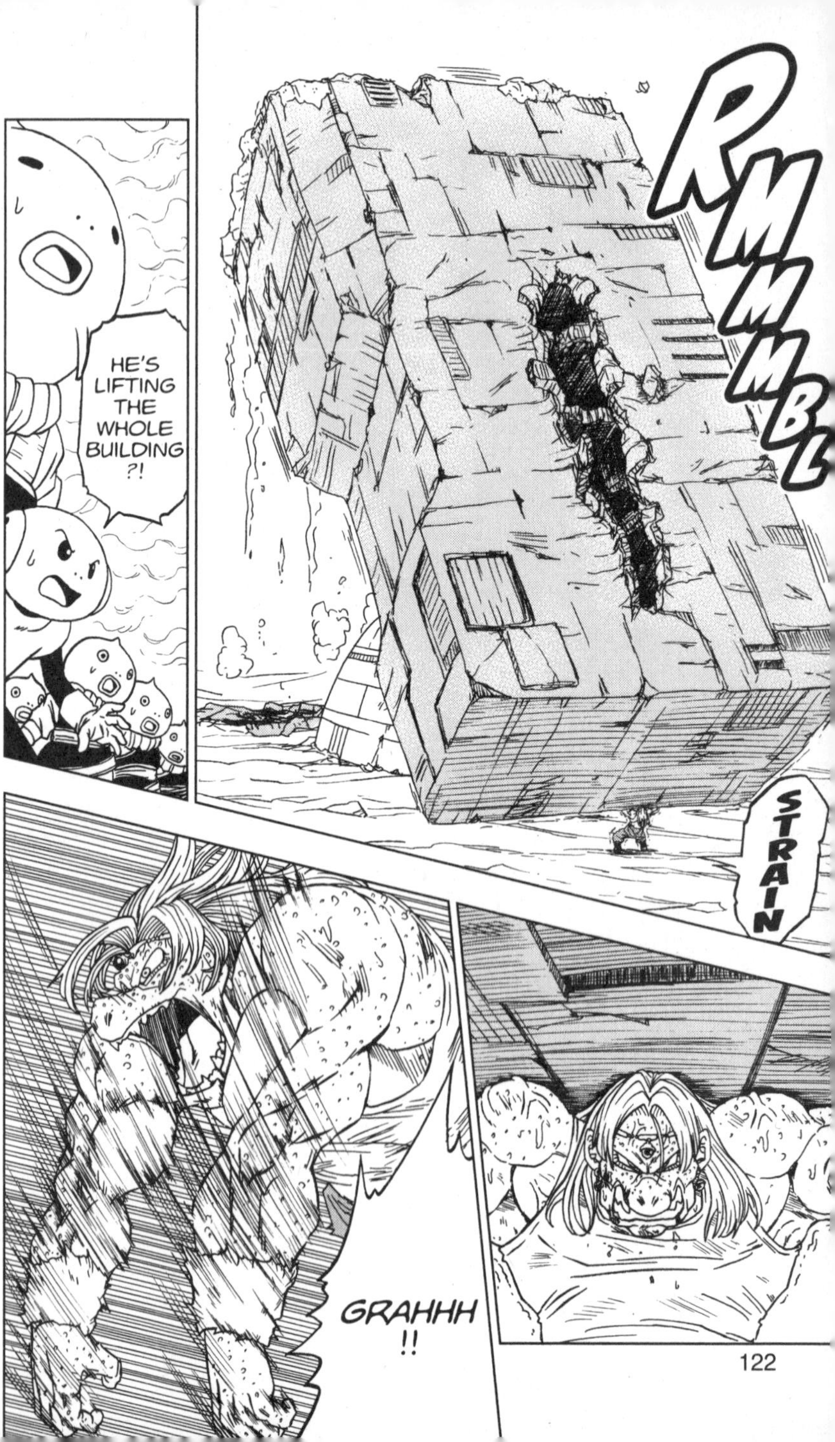
RMMMMBL
STRAIN
HE'S LIFTING THE WHOLE BUILDING?!
GRAHHH!!

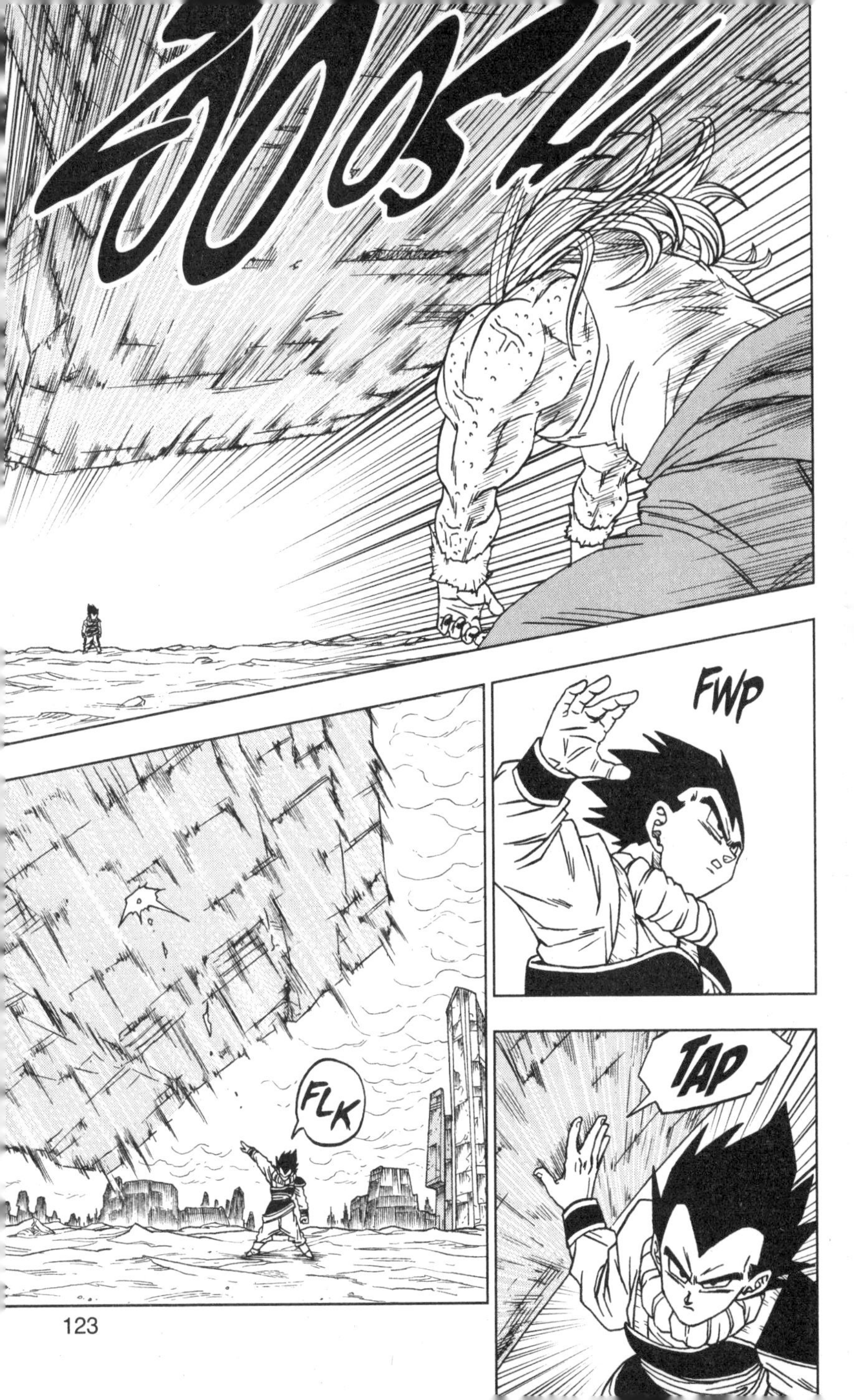
FWP
TAP
FLK

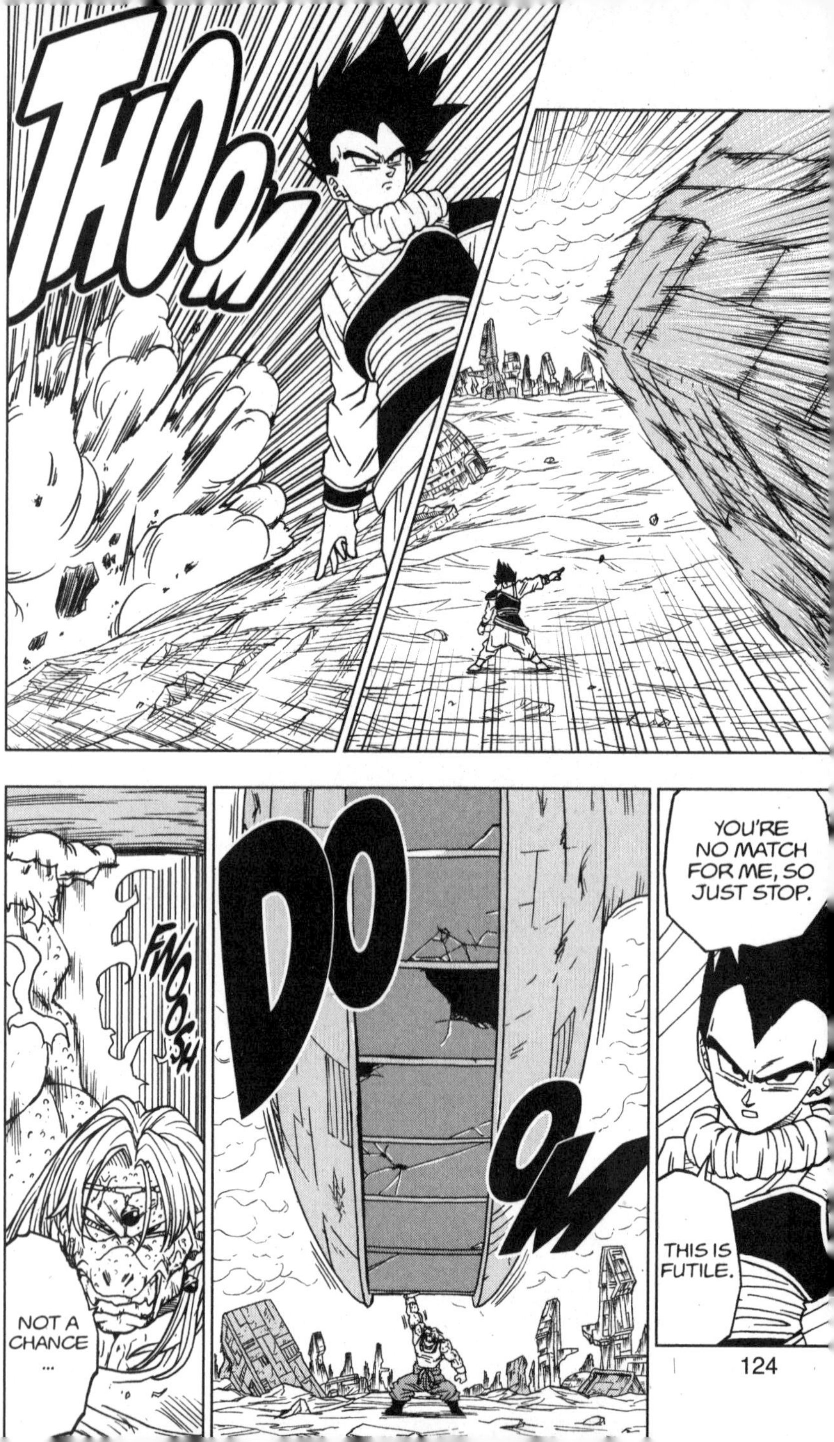
THOOOM
YOU'RE NO MATCH FOR ME, SO JUST STOP.
THIS IS FUTILE.
DOOOM
FWOOSH
NOT A CHANCE ...

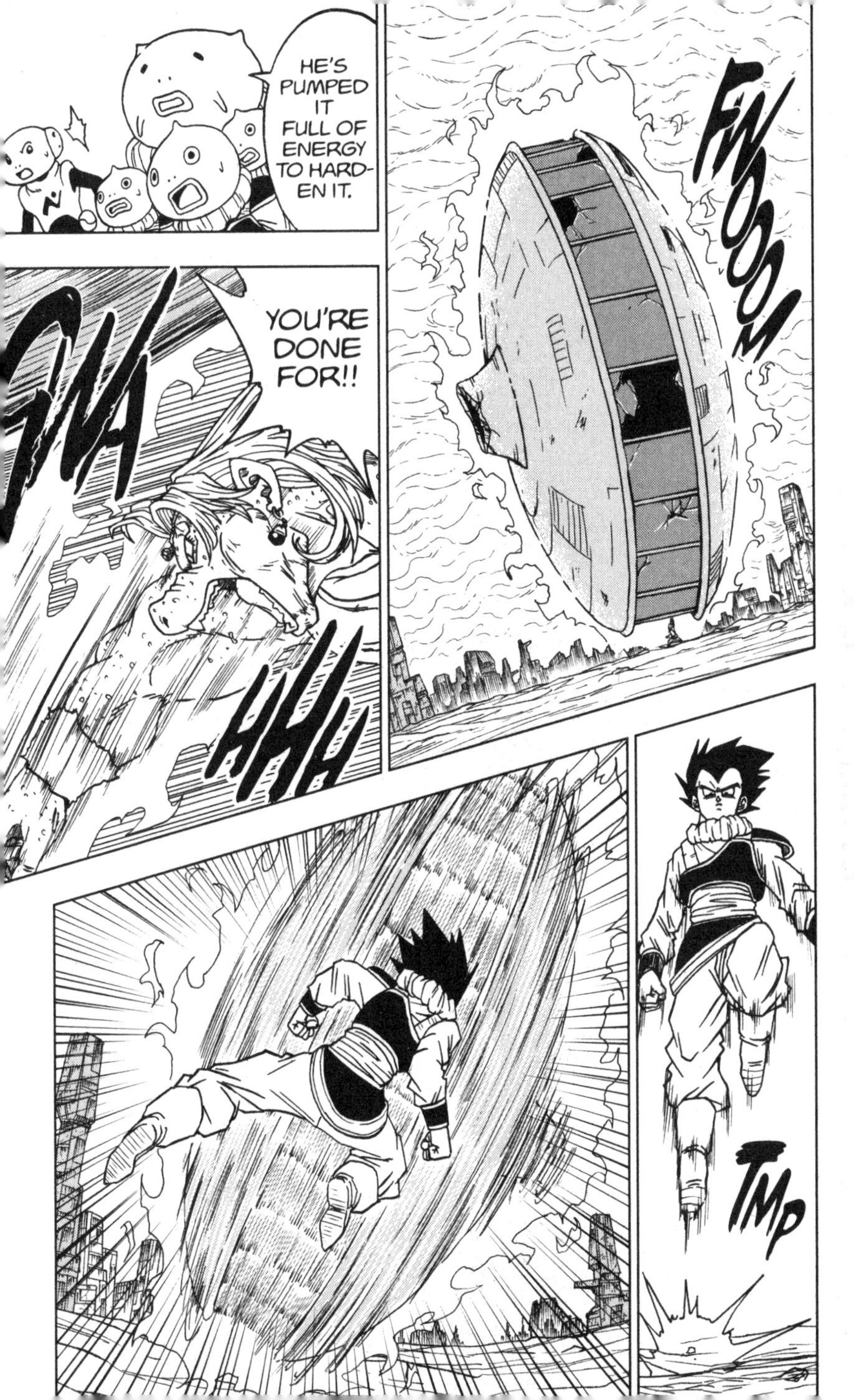
FWOOOOM
HE'S PUMPED IT FULL OF ENERGY TO HARD-EN IT.
YOU'RE DONE FOR!!
GWAHHH
TMP

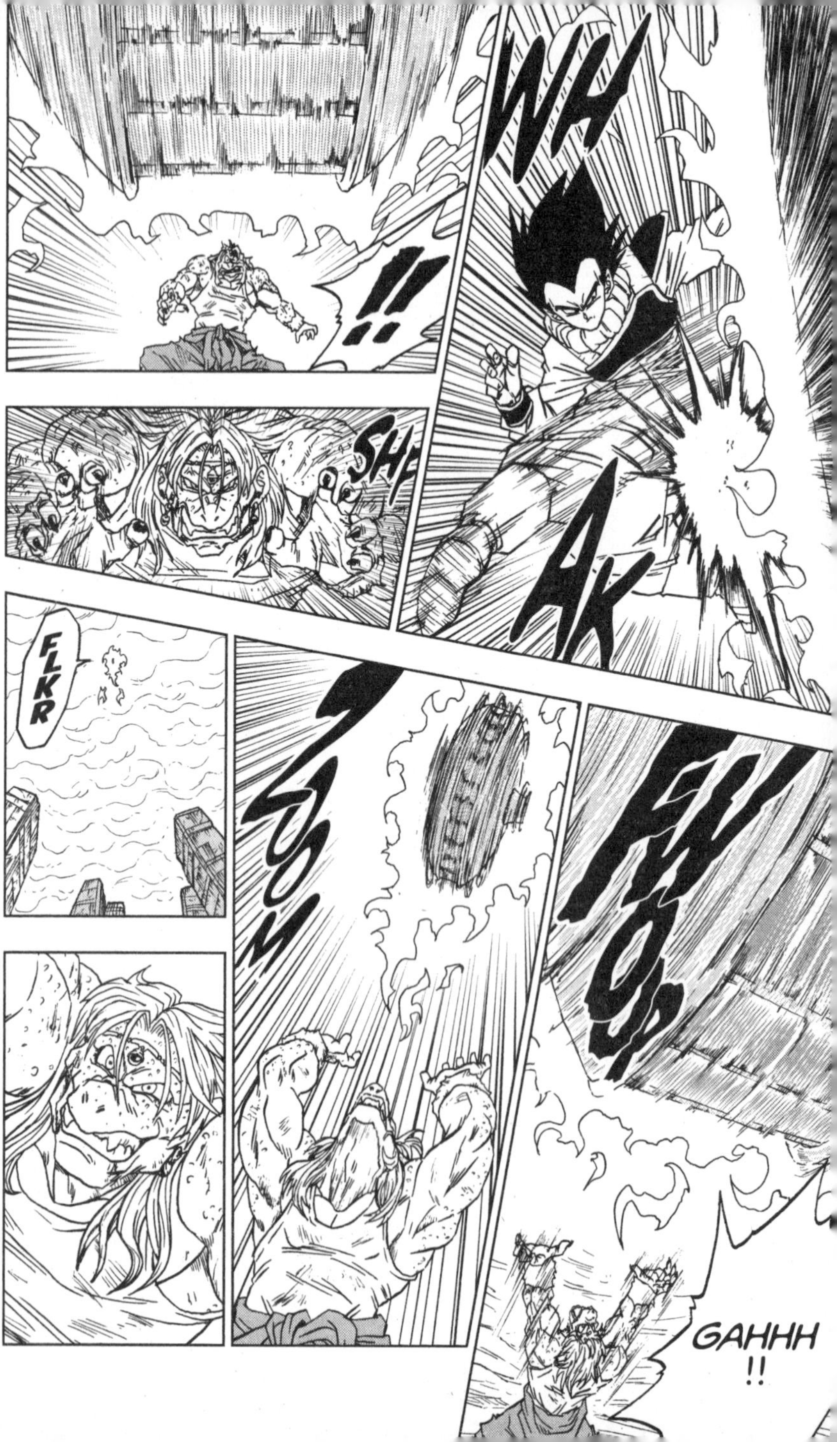
WHAK
!!
SHF
WHOP
GAHHH !!
ZOOOM
FLKR

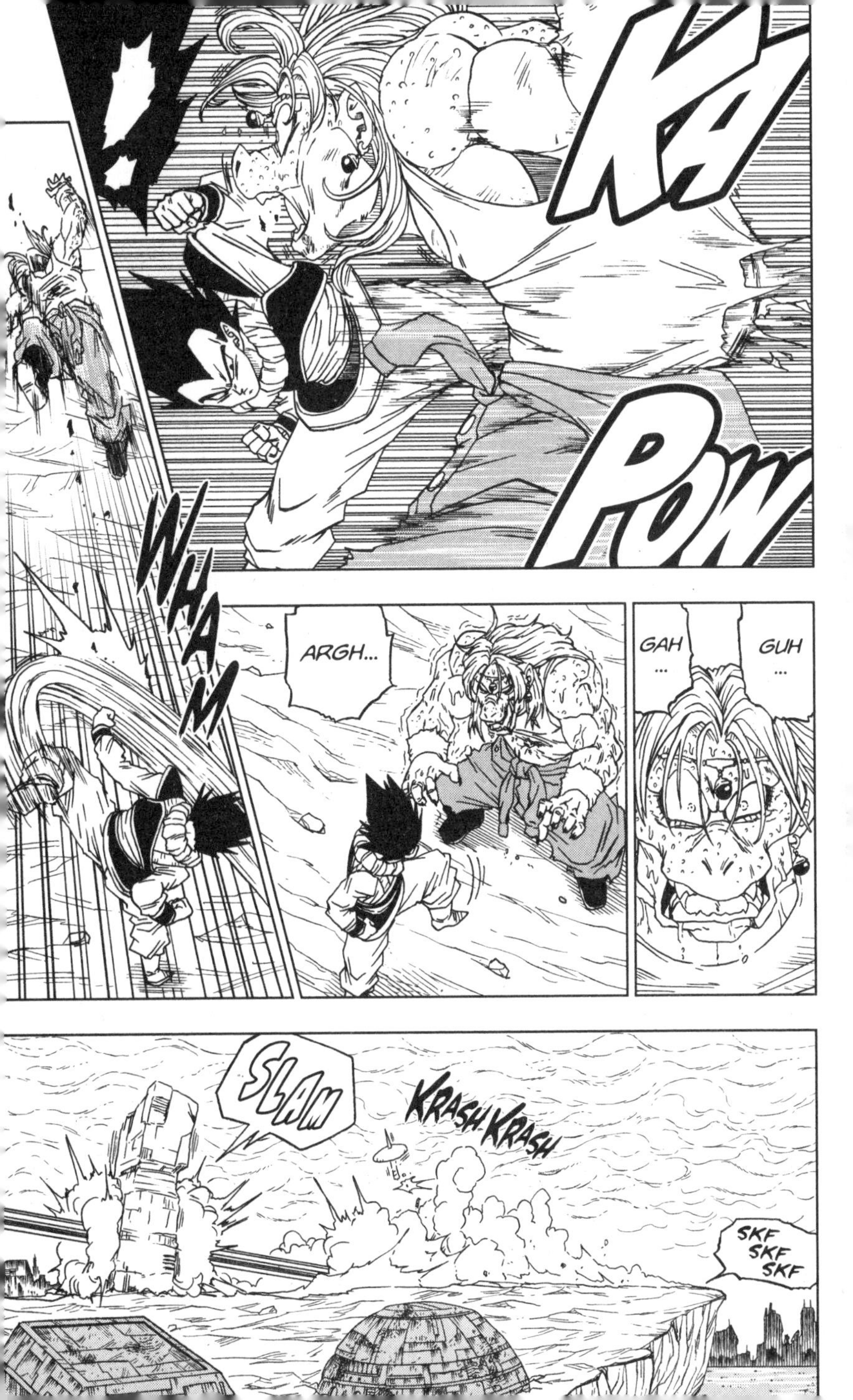
KA
POW
WHAM
GAH ...
GUH ...
ARGH...
SLAM
KRASH KRASH
SKF SKF SKF

HUH?

HOW CAN YOU TELL?

W-WHAT NOW, VEGETA?! SHOULDN'T WE HURRY BACK TO EARTH?!

NO. EARTH REMAINS UNTOUCHED FOR NOW.

AH.

...

INSTANT TELEPORTATION WON'T CUT IT. I NEED A TECHNIQUE CAPABLE OF BRINGING DOWN MORO.

I'M SHORT ON TIME, PYBARA.

HONING YOUR SPIRIT ALLOWS YOU TO SENSE OTHER SPIRITS--EVEN ONES *FAAAR*, FAR AWAY.

FWK

HUH?

THERE'S NO POINT AT ALL IF HE WON'T MAKE IT IN TIME.

FINE.

AND YOU CAN'T GO MESSING AROUND WITH THE ORDER THE LESSONS COME IN!

THAT'S "ELDER PYBARA" TO YOU!

WHOA THERE, BUDDY! SHOW HIM SOME RESPECT!

THAT ONE CALLED VEGETA.

I SEE. HE TRULY HAS GROWN MORE POWERFUL.

WHAT? IT CAN'T BE.

ON THE PLANET YUZUN VENTURED TO, YES. THOUGH YUZUN IS NOW DEAD.

YOU FOUND HIM?

!

IN THAT CASE, I SHALL STOCK UP AND REACH THE UPPER LIMITS OF MY POWER BEFORE TRAVELING TO EARTH.

HEH HEH HEH... WHAT A DELIGHTFUL DEVELOP-MENT.

WHEN HE TRANSFORMS, HE'S SUP-POSED TO BE UNBEATABLE...

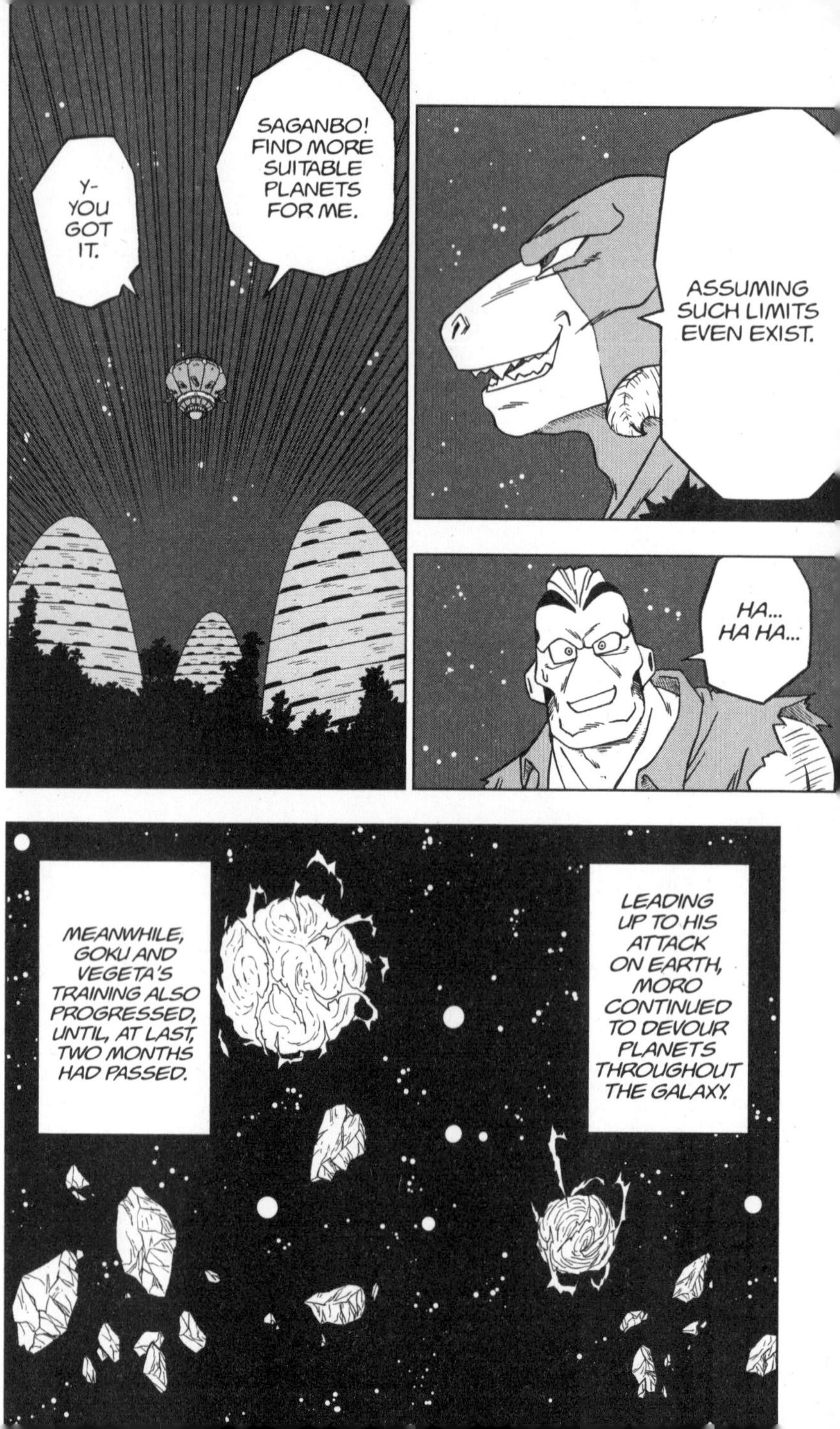
ASSUMING SUCH LIMITS EVEN EXIST.
HA... HA HA...
SAGANBO! FIND MORE SUITABLE PLANETS FOR ME.
Y-YOU GOT IT.
LEADING UP TO HIS ATTACK ON EARTH, MORO CONTINUED TO DEVOUR PLANETS THROUGHOUT THE GALAXY.
MEANWHILE, GOKU AND VEGETA'S TRAINING ALSO PROGRESSED, UNTIL, AT LAST, TWO MONTHS HAD PASSED.

LET US SPAR ONCE MORE BEFORE TAKING OFF FOR EARTH.

TIME IS NEARLY UP.

I'LL JUST HAFTA USE EVERYTHING I'VE LEARNED IN HERE.

SOUNDS GOOD.

I WON'T HOLD BACK EITHER.

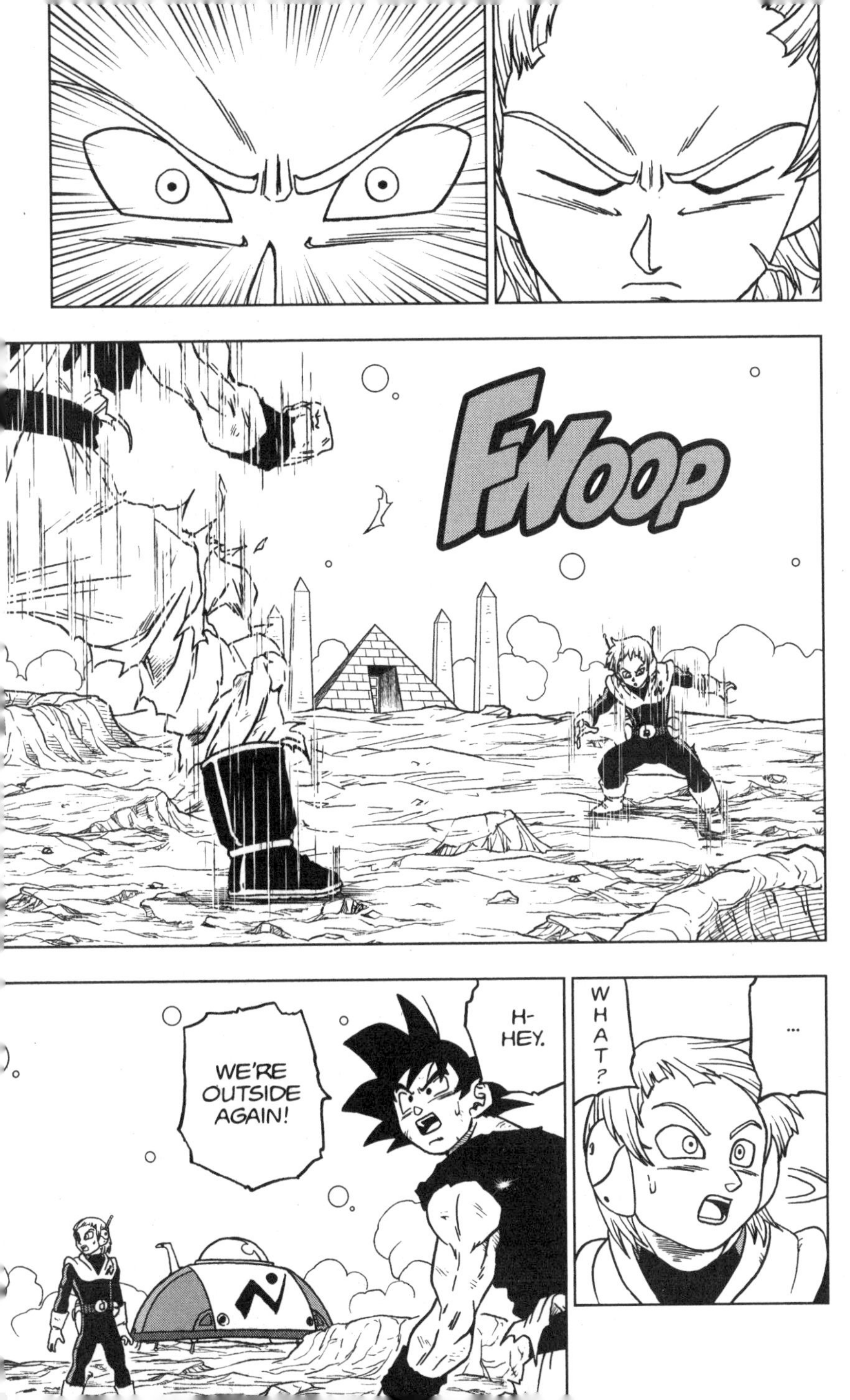
FWOOP
WHAT?
...
H-HEY.
WE'RE OUTSIDE AGAIN!

...QUITE ENOUGH.

THAT'S...

FSSH

BROTHER.

B...

IT'S YOU, WHIS!

HUH?

BROTHER?

HMM?

SO YOU CAUGHT WIND OF WHAT I WAS UP TO?

IT HAS BEEN AGES, MERUS.

I KNEW YOU WERE WEIRD, BUT YOU'RE AN ANGEL, MERUS?

ANGELS?!

... BETWEEN ANGELS.

I'M AFRAID THERE ARE NO SECRETS...

APOLO-GIES.

CLASHING AGAINST EACH OTHER AT FULL STRENGTH CONSTITUTES A BATTLE.

TRAINING CAN ONLY BE JUST THAT-- **TRAINING.**

YES.

Y-YOU KNEW...

...WAS YOUR PLAN TO TRAVEL TO EARTH AND DO BATTLE AGAINST MORO.

EVEN MORE EGREGIOUS...

I APOLOGIZING FOR KEEPING IT FROM YOU...

THAT EXPLAINS A LOT, MERUS.

JUST SO.

OHH, RIGHT. ANGELS AREN'T ALLOWED TO FIGHT EXCEPT IN TRAINING, RIGHT?

WHAT HAPPENS IF YOU GUYS **DO** FIGHT?

BUT WAIT...

...WITHOUT A TRACE.

ANGELS WHO BREAK OUR CODE ARE ERADICATED...

THERE IS NO WAY AROUND THIS TRUTH-- SUCH IS THE NATURE OF ANGELS.

IT IS THE ONLY MEANS BY WHICH AN ANGEL CAN BE REMOVED FROM EXISTENCE.

ERADI-WHAT?! LIKE, POOF?!

I THOUGHT ANGELS COULDN'T DIE!

HUH?

140

UNDERSTOOD.

...

YEESH...

HENCEFORTH, I WILL BE RESPONSIBLE FOR YOU.

ON THAT NOTE, I'VE COME TO INFORM YOU THAT YOUR TIME IN THE MORTAL REALM IS OVER, MERUS.

FLK

MERUS...

FWOOM

BE GRATEFUL THAT I'M NOT DRAGGING YOU RIGHT BACK TO THE GRAND PRIEST.

TAP

141

FLK

! FWOOM TAP

I'M ONLY SORRY I COULDN'T SEE THIS THROUGH WITH YOU.

GOKU...

I'LL FIGURE SOMETHING OUT.

SURE.

I HAVE FAITH THAT YOU WILL DEFEAT MORO.

YES.

IT'S BACK TO THE HEAVENLY REALM WITH YOU.

142

TWNKL

KA*BOOM*

THANKS, MERUS.

UNTIL NEXT TIME, GOKU.

COME BAAACK, WHIS!!

WAAAIT!! I CAN'T DO IT!!

HOLD UP! I GOTTA PILOT THAT THING BACK TO EARTH MYSELF?!

ANYHOO... BETTER GET MYSELF BACK TO EARTH.

...

SAGANBO'S
GALACTIC BANDIT
BRIGADE MEMBER:
YUZUN

DRAGON BALL SUPER

CHAPTER 56: WARRIORS OF EARTH ASSEMBLE

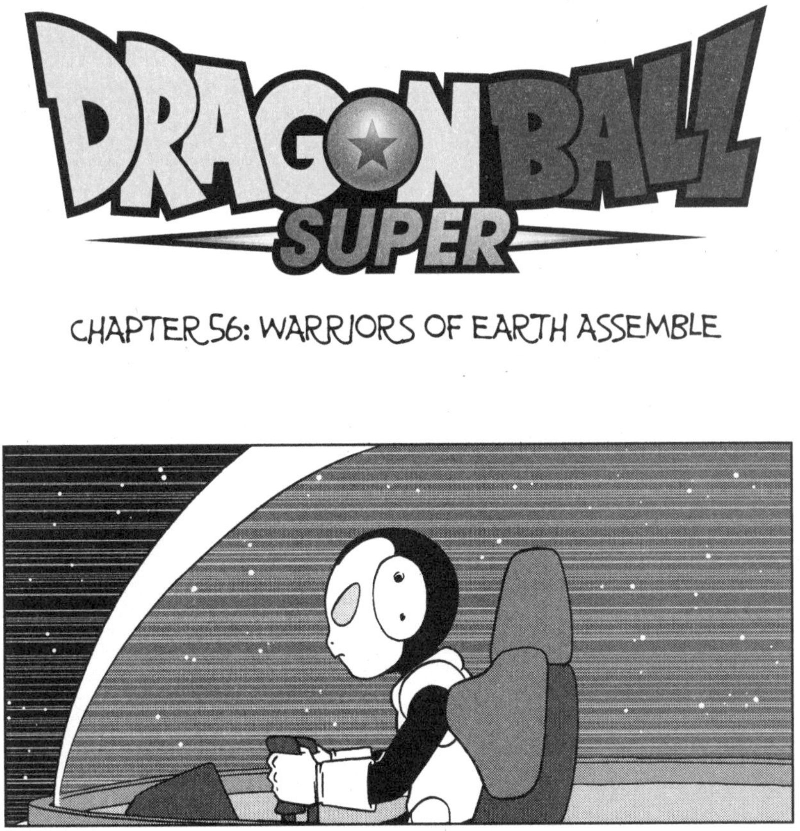

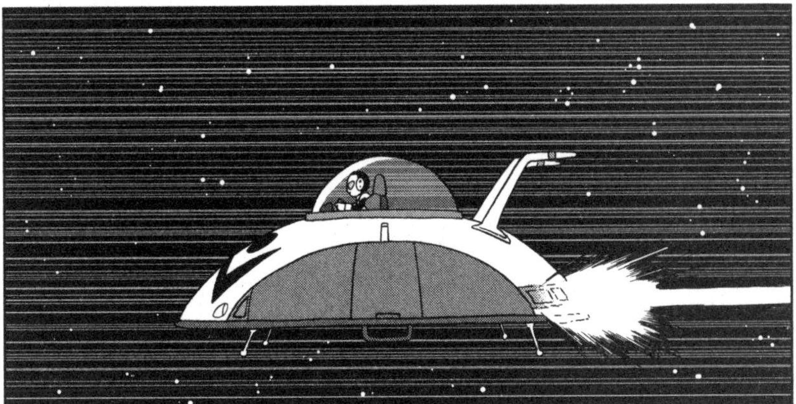

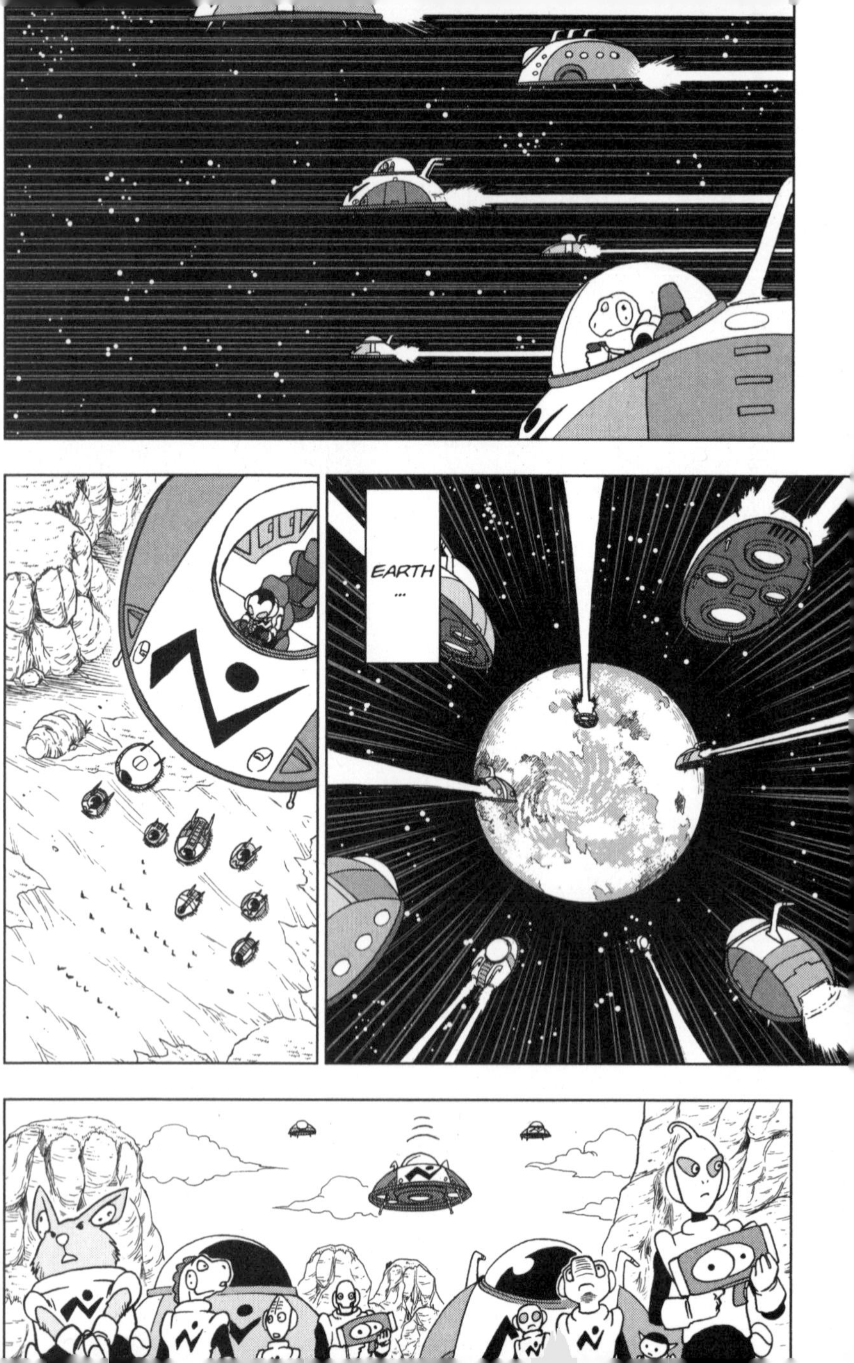
EARTH
...

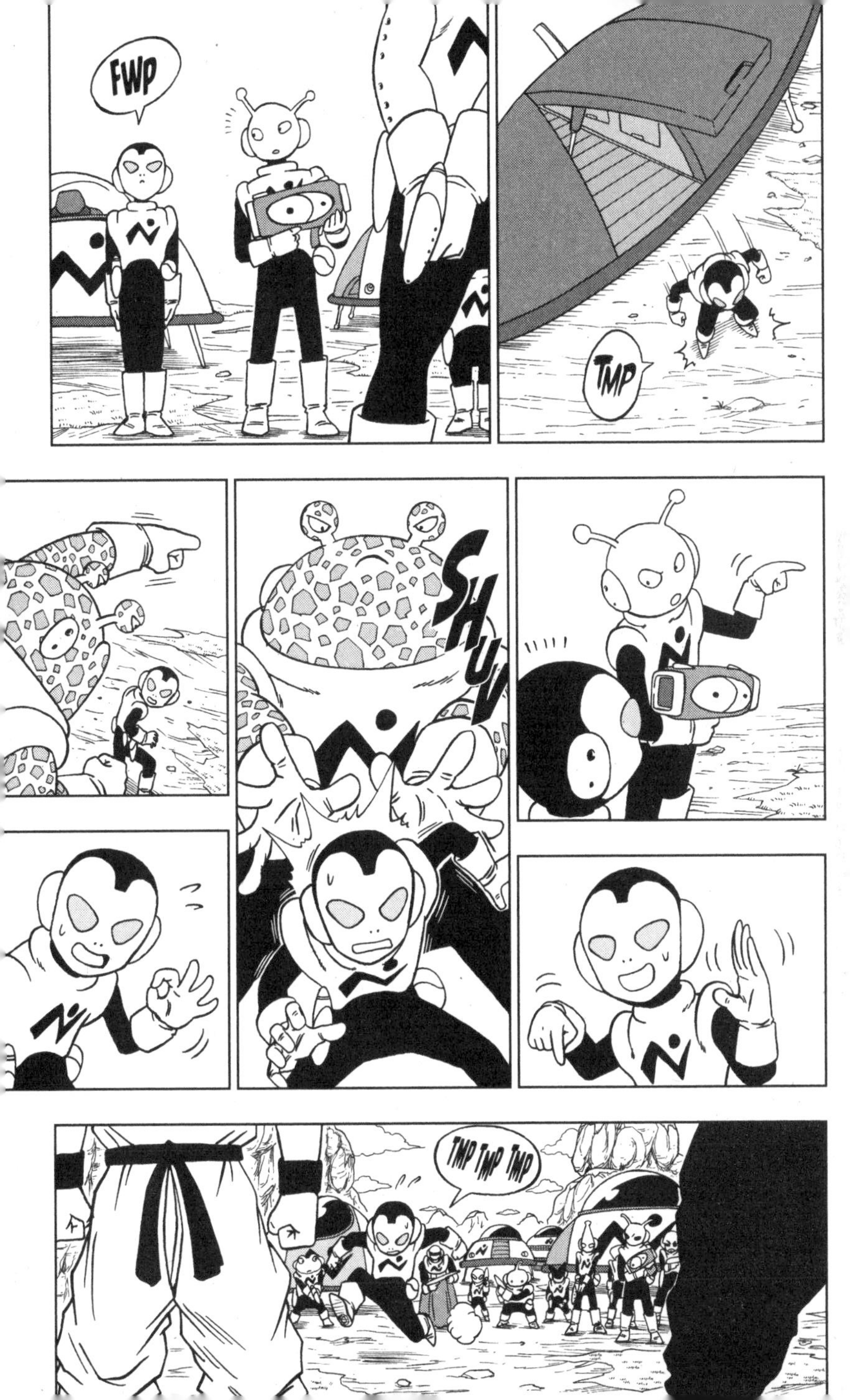
TMP
FWP
SHUV
TMP TMP TMP

HEY, NEW RECRUITS!! LOOK SHARP!

CRUD... WHY'D THEY GOTTA PUT ME IN CHARGE OF EARTH? OF ALL THE ROTTEN LUCK.

IT'S FINALLY MY CHANCE TO SHINE!

IT'S BEEN SO LONG... I HOPE I CAN STILL FIGHT.

...

WE'RE PRETTY MUCH THE VETS OF PROTECTING THE EARTH...

TCH! NEW RECRUITS?

ARE GOKU AND VEGETA STILL NOT HERE, JACO?

YEAH. WON'T BE LONG NOW.

IT'S FINALLY TIME.

...I'M SURE THEY'LL SHOW.

BUT GIVEN THE BEEF THOSE TWO HAVE WITH MORO...

HUH?! THAT'S BAD!

I SENT GOKU A HEADS-UP, BUT WE'VE GOT NO CLUE WHERE VEGETA IS.

SO GLAD YOU'RE OKAY, PAL...

HE'S BEEN FAST ASLEEP SINCE HIS LAST BATTLE.

BOO!

ZZZ ZZZ

VRRRM

S-SORRY ABOUT THAT.

GALACTIC PATROL OR NOT, YOU'LL BE ANSWERING TO ME IF YOU TRY KIDNAPPING BOO AGAIN!

LIKE THAT ONE?

A BIG MOTHER-SHIP SHAPED LIKE A TOP WITH LOTS OF LITTLE SCOUT SHIPS.

WHAT DOES MORO'S SPACE-SHIP LOOK LIKE?

150

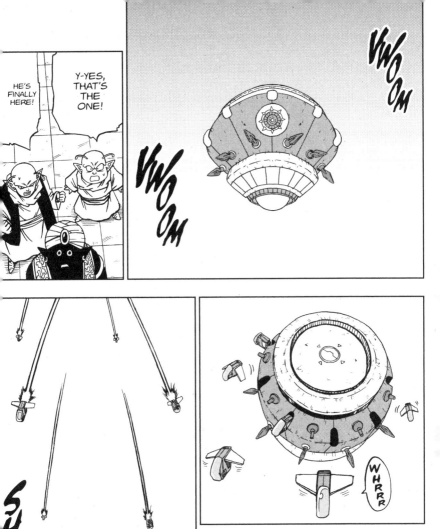

HE'S FINALLY HERE!

Y-YES, THAT'S THE ONE!

VWOOM

VWOOM

SHOOM

WHRRR

FWISH

FWISH

?!

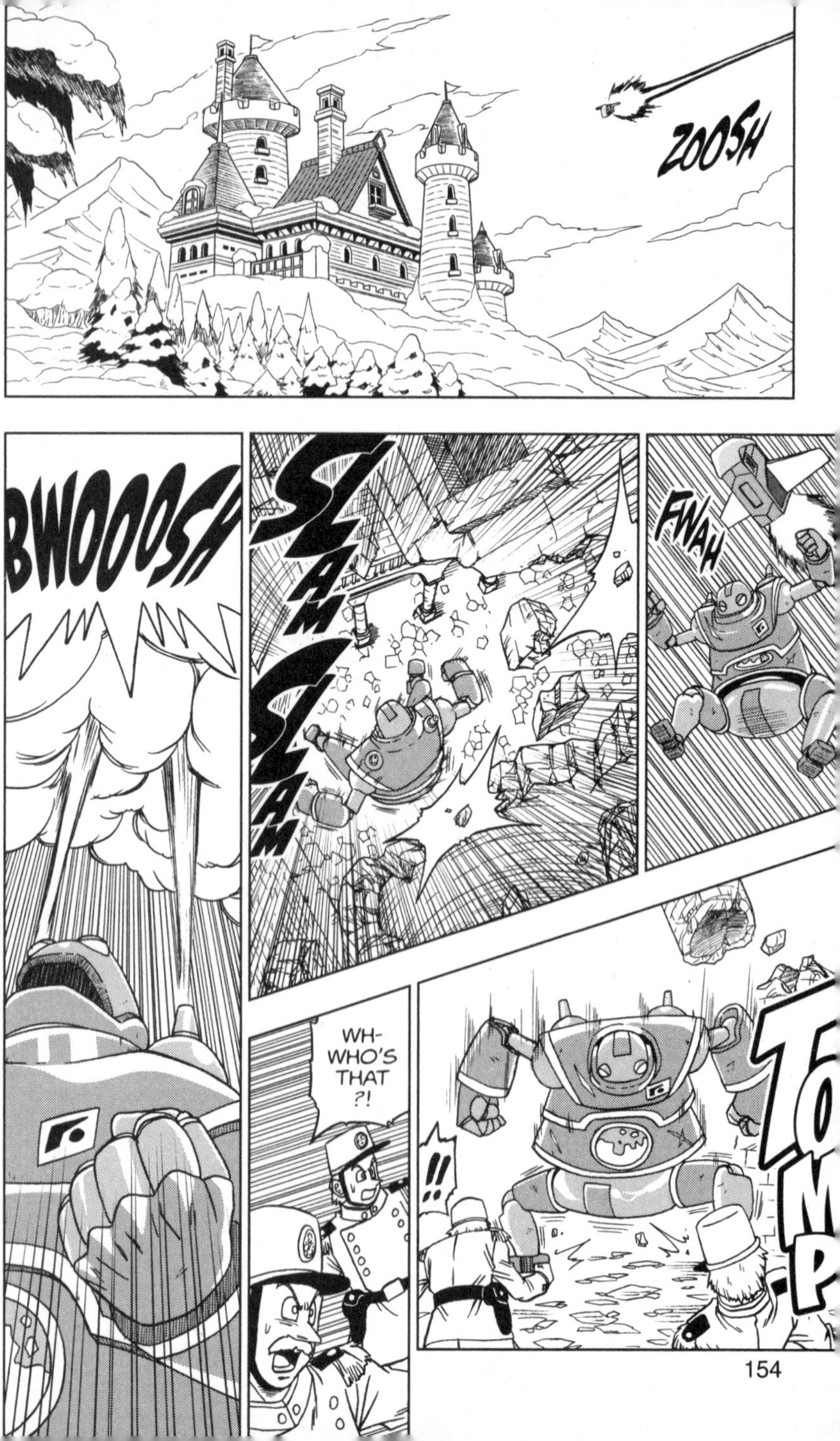
ZOOSH
FWAH
SLAM SLAM
BWOOOSH
TOMP
!!
WH- WHO'S THAT ?!

THE BADDIES'RE FLYING OFF TO EVERY CORNER OF THE WORLD!

PICCOLO! WHAT'S HAPPENING?

BEFORE THE FULL-SCALE ATTACK, THEY'RE PROBABLY PLANNING TO ROB THE EARTH OF ALL ITS TREASURES!!

DANG IT!

!

!!

SHP

TMP

!

TCH... OF COURSE!

CAREFUL OUT THERE! YOU'RE UP AGAINST VICIOUS CRIMINALS!

YUP!

OH... RIGHT.

OFF WE GO, KURIRIN!

...WHILE YOU BOYS FIGHT THE BIG BOSS.

LET'S HANDLE THOSE FAR-FLUNG CONVICTS...

I'LL HEAD THIS WAY.

YEAH!

LET'S GO, CHAOZU.

TMP

TMP

BACK THEM UP!

SPLIT INTO TEAMS AND SUPPORT EARTH'S WARRIORS!

KACHK

KACHK

STP

STP STP STP

VWOOM

VWOOM

157

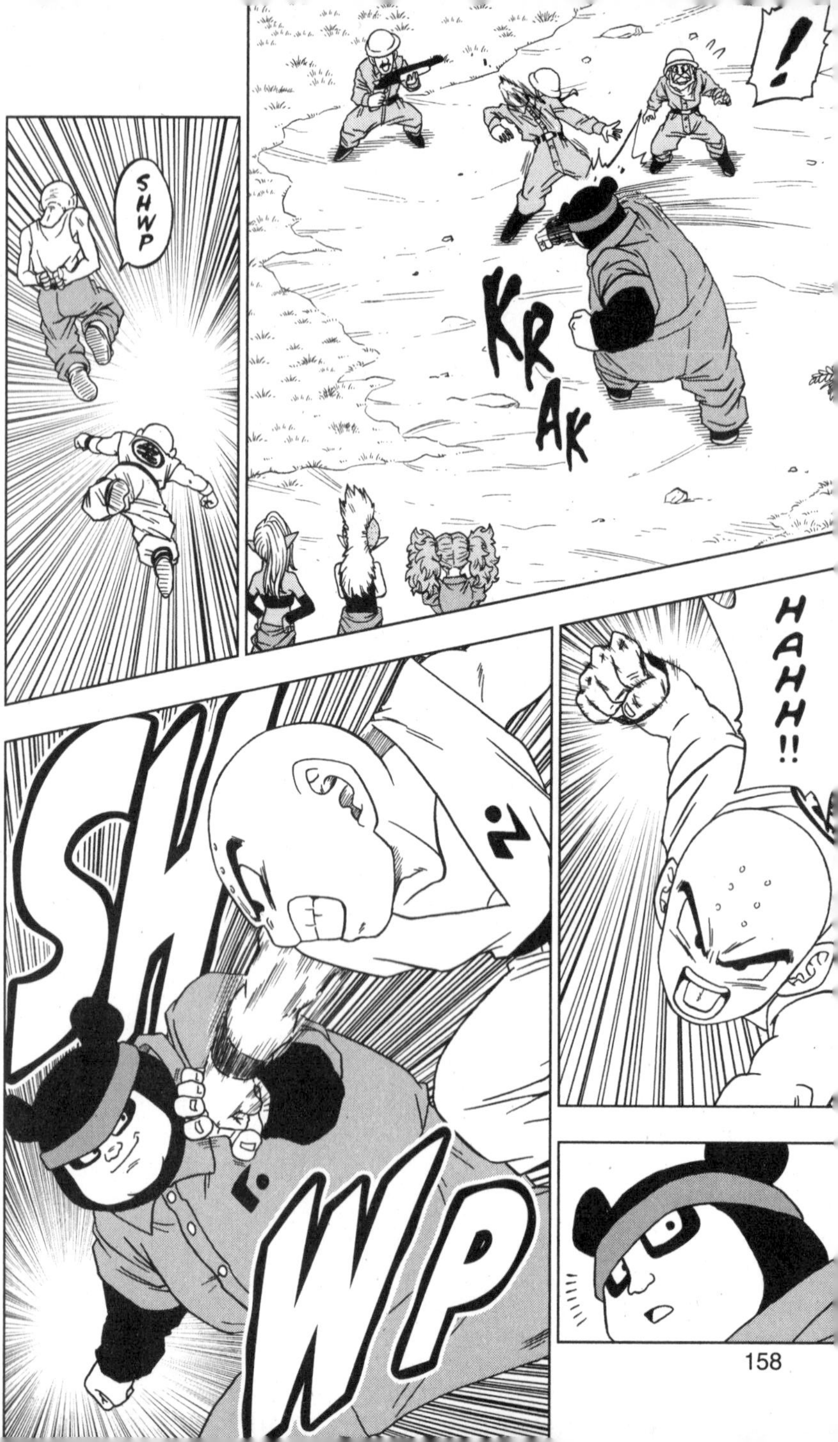
!
KRAK
SHWP
HAHHH!!
SHWP

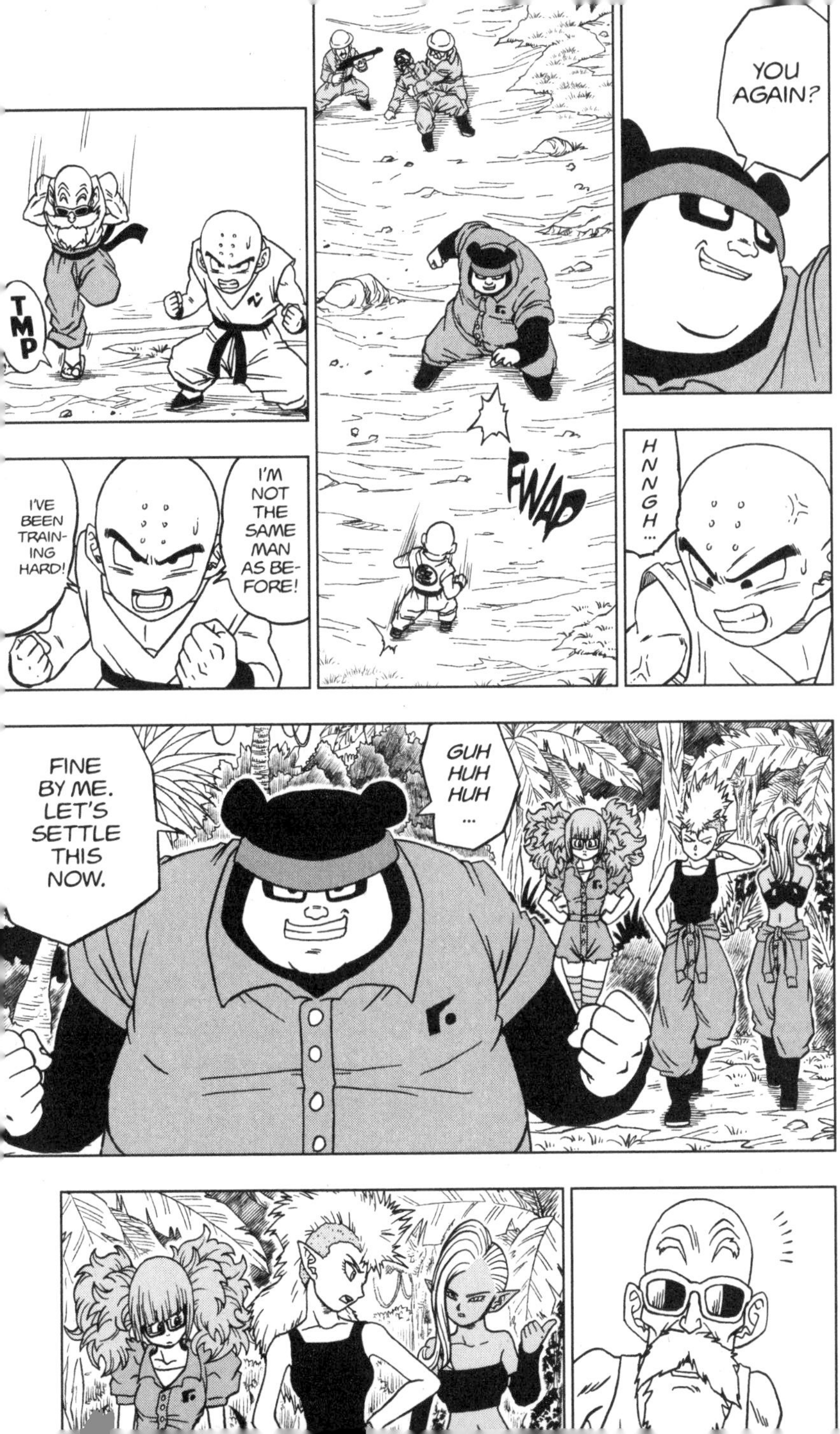
YOU AGAIN?
HNNGH...
FWAP
TMP
I'M NOT THE SAME MAN AS BEFORE!
I'VE BEEN TRAINING HARD!
GUH HUH HUH ...
FINE BY ME. LET'S SETTLE THIS NOW.

ZOOM

...

SURE. GO ON, THEN.

YUNBA! WE DON'T GIVE A CRAP ABOUT THIS DUEL OF YOURS, SO WE'RE GONNA GO WRECK SOME OTHER PLACE.

DASH

DASH DASH

Y'CAN'T GO RELYING ON YOUR OLD MASTER FOR EVERYTHING. I'M BETTING YOU CAN HANDLE THIS CHUMP ALONE.

KURI-RIN...

MUTEN RŌSHI... THIS GUY'S WAY FASTER THAN HE LOOKS, SO LET'S RUSH HIM TOGETHER!

HUH?!

BOING

♪

MEAN-WHILE, I'LL GO WRANGLE THOSE NASTY BABES.

!

I AIN'T WAITING AROUND!

RMMBL

HAHH!!

POW POW POW

DARN YOU!!

OWWW!

162

WHA--

HUH?

FWUNK

ZRM

!!

W-WHEN DID HE--

TCH !!

ZRM ZRM

YOU PEOPLE ARE DUMB AS EVER, I SEE.

THAT MOVE CAME COURTESY OF AN INVISIBLE RACE.

I-IDIOT! YOU DROPPED YOUR GUARD AGAIN!

ANY TRAINING YOU MIGHT'VE DONE? ALL TOTALLY WORTHLESS NOW.

DAM-MIT!!

SINCE SEVEN-THREE COPIES YOU THE WAY YOU ARE RIGHT NOW.

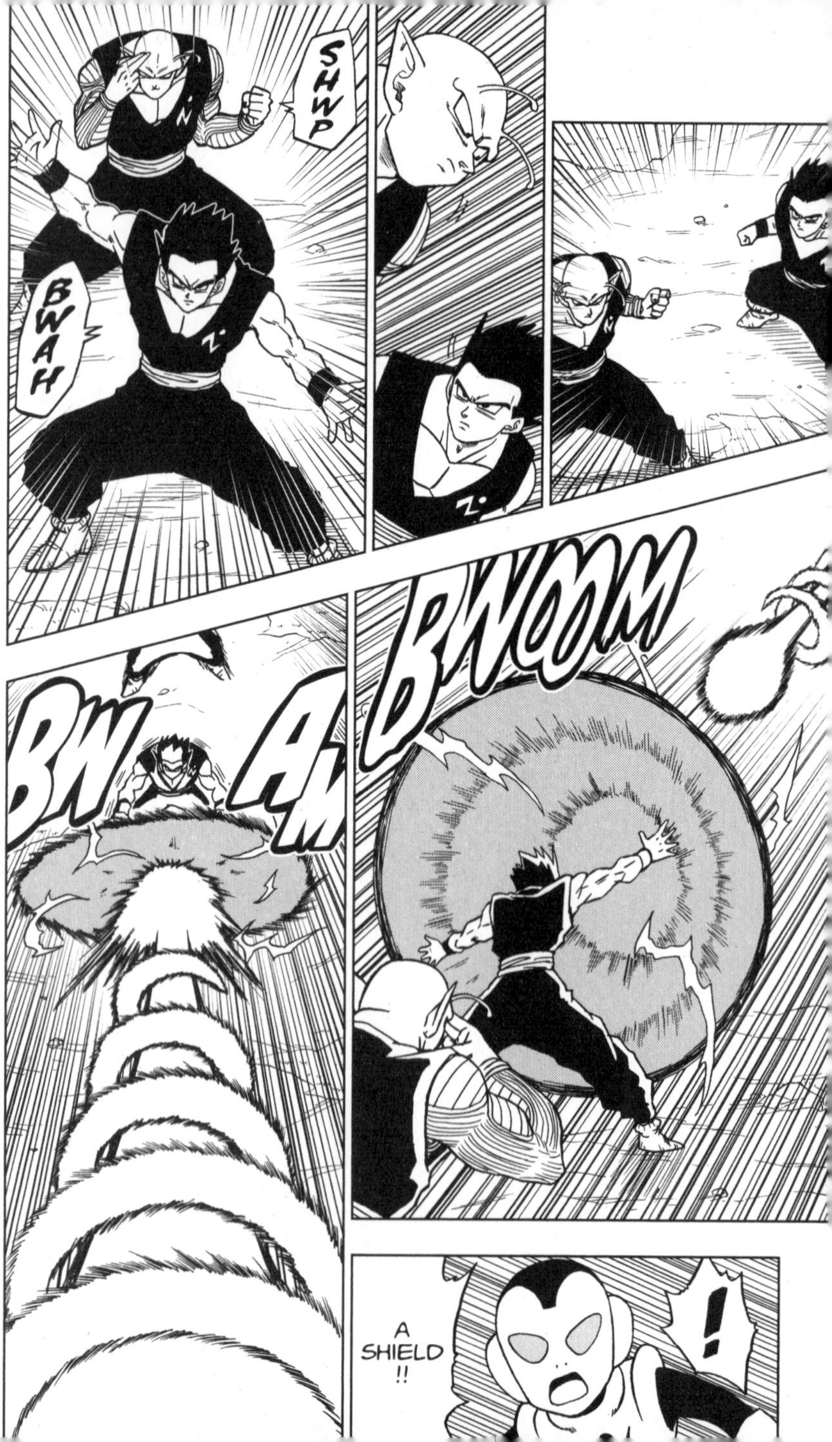
SHWP
BWAH
BWOOM
BWAM
A SHIELD!!
!

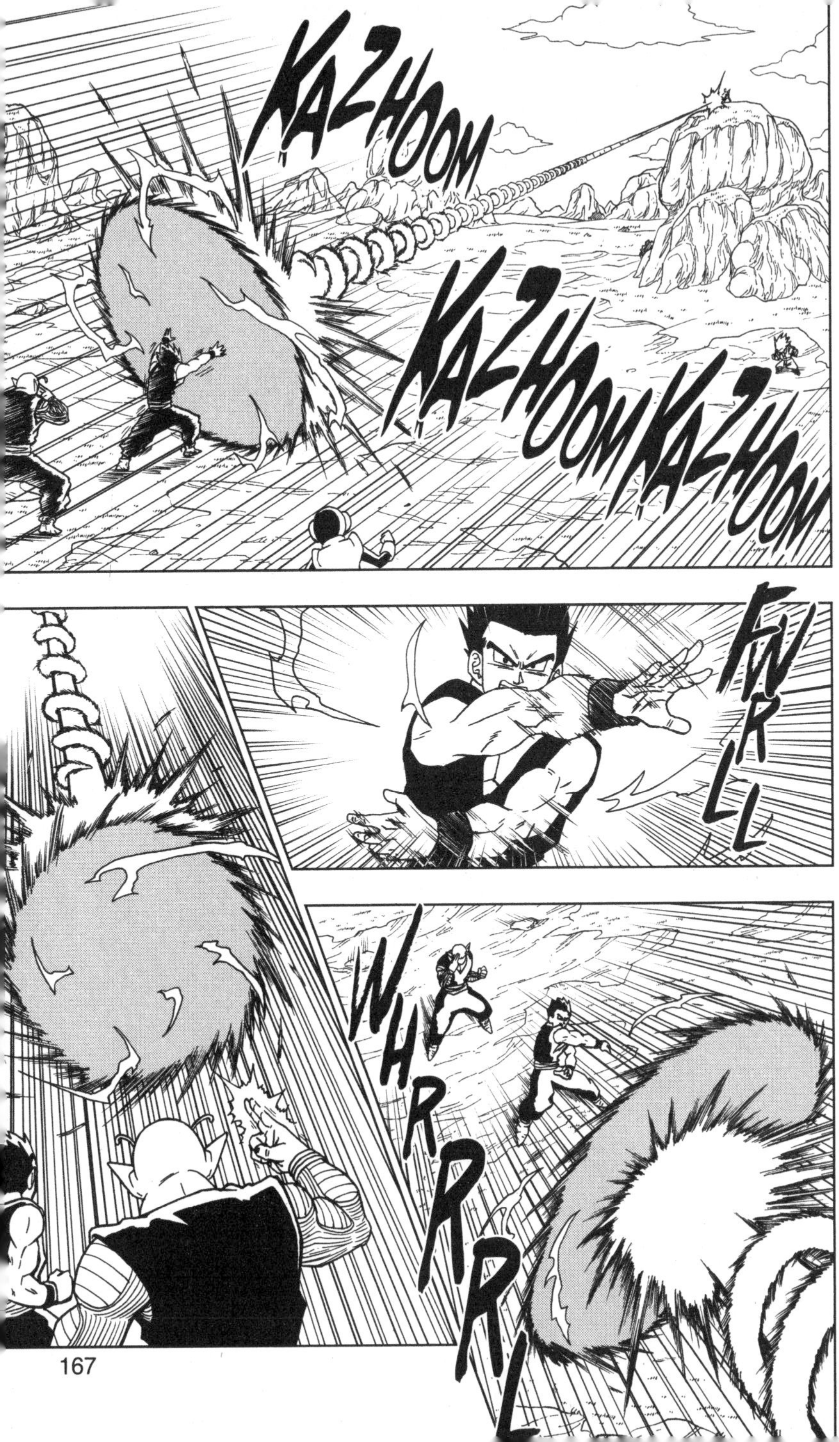
KAZHOOM
KAZHOOM KAZHOOM KAZHOOM
FWRLL
WHRRRRL

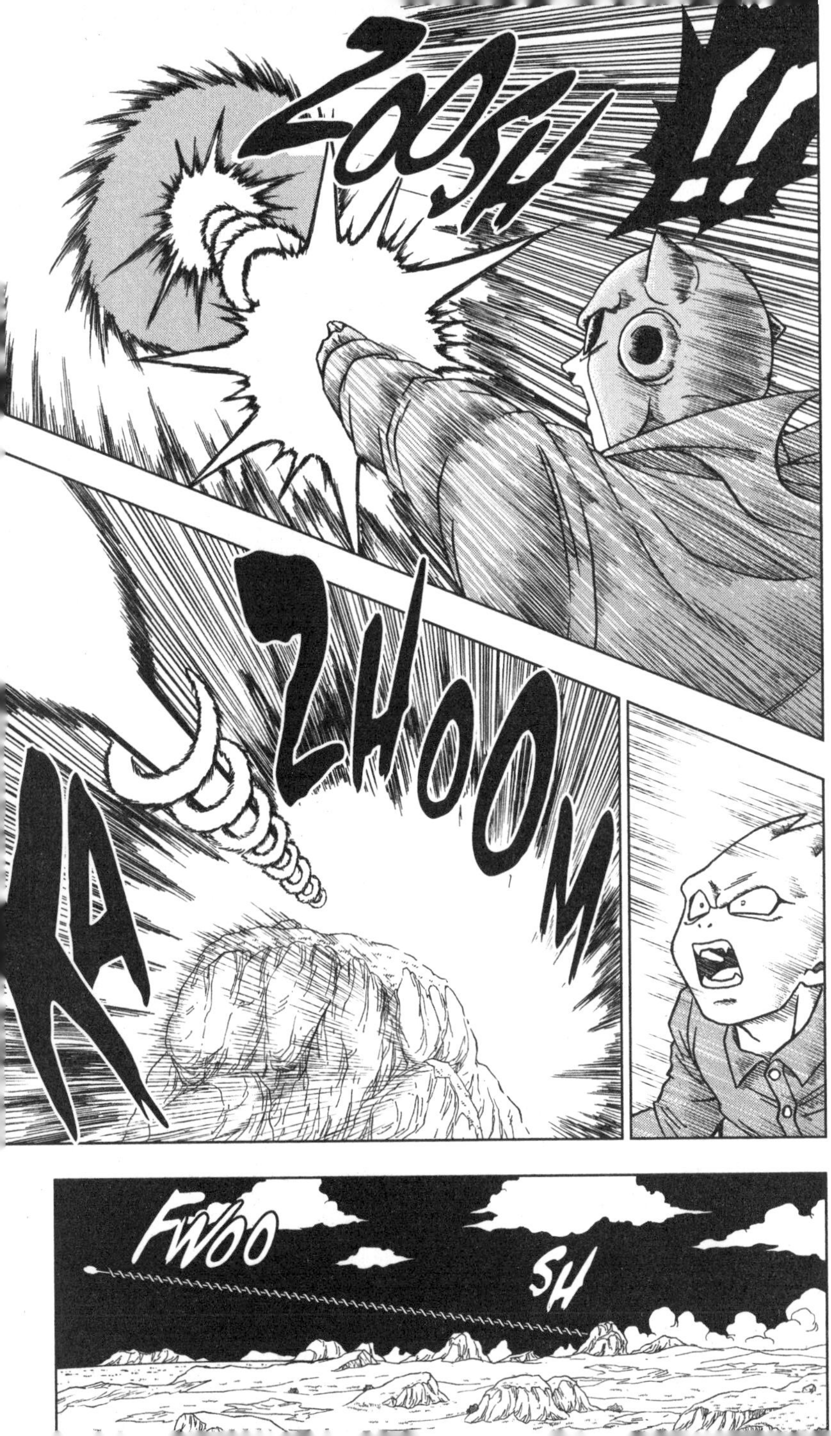
ZOOSH!!
KA
ZHOOM
FWOO
SH

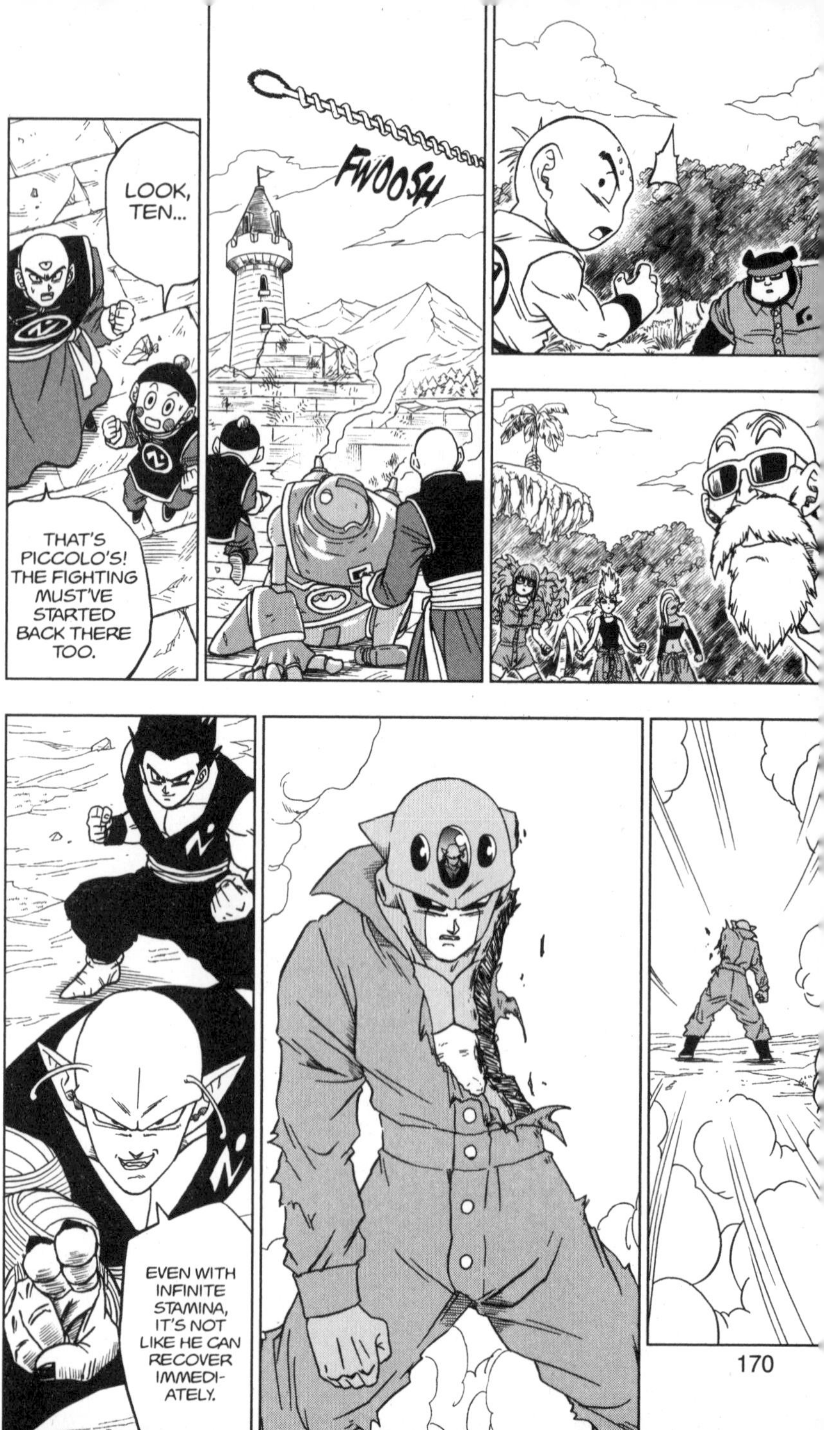
FWOOSH
LOOK, TEN...
THAT'S PICCOLO'S! THE FIGHTING MUST'VE STARTED BACK THERE TOO.
EVEN WITH INFINITE STAMINA, IT'S NOT LIKE HE CAN RECOVER IMMEDI-ATELY.

KRK
KRK

SPLORCH

B-BUT HOW?!

HOW'S THIS HAPPEN-ING?!

BRGL
BRGL

WE WERE TOTALLY READY FOR HIM TO COPY OUR ABILITIES.

RRRIP

SWITCH OVER TO HIM!

SEVEN-THREE, THAT ONE GUY IS STRONG-ER.

VERY WELL.

HMPH! SOUNDS LIKE A BLUFF TO ME.

171

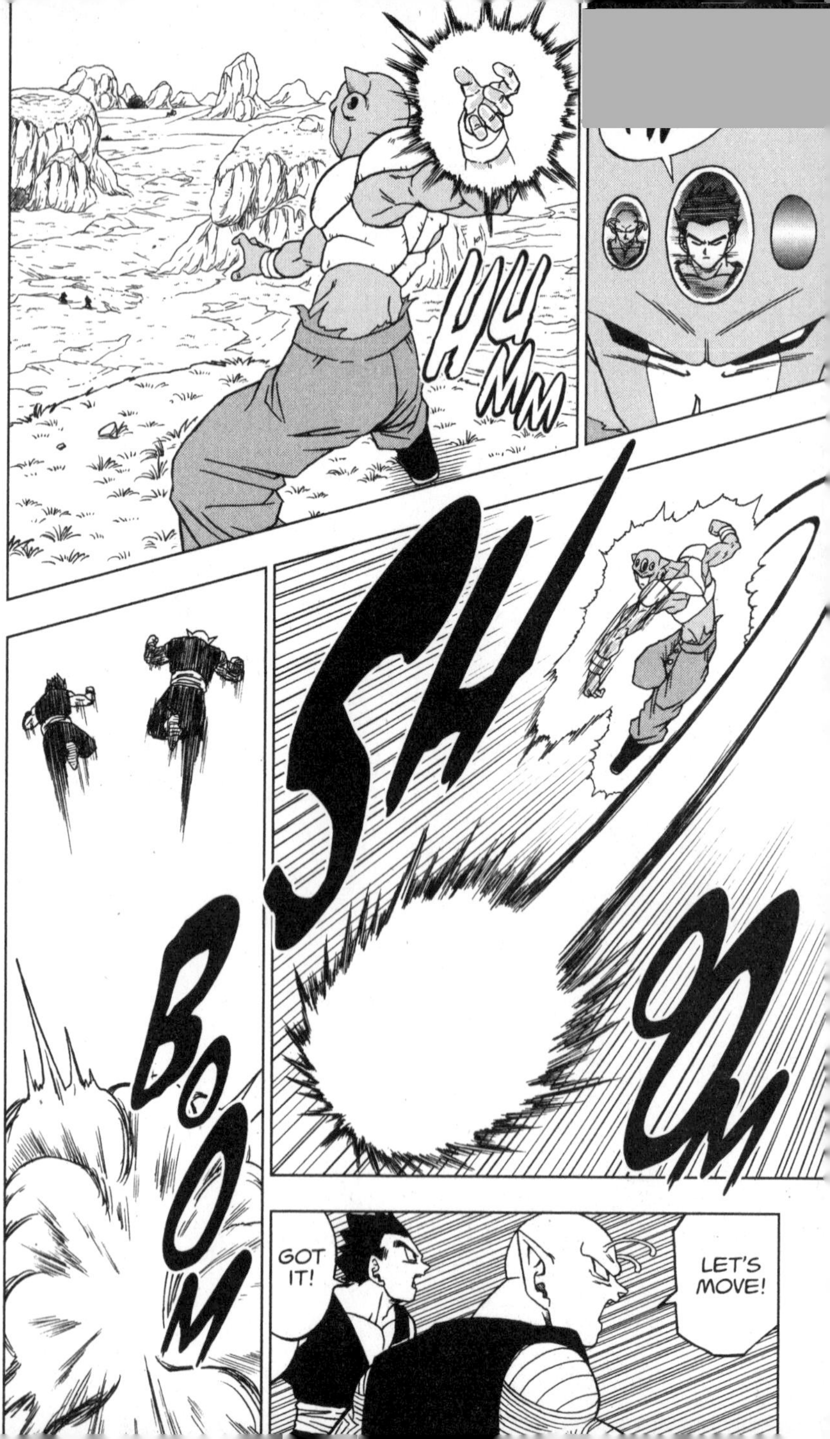
HUMM
SHOOM
LET'S MOVE!
GOT IT!
BOOOM

HUMM
HUMM

TCH!

GOHAN!

ZOOM

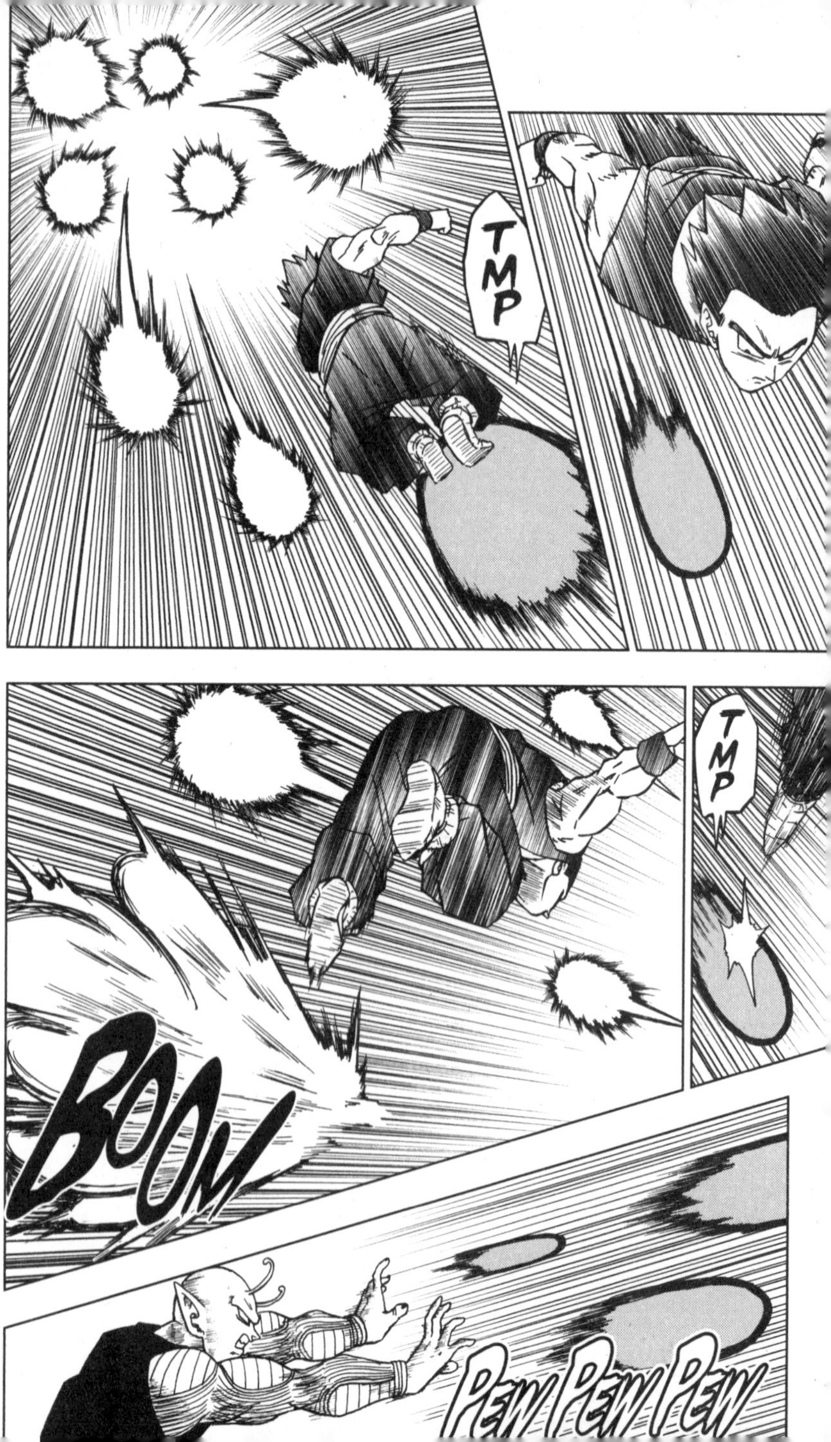
TMP
TMP
BOOM
PEW PEW PEW

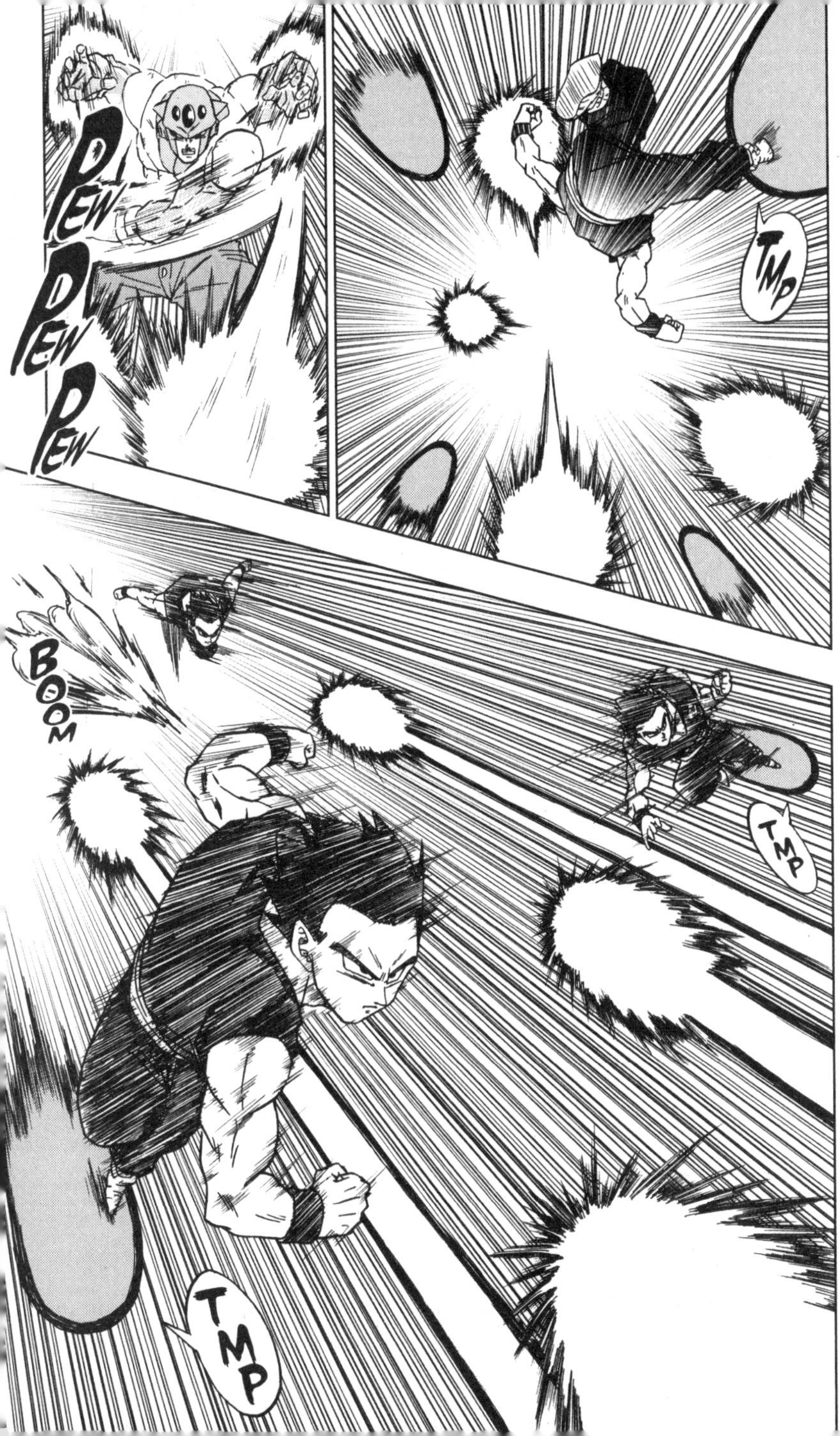
TMP
PEW PEW PEW PEW
TMP
BOOM
TMP

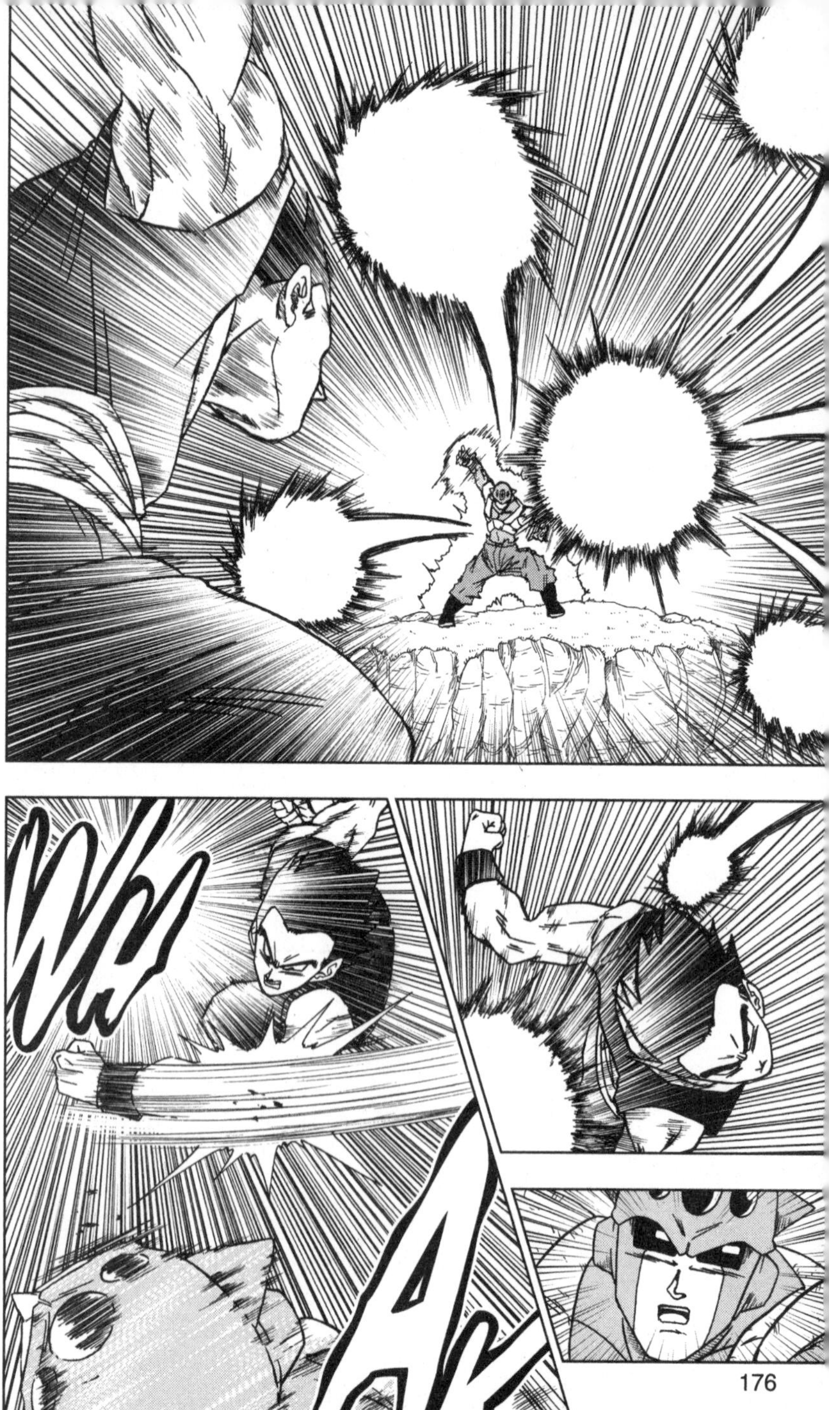

SPLOOSH

GOOD GOING, GOHAN!!

SEVEN-THREE CAN ONLY USE ONE SET OF POWERS AT A TIME...

...SO THERE'S NO WAY HE CAN DODGE ATTACKS FROM A DUO!

TH-THAT CAN'T BE!

WE'LL NEVER LOSE TO SOME COPYCAT.

OF COURSE! COMBO MOVES!!

SPLOOSH

SEEMS LIKE GOHAN AND PICCOLO'S TRAINING IS PAYING OFF.

UGH!

YOU LOOKED SO FREAK- IN' WEAK...

DAMMIT...

GAH!

ACTUALLY, I'M ONE OF THE THREE STRONG- EST EARTH- LINGS AROUND.

AW, YOU THINK?

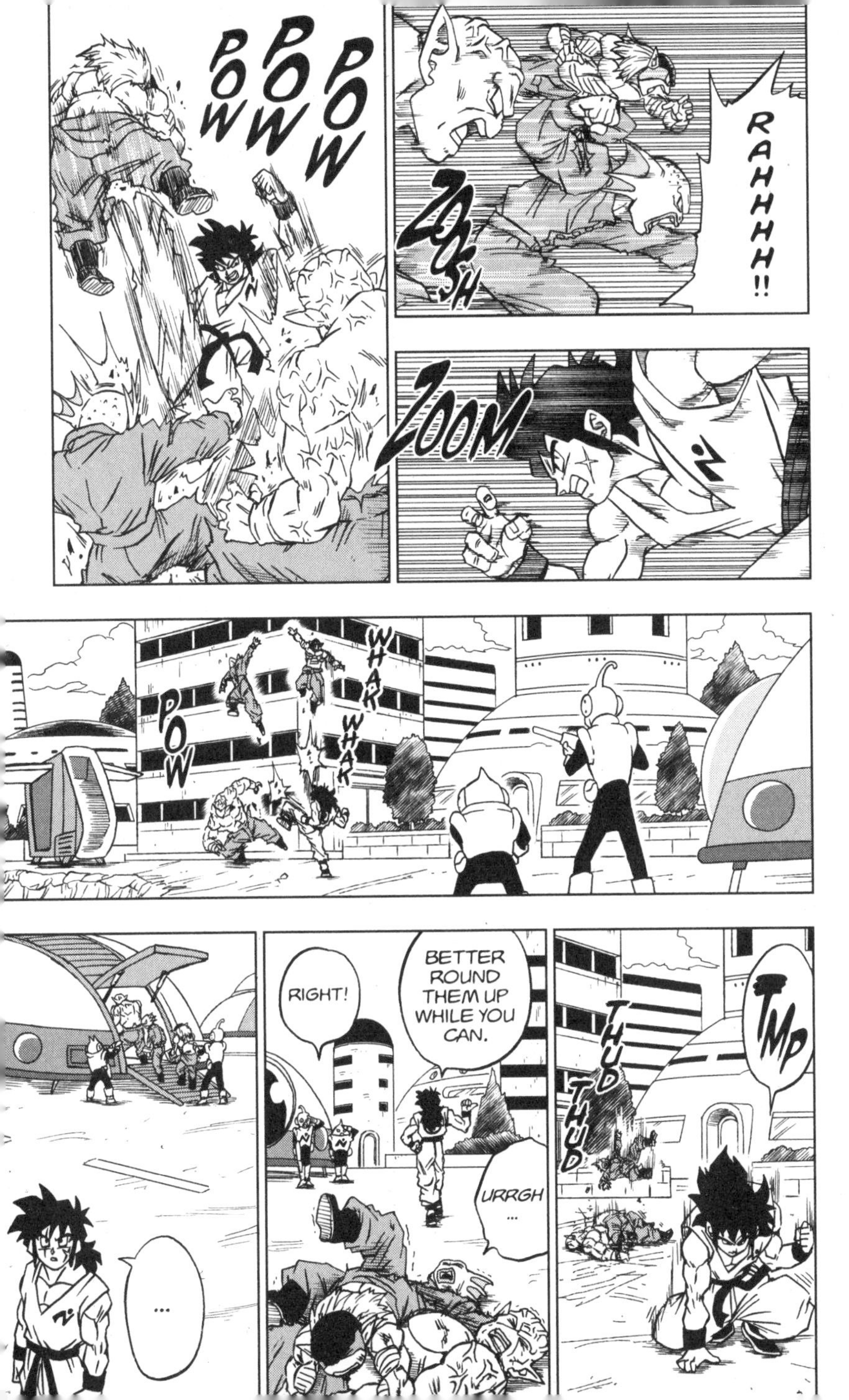
RAHHHHH!!
ZOOSH
ZOOM
POW POW POW
WHAK WHAK
POW
TMP
THUD THUD
BETTER ROUND THEM UP WHILE YOU CAN.
RIGHT!
URRGH ...
...

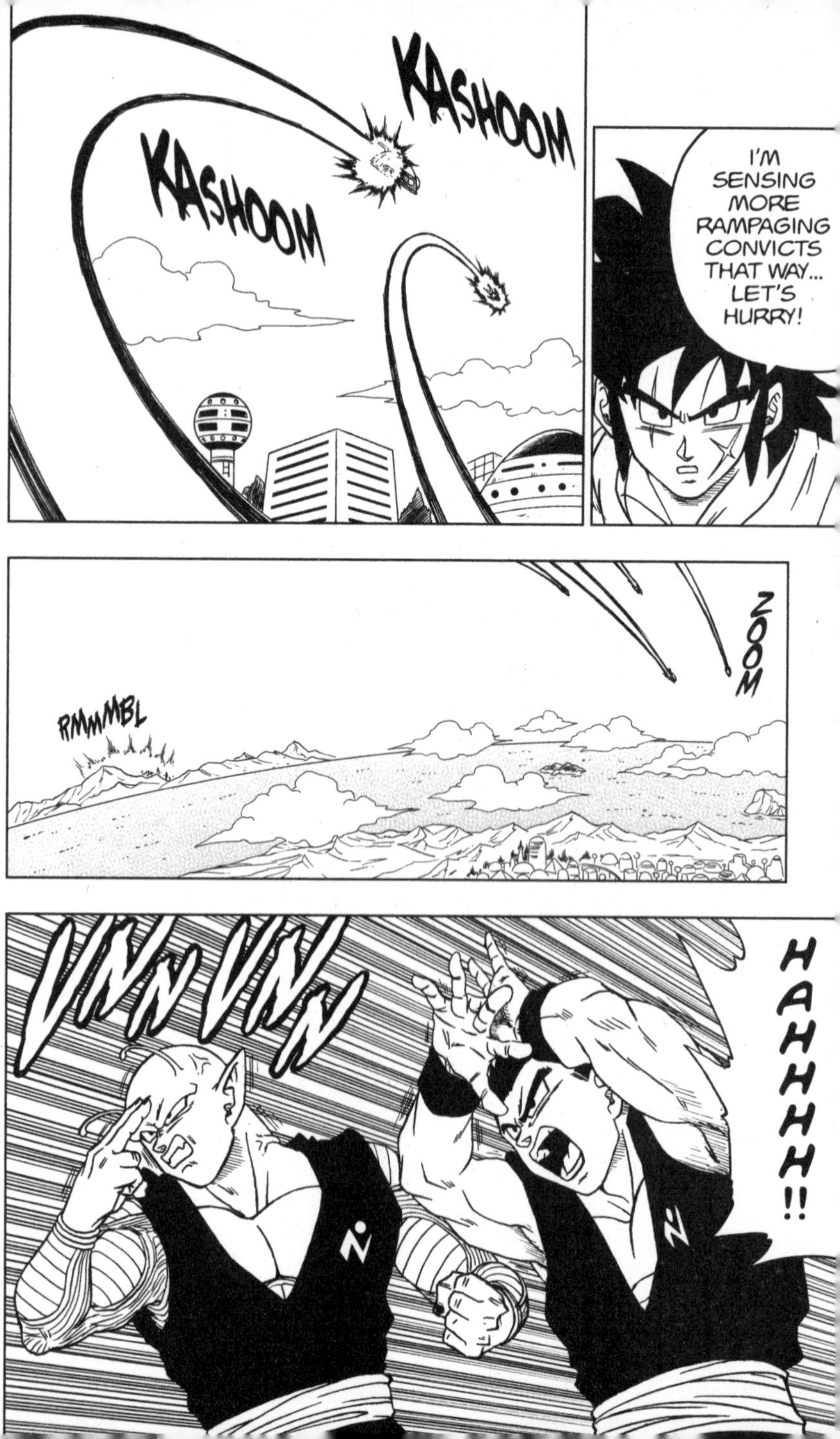
I'M SENSING MORE RAMPAGING CONVICTS THAT WAY... LET'S HURRY!
KASHOOM
KASHOOM
ZOOM
RMMMBL
VNN VNN
HAHHHHH!!

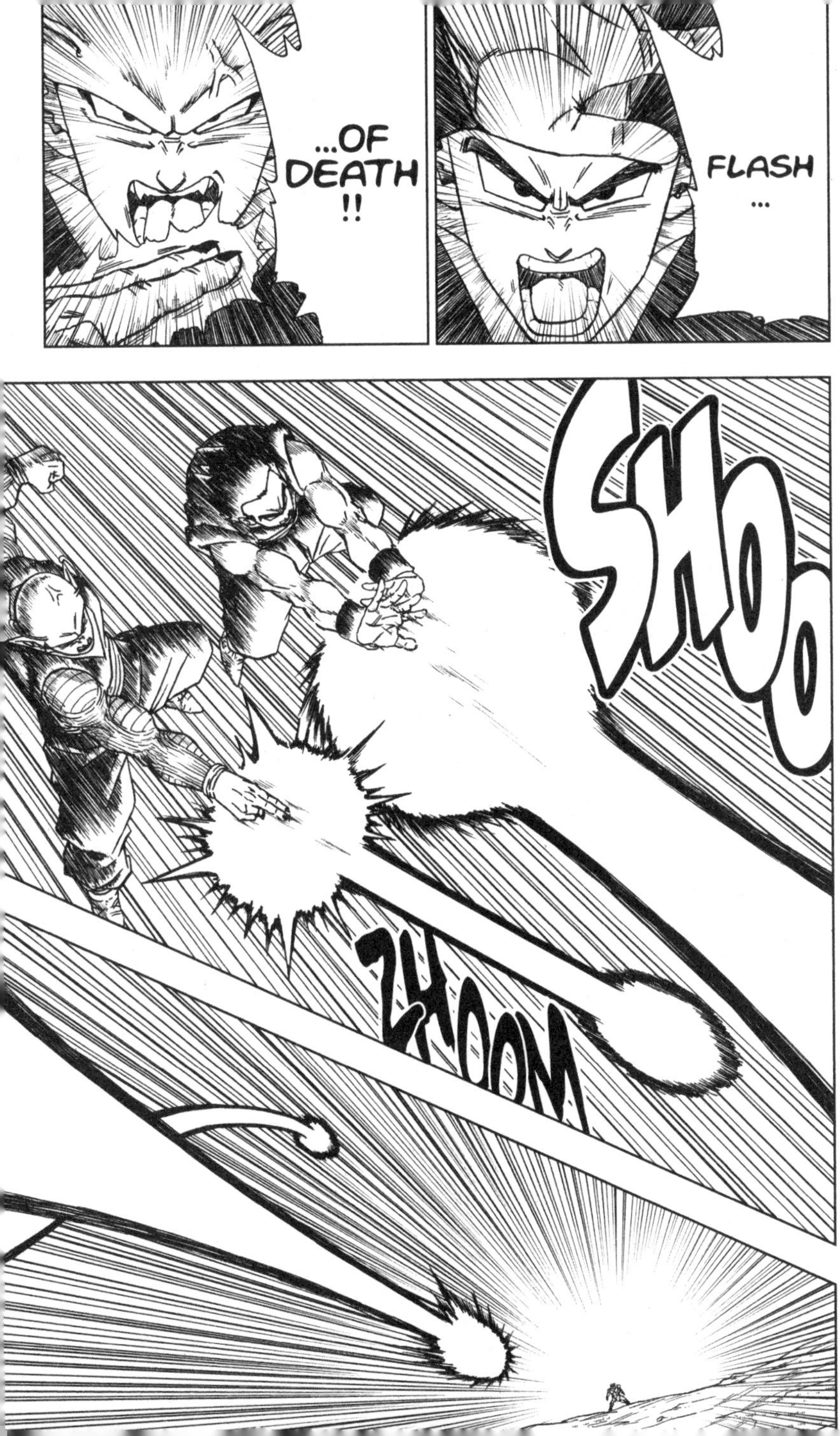
FLASH ...
...OF DEATH !!
SHOOO
ZHOOM

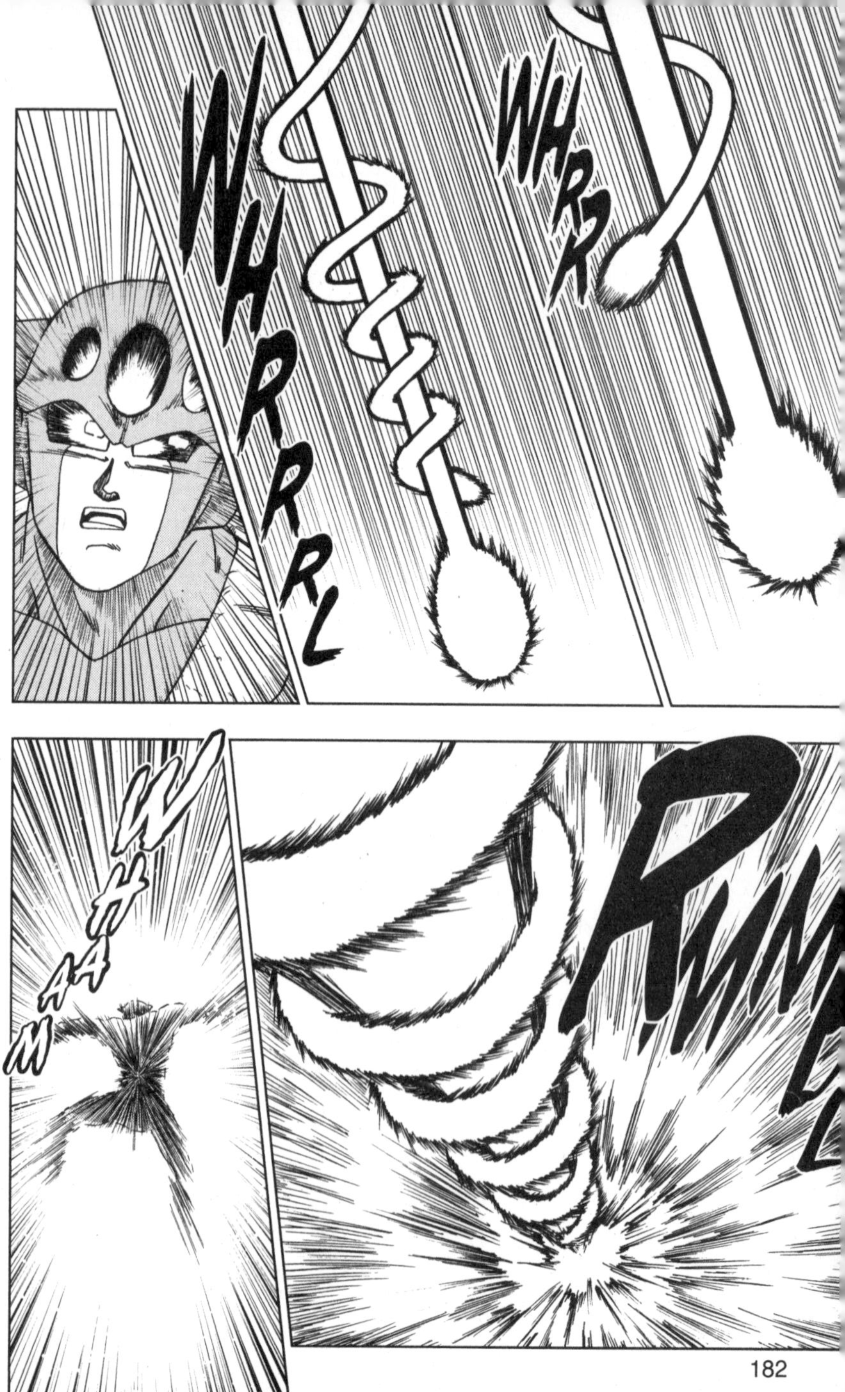
WHRRR
WHRRRRL
WHAAM

KABOOOM

BRGL

BRGL

BRGL

BRGL

RMMMMBL

DID
WE
GET
HIM
?!

HFF!

HE'LL
RESORT
TO MORO'S
POWER
AGAIN...

IF WE
DON'T
FINISH
HIM
OFF...
HE'LL...

NO,
NOT
YET!

...

ZOOM

WHAM

TMP

TMP

SLAM

SLAM

185

THEY SAID HE'S GOT NO EMOTIONS... SO YEAH, PROBABLY.

WHICH ONE'S THAT SEVEN-ELEVEN GUY? WAS HE THE ONE I KICKED?

GAH!

WH-WHO'RE THEY?!

SINCE YOU ANDROIDS DON'T HAVE CHI.

YOU SURE YOU EVEN NEED US, PICCOLO?

YEAH, YOU'RE THE ONLY ONES WHO CAN FINISH THIS FIGHT.

WEIRD. SEEMS PRETTY WEAK TO ME.

...MY LOW EXPECT- ATIONS OF THEM.

TCH... PATHETIC. THESE USELESS FOOLS COULDN'T EVEN MEET...

IT SEEMS LIKE A WHOLE BUNCH OF TOUGH FIGHTERS GATHERED ON EARTH, SOME- HOW...

APOLO- GIES, LORD MORO.

KREEK

NOW... WHO WILL BE FIRST ON MY MENU?

NO MATTER. THERE WOULD BE NO MEANING IN COMING ALL THIS WAY OTHERWISE.

ONE MORE TIME.

DAMMIT! IT FAILED...

ON YAR- DRAT

HFF!

HFF!

YES. THE FIGHTING STARTED NOT LONG AGO.

CAN YOU FEEL THE EARTH'S SPIRIT?

WAIT, VEGETA.

WELL? SHOULDN'T YOU RUSH OVER THERE?

NO POINT... NOT UNTIL I'VE MASTERED THIS TECHNIQUE...

FROM THE TOP, PYBARA.

NOW! ONCE MORE!

IT'S ELDER! ELDER PYBARA!

CUTTING IT CLOSE, HUH?

THERE'S STILL TIME.

BESIDES, MORO HASN'T JOINED THE BATTLE, YET.

...WAS A BIT LOST.

THAT-AWAY.

WHICH WAY IS EARTH?

MEAN-WHILE, GOKU...

TO BE CONTINUED!

WHAT NOW? GO ON, SPIT IT OUT.

LORD FREEZA!

LORD FREEZA!

AT THAT MOMENT, SOME-WHERE DEEP IN SPACE

BONUS MANGA

APPARENTLY, ESCAPED CONVICTS FROM THE GALACTIC PRISON ARE RAVAGING THE PLANET THAT WAS TO BE OUR NEXT TARGET.

THE GALACTIC PRISON, YOU SAY?

A-A THOUSAND APOLOGIES.

NOTHING GOOD CAN COME FROM MIXING WITH CRIMINALS.

C-CRIMINALS...?

...ALSO CRIMINALS...?

UM, AREN'T WE...

LET'S AVOID MEANINGLESS CONFLICT FOR NOW AND SIMPLY MOVE ON TO THE NEXT PLANET.

VERY WELL.

I HAVE HEARD THAT THE PRISONERS INCARCERATED THERE ARE AS NASTY AS THEY COME.

N-NASTY PRISONERS, LORD FREEZA?

PRECISELY AS BERRY-BLUE SAYS.

WE OCCUPY PLANETS AND EXTERMINATE THEIR INHABITANTS IN ORDER TO SELL THOSE PLANETS FOR A TIDY PROFIT TO RACES WHO HAVE LOST THEIR OWN HOMES. **WE ARE RUNNING A BUSINESS.**

WHAT DID YOU SAY?

KIKONO, WE ARE MOST CERTAINLY NOT CRIMINALS.

ACK... NOTHING. NEVER MIND.

IT'S A BIG UNIVERSE, OUT THERE.

THEN GET SEARCHING FOR OTHER PLANETS.

IS THAT A PROBLEM, KIKONO?

Y-YES, LORD FREEZA.

NOPE!

N...

191   END

YOU'RE READING
THE WRONG WAY!

Dragon Ball Super reads from right to left, starting in the
upper-right corner. Japanese is read from right to left,
meaning that action, sound effects, and word-balloon
order are completely reversed from English order.